ATHENS AFTER THE
PELOPONNESIAN WAR

ATHENS AFTER THE PELOPONNESIAN WAR

CLASS, FACTION AND POLICY 403–386 BC

BARRY S. STRAUSS

CROOM HELM
London & Sydney

© Barry S. Strauss 1986
Croom Helm Ltd, Provident House, Burrell Row
Beckenham, Kent BR3 1AT
Croom Helm Australia Pty Ltd, Suite 4, 6th Floor,
64–76 Kippax Street, Surry Hills, NSW 2010, Australia

British Library Cataloguing in Publication Data

Strauss, Barry
  Athens after the Peloponnesian War: class,
faction and policy 403–386 BC.
  1. Athens (Greece) — History
  I. Title
  938'.506   DF285
  ISBN 0-7099-4424-1

Printed and bound in Great Britain
by Billing & Sons Limited, Worcester.

Contents

Preface
Abbreviations
Map
Introduction — 1
Part One: Background — 9
   1. Political Behaviour in Postwar Athens — 11
   2. Society and Economy in Postwar Athens — 42
   3. Athenian Manpower After the Peloponnesian War — 70
Part Two: Politics and Policy — 87
   4. Reconciliation and Recrimination, 403–395 BC — 89
   5. The Politics of War, 395–391 BC — 121
   6. Division and Defeat, 391–386 BC — 150
Conclusions — 171
Appendix: Hoplite and Thetic Battle Casualties in the Peloponnesian War — 179
Select Bibliography — 183
Index — 185

To my parents
and to the memory of my grandparents,
Sylvia and Samuel Signet
and Ida and Meyer Strauss

Preface

This book is intended for the general reader of history as well as the specialist. The non-scholar may wish to consult an introductory book, essay, or encyclopaedia article on ancient Greece before continuing, but he or she will not have to complain of too many Greek words, which I have tried to keep to a minimum; I have transliterated those in the text. The units of Athenian currency are easy to describe: 6 obols = 1 drachmae (dr.), 100 drachma = 1 mina (min.), 6000 drachmae = 60 minae = 1 talent (tal.). Making sense of these units is less easy. As rough guidelines, consider these figures from the late fifth and the fourth centuries BC: a skilled workman on a public project got 1 dr. a day, an unskilled man 3 obols; an assemblyman received 3 obols a day; a woollen cloak cost 5–20 dr.; a yoke of oxen cost 50–100 dr. a head; an unskilled slave cost on the average 150–200 dr.; a man with resources of 4500 dr.−1 tal. may be considered a member of the propertied class; Athens' imperial tribute in the year 413 was $c.$ 900 tal.

The present volume began during my graduate studies in ancient history, when I became interested both in the general question of the relation between principle and power in politics and the specific one of Athens after the Peloponnesian War. To write this book I have thoroughly expanded, updated, rethought and reorganized my 1980 doctoral dissertation; the first chapter is completely new. A young scholar, like a young politician, tends to criticize his predecessors. If I have done so, I hope I may also make clear how much I owe to them.

I have many people and institutions to thank for their help, support, and even a gentle fillip or two. The Department of History of Cornell University supported my research in word and deed, providing a study leave in 1984–5 and travel grants to present early stages of my work as scholarly papers. The Cornell Humanities Faculty Research Grants Committee, the Cornell Peace Studies Program, and the Townsend Memorial Fund of the Cornell Classics Department also supported my work. I am grateful both to them and to the American School of Classical Studies at Athens and the Departments of History and Classics of Tel-Aviv University for their hospitality during my visits in 1984-5, when I wrote most of this book.

Donald Kagan, who directed my graduate studies and my dissertation, deserves my deepest gratitude for setting such high standards of scholarship, teaching, and collegiality. The book manuscript was read by him and by Frederick Ahl, Martin Bernal, Alvin Bernstein, Peter Krentz, and Josiah Ober, who suggested many improvements in substance and style. Colin Edmondson, Donald Kagan, Peter Krentz and Terrence Irwin kindly provided me with unpublished material. My colleagues Isabel Hull, John Najemy, and Joel Silbey provided valuable comments on an early draft of the first chapter. The secretarial staff of the Cornell Department of History, in particular Shirley Rice and Sharon Sanford, prepared the typescript. Vanessa Karahalios, Joseph Kuranda, Laura Linke, Ruth Rothaus, and Lauren Taaffe also helped. I would like to thank them and my editor and the staff of Croom Helm Ltd. I would also like to thank Marcia Mogelonsky, who not only helped in every stage of the work, but ensured that neither footnotes nor fragments, neither papyri nor prosopography would defeat my sense of humour.

JANUARY 1986

Abbreviations

All three-digit dates are BC.
Ancient works are cited by the standard abbreviations in the *Oxford Classical Dictionary*.
Modern works are cited by shortened titles after the first reference; journals are cited according to the style of the *American Journal of Archaeology* 82 (1978), pp. 3–8. In addition, the following abbreviations are employed:

Adkins, *MVPB*	A.W.H. Adkins. *Moral Values and Political Behavior in Ancient Greece* (New York: 1972)
APF	J.K. Davies. *Athenian Propertied Families, 600–300 B.C* (Oxford: 1971)
Beloch, *Bevölkerung*	K.J. Beloch. *Die Bevölkerung der griechisch-römischen Welt* (Leipzig: 1885)
Beloch, *GG*²	Idem, *Griechische Geschichte*² (Strassburg and Berlin: 1912–23)
Beloch, *Attische Politik*	Idem, *Die Attische Politik Seit Perikles* (Leipzig: 1884)
Bengtson, *Staatsverträge*	H. Bengtson. *Die Staatsverträge des Altertums. Vol 2: Die Verträge der griechisch-römischen Welt, von 700 bis 338 v. Chr.* (Munich and Berlin: 1962)
Bruce, *HCHO*	I.A.F. Bruce. *An Historical Commentary on the Hellenica Oxyrhynchia.* (Cambridge: 1967)
Busolt, *GG*	Georg Busolt. *Griechische Geschichte* (Gotha: 1893–1904)
CC	G.S. Shrimpton and D.J. McCargar, eds. *Classical Contributions. Studies in Honor of Malcolm Francis McGregor* (Locust Valley N.Y.: 1981)

Connor, *NP*	W.R. Connor. *New Politicians of Fifth Century Athens* (Princeton: 1971)
Davies, *WPW*	J.K. Davies. *Wealth and the Power of Wealth in Classical Athens* (New York: 1981)
Dover, *GPM*	K.J. Dover. *Greek Popular Morality in the Time of Plato and Aristotle* (Oxford: 1975)
Ehrenberg, *Aristophanes*	V. Ehrenberg. *The People of Aristophanes. A Sociology of Old Attic Comedy* (Oxford: 1951)
FGrH	F. Jacoby. *Die Fragmente der griechischen Historiker* (Berlin and Leiden: 1923–58)
Funke, *HA*	P. Funke. *Homonoia und Arche, Athen und die griechische Staatenwelt vom Ende des peloponnesischen Krieges bis zum Königsfrieden: HistoriaEinzelschrift 19* (Wiesbaden: 1980)
Gomme, *Population*	A.W. Gomme. *The Population of Athens in the Fifth and Fourth Centuries B.C* (Chicago: 1967)
Hamilton, *SBV*	C.D. Hamilton. *Sparta's Bitter Victories: Politics and Diplomacy in the Corinthian War* (Ithaca: 1979)
HCT	A.W. Gomme, A. Andrewes and K.J. Dover. *A Historical Commentary on Thucydides* (Oxford: 1966–81)
IG	*Inscriptiones Graecae* (Berlin: 1924–47)
Jones, *AD*	A.H.M. Jones. *Athenian Democracy* (Oxford: 1975)
Jordan, *Athenian Navy*	B. Jordan. *The Athenian Navy in the Classical Period* (Berkeley: 1975)
Kock, *CAF*	T. Kock, ed. *Comicorum Atticorum Fragmenta* (Leipzig: 1880–8)
Krentz, *Thirty*	P. Krentz. *The Thirty at Athens* (Ithaca: 1982)

Meiggs-Lewis, *SGHI*	R. Meiggs and D.M. Lewis, eds. *A Selection of Greek Historical Inscriptions to the End of the Fifth Century* (Oxford: 1969)
Ober, *FA*	J. Ober. *Fortress Attica* (Leiden: 1985)
PA	J. Kirchner. *Prosopographia Attica* (Berlin: 1966)
RE	*Paulys Real-Encyclopädie der Classischen Altertumswissenschaft* (Stuttgart: 1894–)
Ruschenbusch, *Innenpolitik*	E. Ruschenbusch. *Athenische Innenpolitik im 5. Jhrhdt. v. chr.* (Bamberg: 1979)
Ste Croix, *CSAGW*	G.E.M. de Ste Croix. *The Class Struggle in the Ancient Greek World* (Ithaca: 1981)
Seager, 'TCAI'	R. Seager, 'Thrasybulus, Conon and Athenian Imperialism, 396–386 B.C.' *JHS* 87 (1967), 95–115
Sealey, 'Callistratos'	R. Sealey, 'Callistratos of Aphidna and His Contemporaries.' *Historia* 5 (1956) pp. 178–203
SEG	*Supplementum Epigraphicum Graecum* (Leiden: 1923–)
SIG[3]	G. Dittenberger, ed. *Sylloge Inscriptionum Graecarum*[3] (Leipzig: 1915–24)
Tod, *GHI*, vol. 2	M.N. Tod. *A Selection of Greek Historical Inscriptions, vol 2: From 403 to 323 B.C.* (Oxford: 1948)
Ussher, *Ecclesiazusae*	R.G. Ussher. *Aristophanes' Ecclesiazusae* (Oxford: 1975)

The Greek World in 400 BC

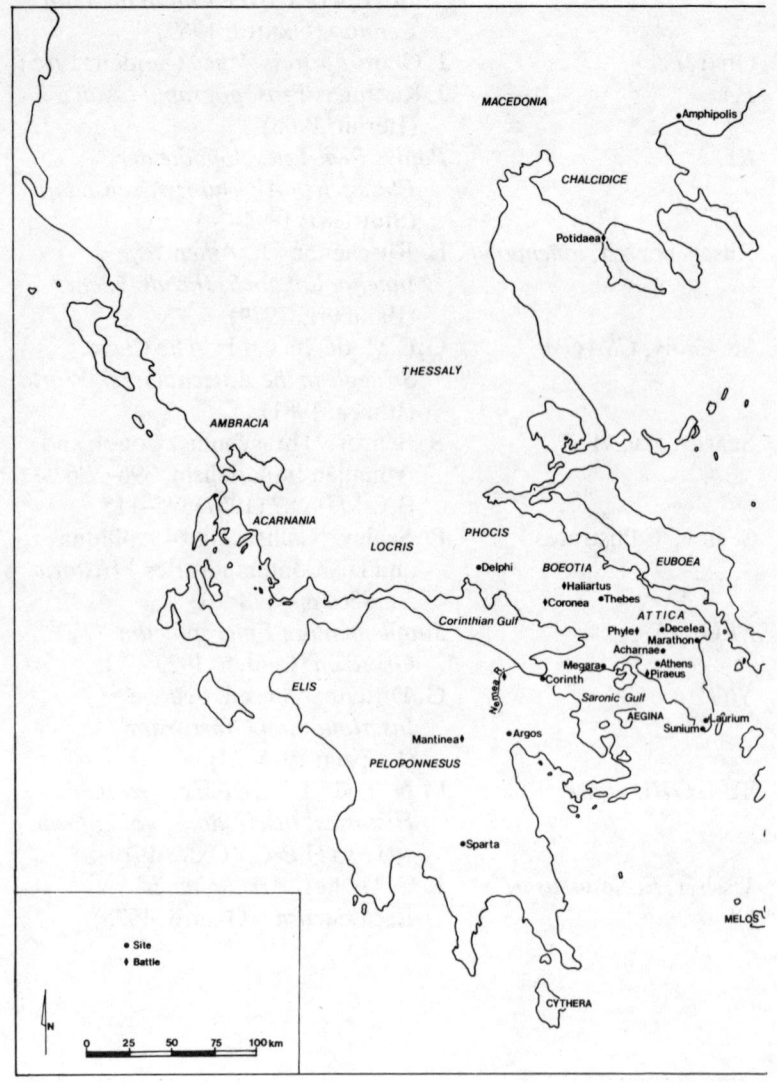

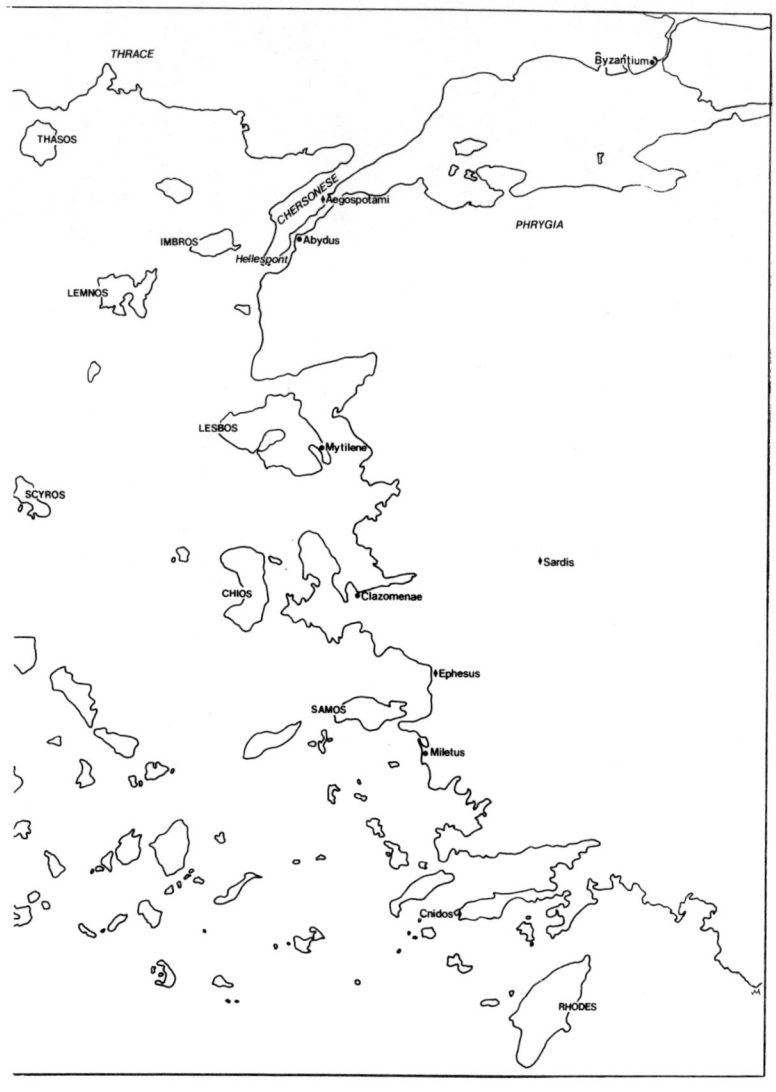

Introduction

A scientist uses a microscope both to examine the details of a single cell and to substantiate theories about the organism as a whole. Likewise, the historian has two purposes in studying Athens after the Peloponnesian War: the inherent interest of the period and the lessons it holds for the general study of politics in classical Athens. As important as it has been misunderstood, this era is rich in evidence about two general topics of significance: the interaction of faction and class in Athenian politics and the power of political demography, specifically, the ruinous losses of the thetes (poorer classes) in the Peloponnesian War.

The period under investigation, from the restoration of Athenian democracy in 403 to the end of the Corinthian War in 386, is a crucial one. It demonstrates the resilience both of Athenian democracy and Athenian imperialism in spite of defeat by Sparta. Nor is this period lacking in drama: the trial and execution of Socrates (399), the continuing political struggle between the democrats who had won in the civil war of 404–403 and the oligarchs who had lost, the Athenian decision in 395 to revolt against Sparta even before the city had been fortified or a fleet raised, and the daily struggles of thousands of Athenians who, in a generation of war and revolution, had gone from riches to rags (or at least from silk to homespun). Although the years after 404 lack a Thucydides as historian, they have important sources of documentation which the earlier period lacks: the forensic speeches of Lysias and the early Isocrates, and the fragments of the Oxyrhynchus historian.

Previous studies raise serious problems of interpretation.[1] There is, first, the nature of Athenian political groups, a question with which ancient historians have wrestled since the 1930s. Nineteenth-century scholars spoke of these political groups as parties, that is, roughly the same as their own political parties.

Historians of the last two generations, however, have rejected this idea. Without platforms, formal structure, mass membership, identification cards, or even names (besides 'the followers of X') Athenian political groups cannot have been parties in the modern sense. Most students of Athenian politics today refer instead to political groups or political friendships.

This model is a great improvement. Yet it says both too little and too much: too little because the term group is so imprecise, too much because of the assumption that friendship groups seek power without any reference to principle. I believe that the term faction is a more precise and accurate description than group. As the word is used by anthropologists and political scientists today, a faction is a small unit of political competition, loosely organized by a leader through a variety of one-to-one ties with his followers and aiming at winning power. Athenian politicians formed just such groups.

The term faction raises further questions. Were factions common to both the political elite and the political community? Do factions necessarily engage in factionalism, i.e., an amoral and no-holds-barred struggle for power? To answer these questions one must consult a wider scholarly literature (in history, anthropology and political science) than ancient historians tend to treat: to understand Athenian categories one must temporarily step outside them. The factional model is necessary to explain Athenian politics but not sufficient. From the fifth century on, if not earlier, appeals to class interest also played an important role in politics. Class did not supersede faction, but in times of crisis especially, factions tended to polarize according to class: for example, the oligarchic and democratic factions of 411 or 404. In ordinary times too, politicians often appealed to class interest to organize a following in the assembly. The historian, hence, must examine both faction and class.[2]

A second broad subject is political culture. The scanty biographical details are not the only means of fleshing out the motives or mentality of Athenian politicians; considerable evidence about the personal and societal values of Athenians is also at hand. If this evidence does not always allow one to determine precisely why so and so did such and such, it can at least narrow the range of choices to a few likely possibilities.

In particular, such a study can avoid the anachronism of ascribing dubiously modern motives to the ancients. Athenian politics were more intensely competitive, more concerned with public appearance, and placed a higher (or at least more overt) premium on vengeance than most modern Anglo-Saxon politics. The student of ancient politics must always keep these and other differences in mind. Several excellent studies of ancient Athenian values have appeared in recent years (for instance, the work of Adkins, Dover, Dodds, Gouldner, and Walcot).[3] I want to apply their conclusions to the analysis of Athenian politics.

A third subject, the question of unity and disunity, is raised by the literature's over-assessment, even mythologising of concord and unity in Athenian politics after 403. The moderation of the restored democracy towards the former oligarchs was virtually proverbial in antiquity.[4] The demos aimed at 'restoring unity and concord in the state,' says Aristotle:

> The Athenians appear to have handled their affairs, both public and private, as well and with as much statesmanship as any people have ever shown in a similar situation.
> (*Ath. Pol.* 40.3)

Funke offers a more complex, though similar, analysis: although the amnesty faced attacks in its first years, by 395, when the Athenians voted unanimously (if Xenophon is right) to fight against Sparta, all tensions between oligarch and democrat had disappeared.[5]

These impressive but incomplete verdicts must be placed in the ancient context. The Athenians ended their civil war much more neatly then most Greeks of the classical period did; one has only to think of Corcyra in 427 (Thuc. 3.69–85). This relative superiority does not turn the Athenians into saints, however. For example, the moderate Athenians are known to have convicted at least twelve politicians, generals, or ambassadors on various charges of misconduct between 403 and 386; at least three were executed. These are the Athenians who, however gentle their ordinary constitution, gave vent to the darkest anger from time to time: in 399 they sentenced Socrates to drink hemlock.[6] One of the reasons for his conviction was his connection, however tenuous, to the oligarchy. As Aeschines said in 345:

> you put to death Socrates the sophist, fellow citizens, because he was shown to have been the teacher of Critias, one of the Thirty who put down the democracy.
> (Aesch. 1. 173)

Moreover, tensions between oligarchs and democrats did not disappear in 395, but are attested in a legal speech as late as 382 (Lys.

26). The Athenians did not violate their amnesty outright, above all because renewed civil strife would only have invited Spartan intervention. Nevertheless, the civil war left a legacy of bitterness. The lame and stitched up Athens of Lysias and Xenophon was not a reborn city of Pericles.[7]

A fourth, and related, subject is the tendency of some to begin the history of Athens in 403 *de novo*, with no connection to the previous period. But to understand the political rivalries of the 390s, one must go back to the civil war and earlier, to the last decade of the Peloponnesian War. For example, the rivalry between Conon and Thrasybulus, so prominent in 393, goes back to a factional dispute of 407. Indeed, the Corinthian War (395–386) itself was in many ways nothing more than a continuation of the Peloponnesian War after a brief time out.[8]

The fifth subject is the Athenian economy and society, so important for politics. Broadly speaking, two opposing points of view have appeared in the literature recently. Claude Mossé and Gerhardt Audring (following Paul Cloché) argue that the invasions and defeat of the Peloponnesian War left a deep split in the structure of Athenian citizenry. The *penetes* — that slippery term often translated as 'the poor' but more accurately 'the people who have to work for a living', i.e., most Athenians — were enthusiastic for war and empire and indifferent to the threat of a Spartan invasion, especially if they lived in Athens or Piraeus. The *plousioi* — the so-called 'rich', but more accurately the leisure or rentier elite — were afraid of Spartan invaders and Athenian war tax and saw little to gain in a revived empire.[9]

Some scholars deny this supposed division. Funke, for example, argues that a broad, property-owning middle class continued to exist in Athens after 403, thus obviating social conflict.[10] Similarly, G. E. M. de Ste Croix writes of postwar Athens:

> Once or twice we hear of a division on foreign policy at Athens on class lines, between rich and poor (see *Hell. Oxy.* VI (I) 3; Ar. *Eccl.* 197–8); but on most issues, home and foreign, there is no clear evidence of any such division: there is not the least reason to expect it at this period.[11]

Pace Ste Croix, there *is* reason to expect political differences between the rich and other Athenians after 403: the continued hostility between former oligarchs and democrats. Naturally, the two antinomies are not equivalent, for many prominent democrats were themselves rich.[12] Nevertheless, the civil war had pitted the interests of a few rich and aristocratic Athenians against those of nearly everyone else. Memories of the conflict, therefore, did nothing for social peace.

On the whole, however, Ste Croix and Funke are, I suspect, closer to the truth than Mossé and Audring: the social classes and geographical regions of Attica had relatively harmonious relations in Athenian politics after 403. What remains to be done, however, is to explain the *reasons* for this consensus, reasons which outweighed the unsettled scores of civil war; this study proposes three such reasons.

The first is the significance of population change in the Peloponnesian War. I argue in Chapter 3 that social conflict after 403 might have been sharper if not for the disproportionately large number of thetes killed in fighting in the last decade of the Peloponnesian War. The numbers of thetes and hoplites were roughly equivalent in 431, but thetes suffered over twice as many casualties as hoplites in the Peloponnesian War, particularly in its last years. Moreover, many of the political leaders of the thetes were executed by the Thirty. By the beginning of the fourth century, hoplites outnumbered thetes by 20 per cent or more. The thetes might have spoken up for their interests more vociferously after 403 if more of them or their leaders had managed to survive the war.

Second, contrary to the picture often painted by ancient and modern writers, the *plousioi* had a considerable interest in the Athenian empire.[13] They had made capital, political as well as economic, from the empire and they had every reason to work for its re-establishment after the Spartan dissolution. On this issue, they were at one with the *penetes*. Third, there is very little evidence for significant conflict (as opposed to a friendly, or even a grouchy rivalry) between country and city. To an alarmingly large degree, proof of this conflict has depended on two lines in Aristophanes' *Ecclesiazusae*:

Ships must be launched; the poor man approves,
The wealthy men and farmers disapprove.
(*Eccl.* 197–198)[14]

But this statement provides no evidence of an urban–rural or rich–poor division in Athenian politics at the time (*c.* 391); indeed it is probably most revealing as an indication of, on the one hand,

Athenian tax-collecting methods and, on the other, of Aristophanes' sense of humour.[15]

Four of the following chapters focus on politics and two on society and economy. Chapter 1, 'Political Behaviour in Postwar Athens,' examines some theoretical questions about Athenian politicians, political groups and political culture. Chapters 4, 5 and 6 trace the play of political faction in the period 403–386. Since domestic and foreign policy are intimately tied, particularly in a period of recovery from one war and participation in another, these chapters analyse the relationship of external and internal affairs. Chapter 2 examines Athens' economy and society after the Peloponnesian War, while Chapter 3 turns to demographic change. My conclusions appear in the final chapter.

To sum up, the story of Athenian politics after the Peloponnesian War needs to be told in detail for three main reasons. First, it promises to yield important conclusions about Athenian political behaviour, particularly about the interaction of faction and class. Second, it is an exercise in placing Athenian politics in the larger context of its times, particularly in the context of striking demographic change and of the Athenian value system. Third, the tasks facing postwar Athenian politicians were so dramatic: to restore a consensus after the long and divisive Peloponnesian War and two civil wars, to direct a new war effort (the Corinthian War) after only eight years of peace, and to cope with a drastically poorer economy. I hope to tell a story that is interesting and important, and to tell it, in Ranke's words, 'as it really happened.'

Notes

1. Among the more important studies of Athenian politics in the two decades after 404 are: Beloch, *Attische Politik*, chap. 7; P. Cloché, *La restauration démocratique à Athènes en 403 avant J.-C.* (Paris: 1915); *Idem*, 'Les conflits politiques et sociaux à Athènes pendant la guerre corinthienne (395–387 avant J.-C.)', *REA* 21 (1919), 157–92; S. Accame, *Ricerche intorno alla guerra corinzia* (Naples: 1951); G. Barbieri, *Conone* (Rome: 1955); R. Sealey, 'Callistratos', 178–203; R. Seager, 'TCAI', 95–115; S. Perlman, 'Athenian Democracy and the Revival of Imperialistic Expansion at the Beginning of the Fourth Century BC', *CP* 63 (1968), 257–67; D. D. A. Kounas, *'Prelude to Hegemony: Studies in Athenian Political Parties from 403 to 379 BC Pertaining to the Revival of Athenian Influence in Greece'* (Diss. Illinois: 1969); G. L. Cawkwell, 'The Imperialism of Thrasybulus', *CQ* 26 (1976), 270–7; C. Mossé, *Athens in Decline, 403–86 BC*, trans. Stewart (London: 1976), chap. 2; B. S. Strauss, 'Thrasybulus and Conon: A Rivalry in Athenian Politics in the 390s BC.', *AJP* 105 (1984), 37–48; H. Funke, *HA*.

Introduction   7

2. For class and faction in Greek political strife, see the recent discussion of A. Lintott, *Violence, Civil Strife and Revolution in the Classical City* (Baltimore: 1982), 253–61.
3. E. R. Dodds, *The Greeks and the Irrational* (Berkeley: 1960); A. W. H. Adkins, *Merit and Responsibility, A Study in Greek Values* (Oxford: 1960); *Idem, From the Many to the One* (Oxford: 1970) and *MVPB*; A. W. Gouldner, *Enter Plato, Classical Greece and the Origins of Social Theory* (London: 1967); P. Walcot, *Greek Peasants Ancient and Modern* (Manchester: 1970); Dover, *GPM*.
4. For a list of sources, see Funke, *HA* 25, n. 26.
5. Funke, *HA* 69, cf. 163, rejects Cloché's analysis ('Conflits', 170) of 'l'unanimité factice et superficielle'; he takes Xenophon at his word.
5. Arist. *Ath. Pol.* 22.4 cites the 'customary mildness of the people' of Athens. Convictions: Onomasas, Ergocles, Epicrates, Andocides, Cratinus, Euboulides, Pamphilus, Agyrrhius, Aristophanes, Nicophemus, Dionysius, Thrasybulus of Collytus. Executions: Ergocles, Aristophanes, Nicophemus. For references, *infra*, chap. 1, n. 88.
7. A more recent Greek Civil War, that of 1944–9, still leaves its mark on Greek politics in the 1980s. Adherence to amnesty: Funke, *HA* 17–26. Recriminations as late as 382: Krentz, *Thirty*, 119.
8. Rivalry: Strauss, 'Thrasybulus and Conon', 37–48; *infra*, chap. 4. Continuation: J. K. Davies argues that in Greek political and military history, the years 413–380 BC form a single period and should not be broken at 404. Davies, *Democracy and Classical Greece* (Glasgow: 1978), 129, 147.
9. See C. Mossé, *Athens in Decline*, 12, 30, and 'Les classes sociales à Athènes au IVe siècle', *Ordres et classes, colloque d'histoire sociale* (Paris: 1973), 25–6; G. Audring, 'Über Grundeigentum und Landwirtschaft in der Krise der athenischen Polis', in *Hellenische Poleis, Krise-Wandlung-Wirkung*, vol. 1, ed. E. C. Welskopf (Berlin: 1974), 108–31; Cloché, 'Conflits', 151–2, and *La politique étrangère d'Athènes de 404 à 338 avant J.-C.* (Paris: 1934), chaps. 1, 2. On the terminology, *infra*, chap. 2, n. 1.
10. Funke, *HA* 6–7.
11. Ste Croix, *CSAGW* 292.
12. It is important to separate personal wealth and political opinions. Funke, *HA* 10, for example, argues that the continued hostility after 403 between the supporters of oligarchy ('the men of the city') and the supporters of democracy ('the men of the Piraeus') was not a conflict between rich and poor, because many of the democrats were themselves rich. But this misses the point; one can be rich and nevertheless defend the political interests of the poor — consider the cases of Pericles, Julius Caesar, or Franklin Roosevelt.
13. The rich gained relatively little from the Athenian empire: *infra*, chap. 2, n. 89.
14. Translation: *infra*, chap. 2, n. 108.
15. Conflict: *infra*, chap. 2, n. 93.

PART ONE
BACKGROUND

1 Political Behaviour in Postwar Athens

A history of Athenian politics from 403 to 386 is necessarily specific, but it needs to begin by asking general questions about the political process in Athens both during those 17 years and more broadly from c. 425 to c. 350. Despite the advances of recent scholarship, some basic questions are still unasked, certain assumptions unchallenged, some key concepts muddy. Before describing what happened in Athenian politics 403–386, it is necessary to explain how Athenian politics in those years worked.

This chapter addresses three basic questions: who ruled, how did they rule, and what were the rules of the game? In other words, the topics are politicians, political groups and the pursuit of power. Power, of course, is pursued by all politicians everywhere. A specifically Athenian analysis is nevertheless necessary, because the intensity with which politicians pursue power, the means they consider acceptable, the ends to which they apply power vary considerably from one society to another. In other words, politics is culture-bound. Yet previous studies rarely appreciate how Athenian politics were 'desperately foreign' from our own.[1] Athens was a closed society whose members played private tunes and played by ear.[2] Only after grasping the peculiar spirit and particular rules of Athenian politics — an investigation that necessarily draws on anthropology — can one write Athenian political history.

In each of the following parts, a date c. 400 is assumed. As much as possible, examples have been chosen from the period 403–386, but examples from other periods are sometimes appropriate or, given the state of the evidence, unavoidable.

Politicians

A half-century earlier, democratic Athens was governed by the sons of aristocratic families, many of which had monopolized political power long ago, before the reforms of Solon. Even Pericles, eulogist of democracy, came, on his mother's side, from the proud and ancient house of the Alcmeonids. Now in 400, after the social and economic changes that came from empire, world war, defeat and revolution, aristocrats in Athenian politics were the exception, not the rule.[3]

The men who governed Athens c. 400 generally made up in wealth what they lacked in lineage. They were men who could afford to subsidize the cost of a warship or a statue in a temple, who knew how to hobnob with kings, who could afford to be educated by sophists. Often they came from families that had made their money in commerce or manufacturing, which led to the ancient slander that they were mere potters or lampmakers or lyremakers or tanners — this last a godsend to the writers of political jokes, because of the use of urine in the tanning process. In other cases their fortunes rested on the traditional source of Athenian wealth — the land. Whatever its source, money was something Athens' leading politicians needed to have — enough at least to free them from making a living as a politician, if not to render them wealthy.[4]

Who ruled in Athens? The prosperous or wealthy farmers, traders and owners of slave manufactories most of whom lived within a 10 km radius of the Acropolis. Beginning with Cleisthenes, the elite had begun vying for the support of that class one step down on the social ladder, the so-called hoplite class, to whose *amour propre* and purses they made incremental concessions in exchange for political support. With Pericles and Ephialtes, the elite reached one step further down on the ladder, to the thetes, similarly exchanging public 'gifts' for political support.[5] Finally, Cleon took the process even further by escalating the rhetoric against his own class and encouraging the thetes to demand even greater 'gifts'.[6] The military failures of the Peloponnesian War made way for the counter-revolutions of 411 and 404. Now that they too had failed, the shape of the political system was open to question. On the whole, the situation returned to the *status quo* of the late fifth century, but with a distinctly more moderate tone. There were, as will be argued, both political and social reasons for this development.

Athenian democracy allowed the average man to play a direct part in government when the spirit moved him. The farmer from Sunium or the shoemaker from the Piraeus could go to Athens for an assembly meeting or a court session or two a year or even hold a minor magistracy and pride himself on a job well done. The man who aspired to political prominence, on the other hand, had a full-time task. The assembly, the heart of the Athenian government, the arena for decision-making and debate, met at least 40 days a year. The council, which prepared the assembly's agenda, met some 250. While no politician could count on a council seat in any year, he always had to follow the council's deliberations closely and, if he could, place a colleague in it. Then there were the courts, where many a political — and not merely legal — battle was fought out; one scholar aptly refers to the Athenian courts as 'virtual subcommittees of the assembly'.[7] Political trials were common in Athens: Pericles the statesman, Phidias the sculptor and Socrates the philosopher are just three prominent examples of defendants in politically motivated trials. A conscientious Athenian politician had to keep his eye on the busy court schedule of 150–200 days a year. Add to these demands on one's time the need to have expertise in Athens' economy, military, and foreign policy, and to have personal contacts in these fields abroad as well as at home, and it becomes clear how time consuming a political career in Athens was.[8]

The aspiring politician *c.* 400 had a number of paths to success from which to choose. The old-fashioned way to win power was by spending one's own money or by sponsoring the expenditure of public money to benefit the citizenry in general or specific groups within it, for which one might hope to be rewarded with 'favour' (*charis*) in the courts or assembly. J. K. Davies, among others, has described the system admirably, arguing however that, as a way of winning office, it had been largely supplanted by the end of the fifth century.[9] Yet, on the contrary, munificence was still of considerable political, and not solely forensic importance in postwar Athens. A speaker *c.* 390 asserts that 'There are, indeed, persons who spend money in advance . . . to obtain a return of twice the amount from the appointments which you consider them to have earned' (Lys. 19.56). One example is the speaker's late brother-in-law Aristophanes of Rhamnus, who spent whatever money he had 'in pursuit of *timé*', i.e., honour or office or pay (Lys. 19.18). Another is Conon, who built in Piraeus a temple to Aphrodite (goddess of Cnidos) and underwrote a festival liturgy (*hestiasis*) for the entire citizenry (and not merely, as was customary, for one tribe). *Pace* Davies, Conon probably expected political as well as forensic *charis* in return. Moreover, politicians continued enthusiastically to take the credit for public political munificence: e.g., ecclesiastic pay, with which Heraclides of Clazomenae and Agyrrhius were associated; the rebuilding of the Long Walls, to which Conon's name was tied; the support for orphans which Theozotides shepherded through the assembly.[10]

A second path to political success was the generalship. Such scholars as Jones and Davies have noticed the growing divorce between generals and politicians in the fourth century; in the 390s, however, this was far from the case.[11] Thrasybulus, for example, owed the political power he enjoyed in 400 largely to his military victories at Phyle and Piraeus in 403 — and to the absence of other experienced generals in Athens after the upheavals at the end of the Peloponnesian War. After Thrasybulus' defeats at Nemea and Coronea and Conon's victory at Cnidos, all in 394, the wheel turned. Four other politicians of the period, Agyrrhius, Anytus, Archinus and Thrasybulus of Collytus, are known to have commanded in the field.[12]

Recent scholarship has rightly emphasized the growing importance after 450 of administrative and financial skill, oratorical ability, and sympathy with the common man as claims to political office — that is, the growth of something roughly akin to politics as we know it.[13] Indeed, these factors were a central — but not exclusive — part of postwar Athenian politics. Among contemporary politicians, Archinus and Andocides were famous for their oratory, Agyrrhius and his rising young nephew Callistratus for their financial expertise. Cephalus and Epicrates were the heirs of Cleon and Cleophon, the leaders of the populist tendency; Archinus, Phormisius and others guarded what was left of the Therameneans. To return to oratory, Callistratus too was no mean speaker. The future architect of the Second Athenian Confederacy began his career by prosecuting Andocides and his fellow-ambassadors in the peace negotiations of 392. Such giant slaying was common in Athenian politics, as in other cultures: it bears much in common with, for example, the ritual of the first public quarrel among the Sarakatsani shepherds of modern Greece.[14]

Oratory, technical expertise, class or interest politics, military success, munificence — these were the roads to power in postwar politics. A man with the military record of Conon or Thrasybulus — and, in Conon's case, the wealth — may perhaps have gotten by with only mediocre oratorical skill or with bland promises to be above class interests. For most politicians, however, the other roads had to be travelled. Moreover, even in a country of would-be heroes, no politician could win success on his own.

Political Groups

Party

A century ago, historians spoke of the rival political groups of ancient Athens as parties, in roughly the sense of political parties of their own day. L. Whibley, for example, in his *Political Parties in Athens During the Peloponnesian War* speaks of 'party government,' dividing Athenian political groups into three parties: the oligarchs, the democrats and the middle party ('mainly composed of moderate or opportunist democrats, but including also some moderate oligarchs').[15] He makes the three groups broadly analagous to the rich, the poor and the middle class. Other nineteenth-century scholars, in England G. Grote, and in Germany K. J. Beloch and G. Gilbert, offer similar schemata.[16]

Thanks to incisive scholarship beginning some 50 years ago, the picture today is very different.[17] A wide consensus now prevails that Athens had no political parties in the modern sense.[18] A comparison of the modern party and ancient conditions demonstrates the wisdom of this reassessment. Consider this definition of a modern political party by the political scientist W. N. Chambers:

> Stated broadly, a political party in the modern sense may be thought of as a relatively durable social formation which seeks offices or power in government, exhibits a structure or organization which links leaders at the centers of government to a significant popular following in the political arena and its local enclaves, and generates in-group perspectives or at least symbols of identification or loyalty.[19]

Chambers' definition fits the American Republicans or Democrats or the British Labour Party or the Communist Party of modern Greece.

Ancient Athenian political groups, on the other hand, were not relatively durable; take away the leader and the group dissolved. Each leader had followers among the people, but the ties were loose and fluid, showing little structure or organization. Nor were the followers very numerous. Modern parties often have millions of members; in contrast, normal attendance at the Athenian assembly seems to have been c. 6,000, and the total citizen body in 400 BC was less than 20,000.[20]

Athenian political groups rarely generated 'symbols of identification or loyalty' beyond the name of the leader, e.g., 'Thrasybulus and his friends' or, in a hostile version, 'Thrasybulus and his flatterers' (Lys. 28.4,6). They had, moreover, precious little of the respectability of modern political parties. Athenians purported to be somewhat embarrassed by their political groups; their thinkers emphasized the need of the state to stand outside class or factional interest. This may help explain why Attic Greek has no neutral word for party — the closest is *stasis*, which usually refers to a seditious group in a civil war.[21]

Methodology

What then were Athenian political groups if not parties? Contemporary scholarship has sidestepped this question: the most common term for an Athenian political group is 'group'.[22] Nor is the problem merely terminological. Current scholarship tends either (a) to have an unnecessarily vague and amorphous notion of an Athenian political group or (b) to focus narrowly on one aspect of the group. Many scholars, for example, write of these groups as if they were solely based on personal association, without considering such unifying principles as class or policy (see below, sect. 'Followings'). Another example is Connor's cogent demonstration of the importance beginning in the 420s of oratory and 'issues politics' to build up mass followings. Unfortunately, Connor has exaggerated the break with the old clientelist politics, which continued in importance, if not exclusive importance. For example, Connor has argued that since Cleon began his political career with a dramatic renunciation of his *philoi*, he relied exclusively on oratory to build a political following; he was the perfect 'new politician'. Cleon was too shrewd, however, to give up so valuable a political tool as *philia*, and it is not surprising to find him in Aristophanes' *Wasps* at a symposium with four friends, or to find two other friends mentioned in other sources. It was brilliant propaganda to proclaim that one's only *philos* was *demos*, but dangerous to mean it.[23]

Common to these various misinterpretations is the failure to subject ancient categories to modern scrutiny. For example, Connor and others have demonstrated the central importance of friendship in traditional — and I would add, postwar — Athenian politics, but they have not gone far enough. By consulting the modern literature — historical, anthropological and political scientific — on friendship, the clientelist and instrumental nature of the Athenian variety becomes clear. Similarly, this modern literature makes it possible to understand more precisely the nature and variety of Athenian political groups.

The following pages offer, I hope, a more precise typology of Athenian politics. This typology is based on scholarly literature that focuses mainly on contemporary, not ancient, examples; hence we must take care to avoid anachronism. Applied sensitively, however, this approach makes it possible for each era to illuminate and clarify the other.[24]

Certain distinctions are fundamental. First, there is a difference between (a) an organized political group and (b) a body of common sympathy, broad similarity of outlook, or shared interest. The first is a cohesive unit, for example a political party; the second lacks structure — it may refer to a group within a party, to sentiments shared by members of several parties, or to interests not organized into any party. Scholars refer to such a loose body as a 'tendency'.[25] In Athens, one should speak for example of an oligarchic tendency but not an oligarchic party, likewise pro-Spartan or imperialist tendencies but not parties.

A second basic distinction is that between professional politicians (the political elite) and the people (the political community) — in Athenian terms, between *hoi politeuomenoi* and *ho demos*. Both groups can be divided further: the first, between a few leaders and other so-called 'lesser orators'; the second, along an informal spectrum ranging from the politically active (e.g., those who frequently attended the assembly) to the occasional participants to the non-participants (*idiotai*). Both professional politicians and the *demos* may have belonged to organized political groups, but the respective groups are likely to have varied considerably. I therefore shall adopt a distinction between (a) the groups of professional politicians, henceforth called elite groups, and (b) the even less-structured units in the political community, henceforth called followings. Let us consider the elite groups first.[26]

Faction

In a non-technical sense, the term faction is no modern invention: it has a long history. An unhappy history, one might add, for faction has been a term of opprobrium since the Romans, 'connoting illegitimacy, if not malevolence and pathology'.[27] Voltaire speaks for many when he defines a faction as 'a seditious party in a state,' adding, with his usual wit: 'The term party is not, in itself, loathsome; the term faction always is.'[28]

In recent years, however, many scholars have argued that the term should be used in a neutral, specialized sense. They define faction not as a seditious party but as either (a) an organized group within a modern political party or (b) an independent unit of political organization that is fundamentally different from a party.[29] If we focus on (b), since ancient Athens had nothing like a modern political party, we shall see how very appropriate the notion of faction is to an Athenian elite political group.

There are various definitions of faction in the literature.[30] One definition, derived from anthropology, fits Athens well. The model has been elaborated by the anthropologists R. W. Nicholas and J. Boissevain (the latter working in Malta) and the political scientist A. J. Nathan (studying Republican China).[31] Nicholas, on whose work Boissevain and Nathan draw, identifies five essential characteristics of a faction: it is (1) a conflict group, (2) a political group, (3) a non-corporate group, whose members (4) are recruited by a leader and (5) are recruited on diverse principles. The first two characteristics are common to all political groups, although factions are particularly prone to conflict.[32]

As for the third, Nathan explains that a faction is made up of one-to-one relationships between leaders (or subleaders) and followers, rather than by such corporate ties as lineage relations, co-membership in an association, or co-membership in a group of more than two blood brothers. It follows that a faction depends upon its leader in a way that a corporate group does not. Only the leader can organize the faction, he has more political power than any of his followers, and his presence is essential: when the leader retires or dies, the faction dissolves. It follows too that the size of a faction is necessarily limited, since there is a limit to a leader's personal connections. On the other hand, these connections might be quite heterogeneous: the leader may draw on, e.g., kin ties, patron-client relations, educational ties, common geographical origins, religious ties, politico-economic ties, shared interest or philosophy, or any combination of these.[33]

The elite groups of Athenian politics may be described with considerable accuracy by these five characteristics. That the groups engaged in constant, at times self-destructive, political conflict will be demonstrated by the narrative of the following chapters. That the leader was essential to the group, that its members felt a personal loyalty to him rather than to a corporate entity, is strongly suggested by ancient terminology, which prefers to any corporate title such names as 'the friends of Pericles' (Plut. *Per.* 10.1–2) or 'the men among whom Theramenes stood out especially' (Arist. *Ath. Pol.* 34.3) or 'those around Thrasybulus and Anytus and Aesimus' (*Hell. Oxy.* 1.2). As Connor argues, moreover, the institution of ostracism also demonstrates that personal not corporate ties were the essence of the Athenian group: why else attack a man rather than an organization?[34]

The members of an Athenian elite group were recruited on diverse principles: Conon's, for example. Even before his return to Athens in 393, Conon employed the family of Nicophemus, his fellow demesmen from Rhamnus, on diplomatic and military missions. It is possible that the family was quite poor before acquiring booty in the Corinthian War (although the source has reason to exaggerate).[35] Other associates of Conon were, however, wealthy. Eunomus, for instance, co-ambassador (with Nicophemus' son Aristophanes) to Dionysius of Syracuse in 393, was a wealthy liturgist who could afford to study with the orator Isocrates and keep up a guest-friendship with Dionysius. Isocrates was a strong admirer of Conon, although it is not clear whether he shared his political counsels. Conon's associates Callias of Alopece and his half-brother Hermogenes were of a family both wealthy (if poorer than in the fifth century) and aristocratic, cult priests at Eleusis. Another political associate was Epicrates of Cephisia. His personal wealth is unknown, but Epicrates' politics favoured the poorer part of the economic scale, the *demos* — a useful constituency to which Conon might be granted access.[36]

Other associates of Conon may be considered later; at this point it is worth examining another case, Alcibiades. Although dead by 403, Alcibiades had made associations that continued to influence politics afterwards. Among Alcibiades' closest associates were his uncle Axiochos and his fellow demesman, Adeimantus, both members of the 'fast set' accused in 415 of parodying the Eleusinian Mysteries.[37] By 411, Alcibiades had begun a lasting association with an untainted and ambitious young general and orator, Thrasybulus, like himself an opponent of the narrow oligarchy of the Four Hundred.[38]

Hence the Athenian political leader enjoyed several different kinds of connections with his followers.

To be sure, there were corporate elements in Athenian elite groups. Kinship ties and common deme membership were not infrequently evoked as a basis of political association, although neither was of overriding importance. A group formed to advance a common financial enterprise might play some political role, such as the group of tax-farmers to which Agyrrhius belonged in 400. In times of revolution, groups of co-conspirators (*synomosiai*) who had sworn oaths to their cause were common.[39]

The most significant corporate element, however, was that of the *hetairiai*. In origin, these were primarily social institutions, lasting associations formed in youth between boys of similar age and class and displaying some affinity to the male fraternities of primitive warrior societies.[40] By the fifth century they had taken on an important political role, becoming, as Thucydides (8.73.3) says, 'associations for the management of lawsuits and elections'.[41] In the late fifth century they seem to have been primarily ologarchic, groups of *gnorimoi*, 'notables,' as Aristotle says (*Ath. Pol.* 34.3), and they organized conspiracies in 411 and 404. After 403 they continued to play a political role, but rarely a secret or subversive one.[42]

It seems unlikely that a majority of Athenian citizens belonged to *hetairiai*, and equally unlikely that many of the political leaders of the period 403–386 formed a political group around a *hetairia*.[43] Even those who did, however, would have found that the group was organized under a leader or leaders for whom the *hetairia* would be named, e.g., 'Charicles and Critias and their *hetairia*' (Lys. 12.55). Even in the exceptional case of a *hetairia*, the tie between member and leader probably mattered more than the ties between individual members.

Thus far, then, Athenian elite groups approximate what modern writers refer to as factions. Before accepting the term, however, three important points remain to be considered: (a) the precise nature of the ties between leader and follower, (b) the size of the group, and (c) the relative importance of policy and pragmatism.

Philia. The leader-follower tie will be considered first. Nathan refers to the one-to-one relation between leader and follower as a 'clientelist tie'. Such a relation between two people sets up well-understood ('although seldom explicit') rights and obligations.

The parties to the tie are dissimilar, often unequal in wealth, status or power. The tie can be abrogated, and is not exclusive; it does not preclude other, similar ties.[44]

In recent years, a host of scholars has recognized the existence of such one-to-one ties, applying various names to them and subsuming a variety of different relationships. G. Foster, for instance, writes of 'the informal, unnamed principle of reciprocity' in a Mexican peasant village, 'serving as the glue that holds society together'. He subdivides this 'dyadic contrast,' as he calls it, into two basic types: 'colleague contracts' between approximate equals and 'patron-client contracts' between unequals.[45]

Similarly, other scholars have focused on one kind of dyadic contract, friendship. Friendship is a universal and variegated phenomenon. In English, the word usually connotes warmth and affection, but it also connotes mutual obligation. It is important to separate the two basic aspects of friendship: (a) the expressive or emotional and (b) the instrumental.[46]

Of the various dyadic contracts, friendship is the most relevant to the Athenian case. Friendship was of fundamental importance in Athenian society.[47] Second only to parent-child and kinship ties in the intensity of its obligations, friendship is central to the thought of many ancient Greek writers.[48] *Philia*, as the Greeks called it, is much broader in its meaning than the English 'friendship'. N. R. E. Fisher writes:

> Linguistically, the most general word for what belongs to a person, is in his group or on his side, is *philos* (noun *philia*), which we usually translate 'friend,' but which, when applied to persons, systematically spans both kin and non-kin, those with whom one has links of mutual aid and benevolence.[49]

Similarly, Connor suggests that *philoi* would be better translated as 'one's own people' than as friends.[50] As he has demonstrated, *philia* was the cement of public as well as private life.[51]

Political *philia* had its emotional aspects, not to be underestimated. Some *philoi* for example shared membership in a *hetairia*, and could trace their association back to youthful friendships in the gymnasia. In this milieu, the formation of comradely bonds or homoerotic attachments which later made political friendships (and enmities) was not uncommon. Not all *philoi* belongs to *hetairiai*, however, and whether they did or not, what they expected from their comrades was not merely affection, but tangible and mutual help. The reader of fifth and fourth-century Athenian documents will find no shortage of references to self-interest. One need not be a cynic to conclude that instrumental friendship, the principle of *do ut des*, was paramount.[52]

Consider, for example, the 'true *philos*' (Dem. 53.7, 8, 12) of Demosthenes 53 *Against Nicostratus*. Two men, Apollodorus and Nicostratus, were neighbours and of approximately the same age, as Apollodorus tells it, and so became friends (53.4). What did the friendship consist of? A. helped N. in various ways; for example, by providing him with slaves. In return, N. managed A.'s farm when A. was away on business. Later, when N. was captured by pirates, he begged A. to provide a ransom, which A., 'pitying him,' did (*ibid.*). In this case, affection is not irrelevant, but mutual interest is the key. Nor were the two friends on an equal footing: A. was the richer and more powerful. Similarly in politics the bond between friends was mainly instrumental.

Another example comes from the postwar period, probably during the Corinthian War. The speaker of Lysias 9, one Polyaenus, has been taken to court for alleged failure to pay a treasury fine. He claims that the suit has been brought by his personal enemies, enemies created by a *philia* of Polyaenus. His explanation is instructive, if self-serving:

> I had become a *philos* of Sostratus before their enmity began, because I knew he had become very prominent in the polis. I became well-known (*gnorimos*) through his power (*dynasteia*), but did not make use of it either to avenge myself on an enemy or to serve a *philos*: for while he lived I was necessarily inactive on account of my age; and when he passed away I injured none of my accusers in word or in deed.
> (Lys. 9.14, Loeb trans. modified)

Once again, it is a question of instrumental friendship.

To take the analysis a step further, one must ask whether this bond was collegial or clientelist. After all, there are many polities, including Rome, where friendship is a euphemism for patron and client. But the Athenians, unlike the Romans, did not speak of patrons and clients at all, and the reason was not merely euphemism. Athenian culture placed an extraordinary emphasis on personal autonomy, and the average Athenian had the economic wherewithal to protect his status: for most citizens, whether farmer, artisan or trader, were independent producers. There was nevertheless substantial inequality in Athenian society, and in politics there are always more underlings than chiefs. Hence, when an Athenian politician spoke of his *philos*, the word might sometimes approximate 'colleague' and other times, depending on the person involved, 'client'. In short, there were often considerable inequalities between *philoi*. The Athenian system of instrumental friendship, for all its egalitarian features, shows many similarities to a patron-client system.[53]

One's responsibilities to one's *philoi* were considerable. They ranged from providing a good meal (Lys. 1.23) to forming a posse to witness a *philos* catching and killing an adulterer in bed with his wife (Lys. 1.23, 27). A prosecutor thought it was credible to say that Thrasybulus' *philos* Ergocles urged his chief to escape his enemies at home by keeping his fleet, occupying Byzantium, and marrying a Thracian princess (Lys. 28.6). Socrates' *philoi* were willing to arrange his illegal escape from justice after his conviction (Plato, *Crito* 45–46). These are, no doubt, exceptional cases all, but in daily political life the tasks of mutual support — organizing followers, lending money, advancing a court case, writing a speech, vilifying an enemy, etc. — may have seemed endless.[54]

At every crucial moment one's *philoi* were expected to be at hand. A particularly dramatic case is Alcibiades' return to the Piraeus in 407 after eight years of exile. Xenophon reports:

> Meanwhile Alcibiades, who had come to anchor close to the shore, did not at once disembark through fear of his enemies; but mounting upon the deck of his ship, he looked to see whether his *philoi* were present. (Xen. 1.4.18, tr. Loeb)

Reassured by the sight of *philoi* and kinsmen, Alcibiades finally disembarked.

In less happy moments as well, the presence of one's *philoi* was expected. A particularly vivid illustration comes from Euripides' *Orestes* of 408. After Orestes' conviction in court, his *philos* Pylades walks him home, weeping and mourning — and also agreeing to join in an act of vengeance, the murder of Orestes' aunt, Helen. Orestes' gratified response may represent Euripides' bitter comment on contemporary Athenian politics:

> Nothing in this world
> Is better than a *philos*. For one good *philos*
> I would not take in trade either power or money
> or all the people of Argos.
>
> (Eur. *Orest.* 1155sqq., tr. Arrowsmith)

Size. If *philia* is to be significant, the number of individuals in a *philia* group is necessarily limited; let the group grow too large and the personal dimension is lost. Only in a small group can the members know and trust each other. The *hetairia* seems to have provided a model of smallness: as Connor argues, it was rarely larger than 'a moderate-sized dinner party'.[55] Moving from tradition to cash, the frequent charge of peculation, writes Sealey of the 390s, argues for small political groups:

> 'The practice of finding "jobs for the boys" is financially feasible only if "the boys" are few in comparison with the tax-payers.'[56]

Philia groups are likely to have varied in size from a dozen or fewer members to several dozens, from the size of a dinner party to a university fraternity or sorority. In one case there seems to have been the very large number of a hundred. Plutarch states that Cimon fought at Tanagra with a hundred *hetairoi* — which, as Connor argues, may be a synonym for *philoi*.[57] With the huge sums he could devote to private political munificence, Cimon may indeed have had a hundred *philoi*, or have cultivated the lieutenants to serve as intermediaries (thus forming what some call a 'complex faction').[58] But a group on this scale was probably rare, certainly after Athens lost the wealth of its empire. Among *hoi politeuomenoi*, therefore, *philia* groups were small. Coalitions, of course, were both possible and frequent, as were disintegrations.[59]

Pragmatism and Policy. Before calling these groups factions, there remains one final point. Many students of factions emphasize their pragmatism. Nathan argues that 'factions operate within a broad ideological consensus while exaggerating the small differences that remain among them.' The result is 'doctrinalism, i.e., the couching of factional struggle for power in terms of abstract issues of ideology, honor, and face.'[60] Leites reaches similar conclusions about the factions of the Fourth French Republic. Nicholson goes even further, asserting that factions are interested in power and nothing but — neither ideology, policy nor class disputes matter.[61]

Some of the most influential students of ancient Greek politics have reached a similar conclusion. Sealey, for instance, one of the leading exponents of the personal or prosopographical approach to politics, writes:

> although it has been seen that Athenian political groups sometimes disagreed on immediate details of policy, the evidence has nowhere suggested any deep and lasting difference of programme. It would seem to follow that a political group in Athens was not, as in a modern state, primarily the protagonist of a policy contrasting with that of its rivals.[62]

Dover has identified three 'moments' in Athenian politics: ideological, economic self-interest, and the association of individuals. The first he doubts ever to have been 'the decisive one at any stage, however critical, of Athenian political history'; the third, he believes, usually mattered most.[63]

Funke, author of a monograph on Athenian politics after the Peloponnesian War, blames Sealey for trying to make too much out of scanty evidence; he doubts whether the sources allow the reconstruction of specific Athenian political groups. Nevertheless, Funke accepts Sealey's basic theoretical premise:

> The existence of power struggles for political influence of various groups will not on the whole be debated here. What must be insisted upon is the impossibility of differentiating these groups by means of constitutional or socio-economic categories. They were, rather, struggles for the consolidation or increase of a personal position of power, which do not presuppose a difference in political goals.[64]

These arguments have considerable merit. A politician does not choose his associates the way a philosopher chooses his doctrines, and political success requires expediency. Clearchus, a Spartan mercenary, was a realist not a cynic in explaining why he chose to march under the rebel Persian prince Cyrus in 401:

> The reason why I wanted Cyrus to be my friend was because I thought that of all his contemporaries he was the best able to help those he wished to help.
> (Xen. *Anab.* 2.5.11)

But a dichotomy between ideologues and opportunists will not do. The scholarly consensus which reduces Athenian politics to a personal power struggle is simplistic, and must be corrected. An Athenian entered politics to help his *philoi*, i.e., 'his own people,' and to hurt his enemies (Xen. *Mem.* 2.6). One does not define 'one's own people' without reference to social class or economic self-interest or even, on occasion, ideas. Moreover, like it or not, a politician usually had to identify himself with some policy, because clientelist ties or personal charisma were rarely enough to win votes in the assembly. Sometimes the policy identification was shallow, sometimes deep.

Foreign policy examples come to mind most easily. One thinks, for instance, of Demosthenes' general hostility to Macedon and his rival Aeschines' general support for Atheno-Macedonian rapprochement, or of Cimon's affection for Sparta and Ephialtes' hostility.[65]

There are domestic political examples too. Athenians had an acute sense of class differences, especially after the civil war of 404/403. The leading elite political groups tended to champion a particular class, or to proclaim as Alcibiades had that they represented all the classes.[66]

The postwar sources abound with references to Athenian class consciousness. The Oxyrhynchus historian, for example, writing of Athens in 395, distinguishes 'the democratic many' from 'the men of reason and property' (*Hell. Oxy.* 1.3). Lysias, writing in the 390s, decries prejudice against the long-haired aristocrats of the Athenian cavalry (Lys. 16 *For Mantitheus* 18). Isocrates, writing at about the same time, pits 'a poor man and of the people' against a rich young man whom he associates with the oligarchy (Isoc. 20 *Against Lochites* 10–11, 19).

The politicians mobilized this class consciousness. Throughout his career, Theramenes for example championed the so-called hoplite class (*infra* Chapter 2). After 403 Archinus continued this policy, without, of course, advocating oligarchy. In the same period Epicrates and Cephalus were the leading *demotikoi*, the champions of the lower class.[67] In these years, ideology was not so much a part of Athenian politics as in the previous decade, when oligarchy was a major issue. After 403 the conflict of world-view between 'the Many' and 'the Few' continued nevertheless to mark Athenian politics: consider, for example, the debate over compensation for attending the assembly (ecclesiastic pay) or the decision to go to war against that paragon of oligarchic virtue, Sparta (see the pro-Spartan remarks in Andocides 3 *On the Peace* 18). In each case, an elite group had to decide which side to choose.

Pressed to choose, the Athenian politician would probably prefer his *philoi* to his principles. But he would prefer not to choose, and prefer that the general policies with which he and his friends were associated were to his advantage. Clientelist ties were the building blocks of elite political groups; leadership, oratory, munificence, and the advocacy of specific policies were what these groups offered the political community. More generally, a political system need not be characterized by one exclusive organizing principle, but may display several complementary ones.[68]

That Athenian politicians lavished money on the *demos* presupposes that 'the *demos* voted for people rather than policies,' S. C. Humphreys writes.[69] It would be more accurate to say that the *demos* never voted for policies without considering the people proposing them. The *demos* was not indifferent to policies, but it never abstracted them from personalities.

To write the history of Athenian politics without the competition of policies is to leave out something of immense importance. The pages of the historians and the orators are full of declarations of policy, from Solon's praise of the middle way (Arist. *Ath. Pol.* 11–12) to Pericles' encomium of democracy in his Funeral Speech (Thuc. 2.34–46) to Demosthenes' denunciation of monarchy in his *Philippics* (Dem. 6.25).

Among practising politicians, there were opportunists like Alcibiades, Peisander or Phrynichus, but it is difficult to doubt the sincere conviction of Cimon or Thucydides son of Melesias to a conservative order, of Antiphon or Charmides to oligarchy, of Ephialtes or Pericles or Thrasybulus to democracy. If Athenian politics was never more than a factional struggle, it is hard to understand why Ephialtes' reforms led to his assassination and, not long afterwards, to a plot to betray Athens to a Peloponnesian army. Neither Thucydides (e.g., 2.65, 8.75, 97), nor the 'Old Oligarch' nor Aristotle (e.g., *Ath. Pol.* 28) reduced Athenian politics to opportunism: their authority is decisive.[70]

Conclusion. Postwar Athens had a vigorous political life dominated by the clash of factions. These were small, informal, rival elite groups, loosely organized by non-corporate ties, sometimes collegial, usually clientelist, i.e., the leader-follower or sub-leader-follower relationship was key. Membership was acquired, not ascribed, and membership was temporary — there was no permanent organization. In theory all members were friends and therefore equals, and in practice responsibilities were reciprocal, but power was hierarchical. A faction was too interested in seeking power to tie itself down to an ideology, but Athenians were too class-conscious and the *demos* too watchful of its interests and too attentive in the assembly for a faction not to identify itself with some general policies.

Followings

The Athenian assembly was more like a town meeting than an elected legislature. There were some more or less regular assembly-goers, primarily city residents and peasants from the nearby Attic plain.[71] From the faction leader's point of view, nevertheless, 'an important element of predictability was lacking,' as M. I. Finley writes.[72] He could not count on party discipline to 'bring out the vote'; he could not even be sure precisely who would be in attendance at a given meeting. If he attempted to 'count heads' on the eve of an important vote, he needed to remember that effective oratory (his or an opponent's) might cancel all predictions. The Athenian politician had to reckon with such factors as spontaneity and crowd psychology far more than a modern legislator must.[73]

The assembly was too informal and too fluid for organized parties. Nevertheless, there is evidence of informal groups of supporters in the assembly upon whose support a faction could draw. Indeed, the political elite spent a great deal of time and energy in organizing such groups. Unfortunately, most scholars have a tendency to ignore these groups, emphasizing like Finley the unpredictability of the assembly, or focusing almost exclusively, like Sealey, Pecorella Longo, Funke and others, on the elite groups.[74] This omission is understandable, for the evidence about popular followings is lacunary. Nevertheless, the sources provide several tantalizing hints of their existence.

That existence is *a priori* likely. It would be surprising if like-minded people did not merge from time to time to support or oppose particular policies — that is, to form what anthropologists call action-sets. As an example, take that mobilized body of opinion that forced the assembly to reopen the Mytilenian Debate in 427 and hence saved Mytilene (Thuc. 3.36). Another example is the young men (*hoi neoteroi*) whom Nicias blames for rashly supporting the Sicilian Expedition (Thuc. 6.12.2–13.1, cf. Athenagoras the Syracusan at 6.38.5). Andocides too may be deemed to be referring to an action-set when he mentions the supporters of the proposed peace treaty of 393/92 (And. 3.33). A series of action-sets that regularly unites again and again, but without any formal structure, might be called a quasi-group. The 'democratic many' (*hoi polloi kai demotikoi*) and the 'men of intelligence and some substance' (*hoi epieikeis kai ousia echontes*) whom the Oxyrhynchus historian describes in the assembly in 395 are two quasi-groups (*Hell. Oxy.* 1.3).[75]

The *philia* system is another reason to credit the existence of action-sets and quasi-groups in the assembly. A man with *philoi* could assume that his *philoi* each had other *philoi*, upon whose support he could sometimes rely. The exchange of gifts and the creation of *philiai* were so basic to Athenian society that it would be odd indeed if *hoi politeuomenoi* had not formed some such ties among the *demos*, and if they never drew upon them in the assembly.[76]

Let us consider several examples in detail: first, the acrimonious debate on the generals following the battle of Arginusae in 406. Although victorious, the generals had failed afterwards to save their own shipwrecked. The assembly had met once, without reaching a decision, and the council was reviewing the matter, when Theramenes, who opposed the generals lest they shift blame to him, made a dramatic move. Xenophon writes:

> After this the Apaturia was celebrated, at which fathers and kinsmen meet together. Accordingly Theramenes and his supporters (*hoi peri ton Theramene*) arranged at the festival with a large number of people, who were clad in mourning garments and had their hair close shaven, to attend the meeting of the assembly, pretending that they were kinsmen of those who had perished, and they persuaded Callixeinus to accuse the generals in the council.
>
> (Xen. 1.7.8. Loeb tr. modified)

This remarkable incident occasions many questions. Among other things, one would like to know just how Theramenes' faction procured the co-operation of the mourners. Perhaps they offered money. Perhaps they appealed to a disinterested sense of justice.

Perhaps they called on *philiai*. Whatever the case, Theramenes' faction was able to mobilize an action-set of supporters.[77]

There are several other, though less dramatic, examples of assembly-packing. Demosthenes accuses Aeschines of encouraging his supporters, who sat around him, of preventing Demosthenes from speaking (18.143). In Demosthenes 57 *Against Eubulides*, Euxitheus accuses his opponent of having packed the deme assembly of Halimous (less than 30 men) with his supporters (57.10–14). Plutarch credits Thucydides son of Melesias with organizing 'the aristocrats' in a single body in the assembly (*Per.* 11.2). Again, one would like to know what cement bonded these groups together.

There were no ostracisms, of course, in the postwar period: the last was in 416. But this case demonstrates an organizational skill that is unlikely to have been forgotten in 13 years. In the ostracism of 416 Nicias and Alcibiades agreed to join forces against a third man, Hyperbolus. There could have been no such agreement unless support in the *demos* had been arranged in advance, before the vote.[78]

What one does not have in these cases is perhaps more obvious than what one does. There were no large-scale, competing sets of clients upon whom one could rely, nor even the loose structure of the elite factions. There was, to be sure, a degree of clientelism in the political community: several examples have been mentioned here, and a thorough survey of all the evidence of the classical period will find others. Nevertheless, action-sets and quasi-groups are a long way from the clientage of, say, Rome. Leadership, oratory, munificence, and the advocacy of policy were, as stated above, more important than clientelism when it came to organizing the political community.

The Athenian politician wanted to build up a faction and a following, and to outdo his rivals. How far was he willing to go in the attempt? What did he consider fair play, and what did he rule out? An answer requires stepping outside of politics into the larger culture of which political mores are a part. It requires an examination of what anthropologists and political scientists call the political culture, which may be defined as the system of beliefs, values and symbols which defines political action.[79]

The spadework has been done in the work of literary critics (e.g., Dover), philosophers (e.g., Adkins), cultural historians (e.g., Walcot), and social scientists (e.g., Gouldner). The following inquiry applies their conclusions to postwar Athenian politics. The central question is the relative degree of cooperation or competition in the political culture. The focus is on four main themes: success, reputation, liberty and loyalty.

Political Culture

Like a modern leader, the Athenian politician wanted power — wanted, like Agyrrhius, 'to do the greatest things in the polis' (Ar. *Eccl.* 104).[80] To a much greater extent than in the modern case, however, he wanted recognition of this power: he wanted honour. This was in part merely a practical acknowledgement, a recognition that in Athens one could not succeed without being well spoken of.[81]

Plato's Socrates expresses this very well in a conversation with the young Alcibiades:

> You think that if you come shortly before the Athenian Assembly — which you expect to occur in a very few days — you will stand forth and prove to the people that you are more worthy of honour than either Pericles or anyone else who has ever existed, and that having proved this you will have the greatest power here in the polis.
>
> (*Alcib.* I 105a–b)

The Athenian esteem of honour was not merely a practical matter, however, for to some, honour was an end in itself.[82] When Xenophon in 401 is offered command of the Ten Thousand, for instance, he tells us that he accepted

> because he thought that he would acquire greater honour among his *philoi* and that his name, when it reached the polis, would have increased in stature.
>
> (*Anab.* 6.1.20)

Here, he is echoing the voice of an earlier generation. 'One's love of honour (*philotimon*),' says Pericles,

> is the only thing that does not grow old, and the last pleasure, when one is worn out with age, is not, as the poet said, making money, but having the respect of one's fellow men.
>
> (Thuc. 2.44.4, tr. Warner, modified)

Athenian politicians of course wanted it all — power and success as well as honour. But none of them would have turned up his nose at a fate like that of Pericles himself, who, for all the failures of his last years, ended on his deathbed, surrounded by Athens' leading men and his surviving *philoi*, 'praising his virtues and the extent of his power and recounting his famous exploits and the number of trophies he had set up' (Plut. *Per.* 38.2, tr. Scott-Kilvert).

On the other hand, what every Athenian politician, like Achilles, feared most was dishonour. In Athens the brand of shame burned with greater fire than it does today, for a number of reasons. First, Athens was a Mediterranean society and a small society, in which face-to-face, personal contacts were the rule.[83] Everyone was watching, as the very language shows: Attic Greek uses the verb 'to be regarded as' where English uses 'to be'. Politics was intensely personal. Political speeches made frequent use of *ad hominem* attacks, including references to a man's personal expenditures, his parents, his love life.[84]

Second, the individual carried the burden of not only his own reputation, but of his whole family and his *philoi*. So, for example, Alcibiades' son was prosecuted c. 397 for his late father's double-dealing in a chariot race of 416 (Isoc. 16). When Eratosthenes allegedly seduced the wife of the speaker of Lysias 1, he brought disgrace not only upon the woman and the cuckold but also their children (Lys. 1.4).

Third, ancient ethics placed more weight on results than intentions. To use Dodds' now-famous characterization, Athens was a 'shame culture' rather than a 'guilt culture'. The consequences were twofold. On the one hand, the shame of failure was not mitigated by a sense of inner innocence. On the other hand, this created a strong incentive to find someone else to blame, a point that has not received sufficient attention.[85]

An incident in Aristophanes *Ploutos* provides a good example. When the god Wealth miraculously regains his eyesight, he confesses to shame (*aischyne*) for his former deeds, in which he bestowed bounty upon the unworthy. At the same time, though, he is anxious for all people to know that the responsibility was not his; no, he was tricked by others (771–81). He feels shame, but not guilt.[86] One suspects that real life Athenians acted similarly. Conon, for example, prosecuted Adeimantus of Scambonidae in 393 for treason at Aegospotami twelve years earlier — hence beating off any questions about Conon's own behaviour at that disastrous encounter (Dem. 19.161).

In Athenian politics, then, reputation was everything. But what was held in the highest repute? The speaker of Lysias 7 helps out by recognizing three possible motives for his opponent's action: greed, patriotism and vengeance upon his enemies (Lys. 7.20). Not surprisingly, the first motive is universally despised in Athenian writings and the second universally praised, but perhaps more surprising is the equal if not greater praise bestowed upon the third.[87] 'The excellence (*arete*) of a man,' says Xenophon's Socrates, 'is to conquer his friends in benefaction and his enemies in harm' (Xen. *Mem.* 2.6.35). Polyaenus, a small-fry politician during the Corinthian War, repeats this well-known Greek maxim to an Athenian jury: 'I believe that it has been ordained to treat one's enemies badly and one's friends well' (Lys. 9.20). It is important to remember that this rule enjoins two kinds of behaviour, and that it makes vengeance a moral obligation, even an inherited obligation (Lys. 32.22, 14.2). The prosecutor of Agoratus, for example, claims to be avenging the late Dionysodorus, both his brother-in-law and cousin, as well as other Athenians. 'I, therefore, gentlemen,' he tells the court, 'consider it an act of justice and piety in all of you as well as myself to take vengeance as far as each of us is able' (Lys. 13.3). Hence, when Conon returned to Athens in 393, the polis would have benefited had he given up his old enmity toward Thrasybulus, but his obligation of vengeance would have been neglected (*infra*, Chapter 4). Alcibiades was no longer alive after 403 to feel his opponents' stings, so they directed them against his son and his former comrades Adeimantus and Thrasybulus. The speaker of Lysias 14–15 *Against Alcibiades* states his point bluntly: to help his *philos*, the prosecutor Archestratides, and to punish his enemy, Alcibiades' son (Lys. 15.12). Had Athenians loved their country more and their desire for vengeance less there would have been far fewer divisive political trials between 403 and 386: as it is, the trials of 10 military men and of at least 15 orators, officials and statesmen, are recorded, as well as of Socrates the philosopher and of Alcibiades' son Alcibiades.[88]

If vengeance undermined patriotism, so did another Athenian trait, competitiveness (*philonikia*), which Lysias (2.16) praises along with love of honour (*philotimia*). The ancient Olympiad had no prizes for second or third place. Nor did the ambitious Athenian wish to become a team player; he wanted to win.[89] 'If you are better than those whom you encounter,' Demosthenes writes to a boy, 'do not cease trying to excel everyone else too; consider that your aim in life should be to become foremost of *all*' (Dem. 61.52). A platitude, no doubt, but not an empty one.[90]

When, for example, Conon returned to Athens in triumph from victories at Cnidos and the Greek cities of Asia Minor, there was no question of his sharing the glory with his seconds-in-command or his men. The assembly voted him, among other honours, two commemorative statues, one in bronze, making Conon the first Athenian so honoured since the tyrannicides of 514, Harmodius and Aristogiton (Dem 20.71). One suspects that Thrasybulus would have been no more modest had he the support of Persian money. He too wanted the limelight: 'salvation peeked out,' says Praxagora in the *Ecclesiazusae*, referring perhaps to the proposed peace of 392, 'but Thrasybulus is angry because he is not sent for' (202–203).

When the political realities demanded generosity, Thrasybulus could be magnanimous: in 403, for example, when, bowing to Spartan power, he offered amnesty to his former oligarchic opponents (Xen. 2.4.42). All too often though, Athenian politicians were not so highminded; they treated the contest of politics as a zero-sum game, in which their victory required another man's defeat.[91] They display again and again a dangerous tendency to press a victory too far or to seek vengeance for a defeat, to place a private quarrel before the public good.[92] Callias of Alopece, for instance, thought nothing of stirring up the wounds of the affair of the Herms of 415 in order to beat Andocides of Kydathenaion to an heiress in 400 (And. 1.117–23). Nor did Conon scruple at reawakening memories of the defeat at Aegospotami when he prosecuted Adeimantus, thereby both protecting his own reputation and attacking the *philos* of his old enemy, Alcibiades. Finally, Thrasybulus himself is open to suspicion for his behaviour in the Demaenetus affair of 395 (*Hell. Oxy.* 1.2). Withholding support from Conon's fleet may have been simple prudence on Thrasybulus' part, but it also prevented undue credit from going to an old rival; Thrasybulus was much more enthusiastic about fighting some eight months later, when he had both the support of his old allies in Boeotia and a command for himself (*infra*, Chapter 4).

Along with the problem of competitiveness goes that of envy (*phthonos*). The audience in an Athenian lawcourt *c.* 400 seems to have believed both that envy was wrong and that it was all too common. For example, the speaker of Lysias 24, a cripple accused of undeservedly pocketing a state pension, argues that his prosecutor's motive is envy of a better citizen, even an infirm one. He is careful to deny that he is the prosecutor's enemy, for enmity would give the prosecution a moral sanction, while envy does not (Lys. 24.2,3). Likewise, Xenophon writes that the jurors who condemned Socrates in 399 were envious of his divine voice (*Ap.* 14). Both charges are self-serving, of course, but they are meant to strike a chord in the audience. It is worth asking whether envy was an element in the rivalries between the major politicians of the postwar period: e.g., Conon and Thrasybulus (*infra*, Chapter 4), Callias and Andocides (And. 1), or the unnamed prosecutor and Thrasybulus' lieutenants Ergocles and Philocrates (Lys. 28–29).[93]

Along with envy of others there was sometimes a proud and oversensitive self-esteem, that strain in the Athenian character that made cooperation into slavery and compromise into cowardice, that made the freedom of a tyrant seductive.[94] True enough, Solon, the great compromiser, was a hero of Athenian history; nor were the Athenians, whom Aristotle praises for their 'habitual mildness' (*Ath. Pol.* 22.4), so violent as some Greeks. But they were harsh enough to drive Aristotle into exile, prickly enough to admire the courage to stake out a difficult position and stick to it against all odds. When Plato's Socrates prides himself (*Ap.* 33a) on refusing to change his beliefs to suit others, he is following in the tradition of Pericles and Cleon and even the Sophoclean heroes Oedipus and Antigone.[95] The Athenian may have understood the importance of compromise, but he was often impelled along another path by powerful motives.

The results of this survey of political culture c. 400 may now be summed up. The Athenian politician was ambitious and aggressive, intent on reaching the top of the mountain and claiming it for his own. His public reputation, his honour, was of immense concern. He was devoted to his *philoi* and equally hostile to his enemies. He would try equally to reward every favour and avenge every insult. Patriotism, intelligence honed by training in oratory, and unflagging energy were his virtues; a taste for vengeance, envy, and the refusal to submit to the rules of others his vices.[96]

In the wake of Athens' defeat in the Peloponnesian War and the civil wars of 411 and 404–403, some of the city's finest minds parted company with the vices and tried to foster the virtues. Sophocles, Aristophanes, Thucydides, Lysias all spoke of the need for unity, reason and moderation.[97]

But great minds move at a faster speed than do those of ordinary men or even well-educated politicians. Socrates knew that the Athenian soul had to be reformed; Anytus had him prosecuted. But it was Anytus who won generalships and a leading position in the assembly; Socrates won only martyrdom. In the political culture of Athens, the cooperative values which hold society together lived in an uneasy symbiosis with the powerful values of atomistic competition: *philotimon, arete, philonikia* and *philia*. Whether Athenian politicians would be able to slip out of the complex cords of jealousy and enmity, tied more tightly than ever after a generation of defeat and revolution, is a major question for the political history of Athens after the Peloponnesian War.

This study of politicians, of factions, followings and political culture, has demonstrated the considerable tensions — the 'flip side' of an admirable vitality — in the Athenian polity *c.* 400. In order to understand these tensions more fully, it is necessary to broaden the context. Let us turn to society and economy.

Notes

1. M. I. Finley, 'Introduction: Desperately Foreign', in *Aspects of Antiquity, Discoveries and Controversies* (New York: 1968), 1–7.
2. The metaphor is D. W. Brogan's, Foreword to N. Leites, *On the Game of Politics in France* (Stanford: 1959), viii.
3. Pericles: *PA* 11811, *APF* 455–60. Decline of aristocrats in Athenian politics: W. R. Connor, *NP* 9–14, 151–62; Jones, *AD* 130.
4. Warship: e.g. the speaker of Lysias 25.12–13 (399?), cf. *APF* xvii–xxxi. Statue: Thrasybulus, Paus. 9.11.6. Hobnobbing with kings: Conon and Evagoras, Isoc. 5.62; Ctesias F 30; Diod. 13.106.6, 14.39.1; Nepos *Conon* 1; Justin 5.6.10. Sophistic Education: e.g., Callias, son of Hipponicus, 'a man who has spent more money on sophists than everyone else put together' (Plato *Ap.* 20a). Sources of wealth: Connor, *NP* 151–62. Tanners: H. Michell, *The Economics of Ancient Greece*[2] (Cambridge: 1957), 170–1. Athenian politicians were men of property: S. Perlman, 'The Politicians in the Athenian Democracy of the Fourth Century BC', *Athenaeum* n. s. 41 (1963), 332–6; *Idem*, 'Political Leadership in Athens in the Fourth Century BC', *PP* 22 (1967), 162. Terminology: M. H. Hansen argues that *rhetores kai strategoi* is the closest Athenian equivalent to our notion of politician; see 'The Athenian "Politicians", 403–322 BC', *GRBS* 24 (1983), 33–55.
5. See B. S. Strauss, 'The Cultural Significance of Bribery and Embezzlement in Athenian Politics: The Period 403–386 BC as a Case Study', *AncW* (1985); *APF* xvii–xxxi; Adkins, *MVPB* 123–5.
6. See, for example, Aristophanes' caricature of Cleon, the Paphlagonian in *Knights*, who squeezes the wealthy *eisphora*-payers. Ar. *Knights* 774–76, 912–18, 923–26; cf. Thuc. 3.19.1; W. E. Thompson, 'Athenian Leadership: Expertise or Charisma?', *CC* 156–7.
7. Adkins, *MVPB* 124.
8. Assembly meetings: M. H. Hansen, 'How Often Did the *Ecclesia* Meet?', *GRBS* 18 (1977), 43–70. Council and Court meetings: *Idem*, 'How Often Did the

Political Behaviour in Postwar Athens 37

Athenian *Dicasteria* Meet?', *GRBS* 20 (1979), 243–6. Cimon: Plut. *Cimon* 14–15. Phidias: Plut. *Per.* 31. Socrates: Plato *Ap.* 326. Political trials: Perlman, 'Politicians', 342. Full-time job: Ibid., 340–39; Jones, *AD* 128.
  9. Davies, *WPW* 91–105.
  10. Conon's expenditures: *APF* 508–9, *infra*, chap. 5. Ecclesiastic pay: Arist. *Ath. Pol.* 41.3, *infra*, chap. 4. Long Walls: Xen. 4.8.9, Diod. 14.85.2–4, Dem. 20.68–69. Theozotides: see R. Stroud, 'Theozotides and the Athenian Orphans', *Hesperia* 40 (1971), 298–9.
  11. Jones, *AD* 128; Davies *WPW* 125–6.
  12. Thrasybulus: Xen. 2.4, 4.8.25–31, Isoc. 18.23, *Hell. Oxy.* 1.2, Nepos *Thrasyb.*, Paus. 1.29.3. Agyrrhius: general 390/89 (Diod. 14.99.5). Anytus: general 410/409 (Arist. *Ath. Pol.* 27.5). Archinus: often a general (Dem. 24.135). Thrasybulus of Collytus: general 387/86 (Xen. 5.1.26, cf. Lys. 26). See J. Roberts, 'Athens' so-called Unofficial Politicians', *Hermes* 10 (1982), 354–62.
  13. E. g., Connor, *NP passim*; Finley, 'Athenian Demagogues', in Finley, ed., *Studies in Ancient Society* (London: 1974), 1–25; Davies, *Wealth* 114–17; Thompson, 'Athenian Leadership', *CC* 153–9.
  14. On these politicians, see *infra*, chaps. 4–5. On Callistratus' prosecution, see Philochorus *FGrH* 328 F 149a. An earlier example is Pericles' prosecution of Cimon, Arist. *Ath. Pol.* 27.1. For the modern Greek case, see J. K. Campbell, *Honour, Family and Patronage* (Oxford: 1964), 280–1.
  15. L. Whibley, *Political Parties in Athens During the Peloponnesian War* (Cambridge: 1889), 38–9, 121.
  16. G. Grote, *History of Greece*, vol. 5 (London: 1870) 130, 210–11, 216–20; G. Gilbert, *Beiträge zur innern Geschichte Athens im Zeitalter des peloponnesischen Krieges* (Leipzig: 1877), 101–4; K. J. Beloch, *Attische Politik* 2–3, 6–8.
  17. T. Walek-Czernecki, 'Les partis politiques de l'antiquité et dans les temps modernes, une comparaison', *Eos* 32 (1929), 199–214. See L. Pearson, 'Party Politics and Free Speech in Democratic Athens', *GRBS* 7 (1937), 41–9; O. Reverdin, 'Remarques sur la vie politique d'Athènes au Ve siècle', *MH* 2 (1945), 200–12; R. Sealey, 'Callistratos', 179–81; Perlman, 'Politicians', 354; 'Political Leadership', 166–7. Connor, *NP* 5–9, 30–2; K. J. Dover, *Lysias and the Corpus Lysiacum* (Berkeley, Cal.: 1971) 48–51; C. Pecorella Longo, '*Eterie' e gruppi politici nell'Atene del IV secolo a.c.* (Florence: 1971), 9; P. J. Rhodes, 'On labelling 4th-century politicians', *LCM* 3 (1978), 207–11.
  18. J. de Romilly, review of K. D. Stergiopoulos, *Ta Politika Kommata ton Archaion Athenon* (Athens: 1955), *REG* 69 (1956) 459; Jones, *AD* 137; Connor *NP* 73–5; M. I. Finley, 'Athenian Demagogues', 10–17; O.Aurenche, *Les Groupes d'Alcibiade, de Léogoras, et de Teucros* (Paris: 1974), 7–9; Funke, *HA* 1 n. 1.
  19. 'Party Development and the American Mainstream', in Chambers and Burnham, eds, *The American Party Systems, Stages of Political Growth* (New York: 1967), 5.
  20. Assembly attendance: M. H. Hansen, 'How Many Athenians Attended the *Ecclesia*?', *GRBS* 17 (1976), 115–34. Population: *infra*, chap. 3.
  21. Finley, 'Athenian Demogogues', 5–6; Pearson, 'Party Politics', 42. On στάσις see Reverdin, 'Remarques', 211+n.6; O. Aurenche, *Groupes* 10–15; Lintott, *Civil Strife* 34, 76.
  22. Sealey refers to 'political groups' in 'Callistratos', 180; Jones, 'groups or cliques', *AD* 131; Perlman, 'political group or political faction', in 'Politicians', 350–3; Connor, 'political group', *NP* 67; Pecorella Longo, '*gruppo politico*', in '*Eterie*', *passim*; Aurenche entitles his book *Groupes*; Funke refers to '*Gruppen*' or '*Gruppierungen*', in *HA* 23–4. Mossé, on the other hand, refers to 'party conflict', *Athens in Decline* 53, although sometimes with quotation marks — '*parti*', *Fin de la démocratie athénienne* (Paris: 1961), 287. Dover recognizes the fluid and personal nature of Athenian politics, but notes that 'it might be pedantic, and sometimes

cumbrous, to do away with the word "party" in all discussion of Athenian politics' (*Lysias* 50).
   23. Ar. *Wasps* 1220–21; Ar. *Knights* 1183 + schol; *PA* 7251–52; cf. Connor, *NP* 130–31. Connor earlier argues that an innovative politician like Cleon could win power 'by direct appeal to the citizenry without the tedious apprenticeship imposed by the system of political friendship without the slow aggregation of alliances and coalitions' (118). This is too absolute a dichotomy, however: Cleon was able to win more by his oratory than most men, but still needed *philoi*.
   24. See the methodological remarks (referring to China) of J. B. Starr, *Ideology and Culture, An Introduction to the Dialectic of Contemporary Chinese Politics* (New York: 1973), 117–18.
   25. Pearson, 'Party Politics', 42; Reverdin, 'Remarques', 212; Jones, *AD* 131; Connor, *NP* 64 n. 4; R. Rose, 'Parties, Factions, and Tendencies in Britain', *Political Studies* 12 (1964), 33–46.
   25. For the distinction between *hoi politeuomenoi* and *ho demos*, see Perlman, 'Politicians', 330. Cf. Aesch. 1.165: οὐκ ὢν δ' ἰδιώτης, ἀλλὰ πρὸς τὰ κοινὰ προσιών. For elite vs. community, see F. G. Bailey, *Stratagems and Spoils, A Social Anthropology of Politics* (New York: 1969), 23. Cf. Hansen's classification of Athenian politicians in 'Athenian "Politicians"', 43–9.
   27. F. P. Belloni and D. C. Beller, eds, *Faction Politics: Political Parties and Factionalism in Comparative Perspective* (Santa Barbara, Cal.: 1978), 6.
   28. Voltaire, article on 'Faction' in the *Encyclopédie* vol. 13 (Geneva: 1778), 765, cited in G. Sartori, *Parties and Party Systems: A Framework for Analysis* (Cambridge, Eng.: 1976), 1–3.
   29. See Beller and Belloni, 'The Study of Factions', in Belloni and Beller, *Faction Politics* 3–17.
   30. Beller and Belloni, 'Study of Factions', 417.
   31. R. W. Nicholas, 'Factions: a Comparative Analysis', in M. Banton, ed., *Political Systems and the Distribution of Power* (London: 1965), 21–61; *Idem*, 'Segmentary Factional Political Systems', in M. Swartz, V. W. Turner, and A. Tuden, eds, *Political Anthropology* (Chicago: 1966) 49–59. A. J. Nathan, *Peking Politics, 1918–1923: Factionalism and the Failure of Constitutionalism* (Berkeley: 1975), esp. 29–43; *Idem*, 'An Analysis of Factionalism in Chinese Communist Politics', in Belloni and Beller, *Faction Politics*, 387–414; J. Boissevain, 'Factions, Parties, and Politics in a Maltese Village', *American Anthropologist* 66 (1964), 1275–87; *Idem*, *Friends of Friends, Networks, Manipulators and Coalitions* (Oxford: 1974), 192–200.
   32. N. K. Nicholson, 'The Factional Model and the Study of Politics', *Comparative Political Studies* 5 (1972), 299, 301–3.
   33. Nathan, *Peking Politics* 29, 32, 36.
   34. Connor, *NP* 73–5.
   35. *Hell. Oxy.* 15.1, cf. *APF* 201–2; Isoc. 9.51; Xen. 4.8.8; Lys. 19.19–21, 28.
   36. Eunomus: Lys. 19.19–20, Isoc. 15.93; cf. Seager, 'TCAI', 104. Isocrates: Ps.-Plut. *Vit. X. Orat.* 837b. Cf. Münscher, 'Isokrates', *RE* 9 (1916) col. 2170. Callias and Hermogenes: Xen. *Hell.* 4.8.12, *Mem.* 4.8.4; Plato *Crat.* 384a, 391b–c; cf. Sealey, 'Callistratos', 182–3. Epicrates of Cephisia: *Hell. Oxy.* 2.2. For further discussion of each case, see *infra*, chap. 5.
   37. Axiochus: Aurenche, *Groupes* 56. Adeimantus: B. S. Strauss, 'Aegospotami Reexamined', *AJP* 104 (1983) 30. Mysteries: And. 1.116.
   38. Strauss, 'Thrasybulus vs. Conon', 42–3.
   39. Kinship: As the following discussion indicates, kinship, although significant, was not as important in Athenian politics as *philia* was. See S. C. Humphreys, *The Family, Women, and Death, Comparative Studies* (London: 1983), 26–8, and H. Hutter's comparison of Greek and Roman society, *Politics as Friendship* (Waterloo, Ont.: 1978), 33–6. Agyrrhius: And. 1.122. Conspirators: Aurenche, *Groupes* 32–41.
   40. Calhoun, *AthenianClubs* 4–9; Hutter, *Politics as Friendship* 26–37.

41. Calhoun, *Athenian Clubs* 97.
42. Aurenche, *Groupes* 25–6, 28–32; Percorella Longo, '*Eterie*' 156.
43. See Connor, *NP* 28 n. 43.
44. Nathan, *Peking Politics* 29.
45. G. M. Foster, 'The Dyadic Contract: A Model for the Social Structure of a Mexican Peasant Village', in J. M. Potter, M. N. Diaz and G. M. Foster, eds, *Peasant Society: A Reader* (Boston: 1967), 214, 216. Cf. J. D. Powell, 'Peasant Society and Clientelist Politics', *APSR* 64 (1970), 411–25.
46. E. Wolf, 'Kinship, Friendship, and Patron-Client Relationships in Complex Societies', in M. Banton, ed., *The Social Anthropology of Complex Societies* (London: 1966), 10. Cf. R. E. Reina, 'Two Patterns of Friendship in a Guatemalan Community', *American Anthropologist* 61 (1959), 44–50. Both are cited by Hutter, *Politics as Friendship* 34.
47. I take Connor's discussion in *NP* 30–66 as my starting point. See also L. Dugas, *L'Amitié antique*[2] (Paris: 1914), 232–70; J. Ferguson, *Moral Values in the Ancient World* (London: 1958), 53–75; L. Pearson, *Popular Ethics in Ancient Greece* (Stanford: 1962), 86–8; Dover, *GPM* 180–4, 273–8; N. R. E. Fisher, *Social Values in Classical Athens* (London: 1976), 18–20; Hutter, *Politics as Friendship*, esp. 25–56 (which, however, overestimates popular participation in *hetairiai*).
48. Dover, *GPM* 273; Dugas, *L'amitié antique* 232–70.
49. Fisher, *Social Values* 5.
50. Connor, *NP* 31.
51. Connor, *NP* 64–5, cf. 30–66.
52. *Hetairiai*: Plato, *Laws* 636 a–b; Calhoun, *Athenian Clubs* 29; Hutter, *Politics as Friendship* 29; Humphreys, *Family, Women, and Death* 27–30. *Philoi* and *hetairoi*: Connor, *NP* 28 n. 43, 29 n. 47, 30–1. Instrumental Friendship: *contra*, Hutter, *Politics as Friendship* 34.
53. On Athenian terminology see Connor, *NP* 18. On personal autonomy, S. C. Humphreys, 'Economy and Society in Classical Athens', *AdSNSdP* 2nd ser. 39 (1970) 1–26. On 'friends' as clients see P. A. Brunt, '*Amicitia*' in the Late Roman Republic, *PCPS* n.s. 11 (1965), 8. On applying the term 'client' to Athenian politics, see Finley, *Politics in the Ancient World* (Cambridge: 1983), 40–1.
54. Connor, *NP* 36–43; Fisher, *Social Values* 18–20; Humphreys, *Family, Women, and Death* 28.
55. Connor, *NP* 27.
56. Sealey, 'Callistratos', 180.
57. Plut. *Cim.* 17; Connor, *NP* 28 n. 43.
58. Nathan, *Peking Politics* 32–7.
59. Connor, *NP* 70–73. Nathan refers to the 'cycle of consensus formation and decline' characteristic of factional politics, *Peking Politics* 39.
60. Nathan, *Peking Politics* 39, 40–1.
61. Leites, *Game of Politics in France* 11; Nicholson, 'Factional Model', 301.
62. Sealey, 'Callistratos', 202.
63. Dover, *Lysias* 9.
64. Funke, *HA* 23–4.
65. For recent discussions, see on Demosthenes and Aeschines, G. Cawkwell, *Philip of Macedon* (London: 1978) 118–23; on Cimon and Pericles, D. Kagan, *The Outbreak of the Peloponnesian War* (Ithaca, N.Y.: 1969), 56–74.
66. E. Lévy, *Athènes devant la défaite de 404: Histoire d'un crise idéologique* (Paris: 1976), 281–2.
67. Theramenes: Arist. *Ath. Pol.* 293. Epicrates and Cephalus: Bruce, *HCHO* 56–7.
68. For a general statement, see G. T. Mavrogordatos, *Stillborn Republic, Social Coalitions and Party Strategies in Greece 1922–1936* (Berkeley: 1975), 16–17.
69. Humphreys, *Family, Women, and Death* 29.

70. Alcibiades: Thuc. 8.48.4. Phrynichus: Lys. 25.9, Thuc. 8.68.3. Peisander: Lys. 25.9. Antiphon: Thuc. 8.68.1–2; *HCT* vol. 5, 170–77. I am grateful to D. Kagan for letting me profit from his discussion of these four figures in his forthcoming book, *The Fall of the Athenian Empire*. Cimon: Arist. *Ath. Pol.* 26.1, 28.2; Plut. *Cim.* 15–16. Thucydides son of Melesias: Arist. *Ath. Pol.* 28.2; Plut. *Per.* 11–12, 14–15. Ephialtes: Arist. *Ath. Pol.* 25; Plut. *Cim.* 15–16, *Per.* 9–10. Pericles: Thuc. 2.34–46; Arist. *Ath. Pol.* 27.1–4, 28.1–2; Plut. *Per.* 9–16. Thrasybulus: *infra* chap. 4. Plot: Thuc. 1.107.4–6.
71. W. G. Forrest, *The Emergence of Greek Democracy, 800–400 BC* (London: 1966), 30–1.
72. Finley, 'Athenian Demagogues', 11.
73. Finley, 'Athenian Demogogues', 11–15; Reverdin, 'Remarques', 212.
74. Finley: 'Athenian Demagogues', 11–15. Sealey: 'Callistratos', *passim*; Pecorella Longo: '*Eterie*', *passim*; Funke, *HA*, *passim*.
75. See A. C. Mayer, 'The Significance of Quasi-Groups in the Study of Complex Societies', in Banton, ed., *Social Anthropology* 97–122; J. A. Barnes, 'Networks and Political Process', in J. C. Mitchell, ed., *Social Networks in Urban Situations* (Manchester, Eng.: 1969), 51–76; J. Boissevain, *Friends of Friends* 186–91.
76. Gifts: Strauss, 'Cultural Significance of Bribery', 72–3.
77. Xenophon's story is doubted by Andrewes, 'The Arginousai Affair', *Phoenix* 28 (1974), 118.
78. Hyperbolus: Plut. *Alc.* 13; Connor, *NP* 79–84.
79. S. Verba, 'Comparative Political Culture', in L. W. Pye and Verba, eds., *Political Culture and Political Development* (Princeton: 1965), 513–17.
80. τὰ μέγιστα πράττει ἐν τῇ πόλει. Cf. the similar expression of Isoc. 18.23, 'Thrasybulus and Anytus are the most powerful men in the city,' μέγιστον μὲν δυνάμενοι ἐν τῇ πόλει.'
81. On the importance of a good reputation in Athenian politics, see Adkins, *Merit and Responsibility*, 154–6; *MVPB* 55–6, 76–7; Gouldner, *Enter Plato* 81–2; Dover, *GPM* 226–9, 236–42. To make honour and shame two of the basic standards of society's judgements remains today typically Mediterranean, as J. G. Peristiany argues in the introduction to Peristiany, ed., *Honour and Shame* (London: 1965), 9–10). Cf. in the same anthology Peristiany 139–70 and J. K. Campbell 173–90; Walcot, *Greek Peasants* 57–76.
82. Honour: Walcot, *Greek Peasants*, 75–6.
83. As Peristiany generalizes,
Honour and Shame are the constant preoccupation of individuals in small scale, exclusive societies, where face-to-face personal, as opposed to anonymous, relations are of paramount importance and where the social personality of the actor is as significant as his office.
(*Honour and Shame* 11).
84. On Attic usage, see Dover, *GPM* 226. Personal expenditures: e.g. Thuc. 6.16.1–4, Lys. 25, 12–13. Parents: e.g., Aesch. 3.171–73, Dem. 18.259–60. Love life: Aesch. 1 *passim*.
85. On Athens as a 'shame culture' see Adkins, *Merit and Responsibility* 154–6, *MVPB* 61; *Enter Plato* 81–5. E. R. Dodds introduced the term to classicists in *The Greeks and the Irrational* (Berkeley: 1960), 17–18, 28, 43. Cf. also Adkins' view that Greece was a 'results' culture, *From the Many to the One* (Ithaca: 1970), 29ff., 42ff.
86. Cited by Dover, *GPM* 240.
87. On greed and patriotism see Dover, *GPM* 171–2, 301–6.
88. Military men: Adeimantus, general 405/404, tried 393 (Xen. 2.1.30, Dem. 19.161); Speaker of Isocrates 18, trierarch 405/404 (Isoc. 18.59); Polyaenus (Lys. 9) and Theomnestus (Lys. 10–11), hoplites in the Corinthian War; Ergocles, general 390/89 (Lys. 28–29); Philocrates (Lys. 29.3) trierarch and purser 390/89; Agyrrhius,

general 389/88 (Diod. 14.99.5, Dem. 24.135; Sealey, 'Callistratus' 140); Pamphilus of Keiriadai, general 389/88 (Xen. 5.1.1–2, 5); Dionysius, general 387/86 (Xen. 5.1.26, Dem. 19.180); Thrasybulus of Collytus, general 387/86 (Xen. 5.1.26, Dem. 24.134).

Orators, statesmen, ambassadors, magistrates: Eratosthenes, member of the Thirty (Lys. 12); Agoratus, alleged informer under the Thirty (Lys. 13); Philon, *bouleutes* c. 403 (Lys. 31.2); magistrate of Lysias 21, 403/402; Andocides, orator 400 (And. 1); Nicomachus, *ton nomon anagrapheus*, 399 (Lys. 30); Epicrates of Cephisia and Phormisius, ambassadors to Persia (*infra*, chap. 4 n. 36); Mantitheus, *bouleutes* between 393 and 390 (Lys. 16); Aristophanes, ambassador to Evagoras and Aristophanes' father, Nicophemus, office unknown, 391 (Lys. 19); the four ambassadors negotiating peace with Sparta 392/91 — Epicrates of Cephisia, Andocides of Kydathenaion, Cratinus of Sphettus, Euboulides of Eleusis (Philochorus *FGrH* 328 F149a); Epicrates (of Cephisia?) and his fellow envoys, now charged with embezzlement and earlier with bribery (Lys. 27); Onomasas the ambassador (Lys. 27); Evandros, archon 382/81 (Lys. 26). Also, possibly Anytus (*infra*, chap. 4).

Alcibiades' son: tried c. 397 (Isoc. 16) and 395 (Lys. 14–15), the latter time a cavalryman.

Contra, Cloché argues for Athenian mildness, 'Les hommes politiques et la justice populaire dans l'Athènes du IVe siècle', *Historia* 9 (1960), 80–95.

89. On Athenian competitiveness, see Gouldner, *Enter Plato* 45–55; Walcot, *Greek Peasants* 77–93; Walcot, *Greek Popular Morality* 229–34. On the Olympic Games, see M. I. Finley and H. W. Pleket, *The Olympic Games: The First Thousand Years* (New York: 1976), 22.

90. Cited by Dover, *GPM* 232.

91. Gouldner, *Enter Plato* 49, 52–3.

92. Cf. Gouldner, *Enter Plato* 13; Adkins, *MVPB* 126–33; Dover, *GPM* 181–4. According to Nathan, Chinese Republican factions of the 1920s observed a 'code of civility' in their conflicts, which limited the harm they might do each other (*Peking Politics* 38). The Athenians were less restrained.

93. On envy see Walcot, *Envy and the Greeks* (Warminster, Eng: 1978), 67–76, who cites Lysias' cripple and Xenophon's Socràtes; Gouldner, *Enter Plato* 55–8; Walcot, *Greek Peasants* 77–93.

94. On the peculiar Greek concept of freedom see Adkins, *MVPB* 68. On the Greek view of tyranny, see A. Andrewes, *The Greek Tyrants* (New York: 1963), 25.

95. Pericles: Thuc. 1.140.1, 2.61.2; Cleon: Thuc. 3.38.1.

96. See Knox, *Oedipus at Thebes* (New Haven: 1957), 67–77.

97. For a thorough analysis of their views see Lévy, *Athènes devant la défaite* 209–22.

2 Society and Economy in Postwar Athens

Athenian politics after 403 cannot be understood apart from Athenian society and the economy, which were affected so drastically by the Peloponnesian War, especially in its last phase (413–404) and by the civil war of 404–403. This chapter considers (a) the effect on society and economy of the Iono-Decelean and civil wars, (b) the consequent class and geographical divisions, and (c) the impact of these divisions on politics. Chapter 3 turns to the demographic consequences of the wars, which themselves had a major political impact.

First it is necessary to define briefly the main terms used in this chapter to describe social and economic classes. Confusion has resulted in the past from the common distinction in the sources between *plousioi* and *penetes*, usually translated as 'rich and poor', but more accurately understood as 'the wealthy, leisured people and the people who have to work for a living'.[1] I employ the following terms:

(a) the liturgical class, the *c*. 300 (or perhaps fewer in the hard times of the 390s) wealthiest Athenians whom Davies has identified as the sole group able to afford liturgies, and the group most frequently referred to in the sources as *plousioi*. In the fourth century, these men each had resources in excess of figure between 3 to 4 tal.[2]

(b) the rentier, leisure, or propertied class: the core is the 1200 (again, in prosperous times) men, roughly equal in 357 to Periander's trierarchic register, who 'owned property of such a value, apparently about 1 tal., that from its income there was any perceptible surplus available which could be tapped for the purposes of direct taxation'.[3] So Davies argues, but the size of the class should be extended to roughly the size of the Three Thousand chosen by the oligarchy of 404/403 (Xen. 2.3.19, Arist. *Ath. Pol.* 36.2). Not only does Thrasybulus equate the Three Thousand with the *plousioi* (Xen. 2.4.40), but the speaker of Dem. 43.2 says that one could live off a capital of 4,500 dr. (that is, three-quarters of a talent). True enough, he says that one could not live off it *easily*, but he is trying to plead poverty. There were differences between the *c.* 1,200 and *c.* 3,000, but compared to the mass of *penetes*, they form a single propertied class.[4]

(c) the *eisphora* payers, estimated by Jones as *c.* 6,000 in the late fourth century, each worth a minimum of 2,500 dr.[5]

(d) the hoplite class, the infantrymen, in 321 the *c.* 9,000 men out of a total adult male citizen population of 21,000 who owned property worth over 2,000 dr. (Diod. 18.18.4–5, Plut. *Phoc.* 28.7. Ctes. *ap. Athen.* 6.272 c).[6]

(e) the thetic class, i.e., the men who did not have sufficient income to furnish the arms of a hoplite (i.e. the rowers) in 321, 11,000 men.

(f) the poor (*ptochoi*), i.e., that indeterminate portion of the thetic class which was genuinely destitute.

These terms are rough, approximate and inelegant, but they are greatly preferable to 'rich and poor' — even our fragmentary data allows better than that.

The Balance Sheet of War

How did a decade of foreign war affect the various enterprises of the Athenian economy? I will examine each of the major Athenian economic enterprises in turn, first domestic (rural and urban) then foreign.

Domestic Rural

Agriculture. The ancient economy was based on land. Even in Attica, which, compared to other *poleis*, seemed to stress commerce and light industry, agriculture was of prime importance. In 403, some two-thirds of Athenian citizens owned land; only *c.* 5,000 did not.[7] This is not to say that all landowners depended exclusively on agriculture for their livelihood. Many wealthy landowners had diversified their investments, turning to nautical loans, real estate, slave-run manufactories or silver mines.[8] Before the collapse of the Athenian empire, a poor landowner (especially if he lived close to town) could easily enough supplement his income by serving as juror, by rowing in the fleet or by working either in the shipyards of Piraeus or on a state building project, but except for the courts (and after 403 the assembly) these opportunities were gone. Nor were there likely to be many opportunities in private industry. Hence, contrary to what some have argued, there is not likely to have been a move to the city in 403.[9] If anything, the country seemed a safer bet, because even the landless could serve as a tenant farmer or as a seasonal labourer.[10] In 431, a majority of Athenian citizens lived in the countryside (Thuc. 2.16.1) and this is not likely to have changed in 403. With the loss of imperial revenues, Athenians depended more on agriculture than in several generations.

The state of Athenian agriculture, then, personally interested a majority of citizens, and in 403 that state was unquestionably bad. The Peloponnesians had been at Decelea for nine years. In their raids they had cut down grain, mutilated olive trees and vines, and carried off sheep, farm animals and slaves.[11] After Athens' surrender, eight months of civil war destroyed more crops. Nor were the buildings of Attica spared. Once the most lavishly furnished countryside of all Greece, Attica had seen raiders so thorough that they dismantled its buildings and carried them back home, 'beginning with the wood and tile of the houses'.[12] Some of Attica's sheep and cattle had probably been sent to Euboea for safekeeping, as in the Archidamian War, but Euboea rose in revolt in 411 (Thuc. 2.14.2, 8.96.1).

Deleterious as these raids were, their effect can be exaggerated. As V. Hanson has recently demonstrated, it is very difficult to do permanent damage to either olive trees, vines or grain fields. Grain could be quickly replanted, and grew again in Attica as early as 403. Vineyards can be trampled or cut, but are too dense to destroy thoroughly, and even a damaged vine will send forth new shoots. Moreover, the tough and hardy olive is both resistant to burning and girdling and very difficult to chop down; individual branches make a more likely target, but within a year they begin to grow back. Attica is too full of hills and dales for raiders to have damaged all of its olive trees. In any case, as Hanson notes, the Peloponnesians much preferred to gather booty than to cut down trees and vines systematically. Finally, the Athenian Plain and even some remote demes were patrolled and protected by Athenian troops.[13]

One should not speak of an irreversible catastrophe, still less of a mass movement to Athens of impoverished peasants (a theory boldly advanced and vigorously refuted).[14] There was, however, a serious depression, if not a universal one, in the postwar/Corinthian War period. Many an Athenian farmer found it necessary to buy seed, lost draft animals, plundered farming equipment and household tools and furniture, not to mention slaves, if his had been among the more than 20,000 Athenian slaves who had escaped to Decelea. If he had sheep or cattle, he would have to replace them, and perhaps poultry, pigs and goats as well. A small number of olive trees and vines would have sustained partial damage, in some cases enough to interrupt production for seven or more years.[15]

An uneven pattern of suffering resulted. A small farmer near Decelea who had lost his household goods, animals and a slave or two to the raiders might have been ruined. His counterpart on the Athenian Plain, however, or a wealthy farmer who had diversified his investments in urban real estate or nautical loans might have suffered little. In Aristophanes' *Ecclesiazusae* Praxagora speaks of such a diverse situation:

> It's all wrong for a man to have too much to spend,
> While others moan, starving; another we see
> Has acres of land tilled prosperously,
> While this man has not enough for his grave.
> You'll find men who haven't a single lean slave
> While others have hundreds to run at their call.
>
> (591–93, tr. Lindsay)

As to individual cases, the landed estate of Ischomachus, a wealthy knight portrayed in Xenophon's *Oeconomicus*, dropped in value from 70 tal. to 20 tal. in his last years, a decline that Davies has plausibly attributed largely to Peloponnesian raiders (to which one might add liturgies and *eisphorai*). On the other hand, several wealthy farmers in the postwar period appear in the sources: the speaker of Lysias 7, a rich farmer with many olive trees (7.26); Plato, who owned land at Iphistiadae and Eiresidae; Crito of Alopece and his son Critobulus; the heirs of Eraton (Lys. 17.2, 7–8); the prosecutor and defendant of Lysias 4.[16]

Mining. From Themistocles' day to that of Demetrius of Phalerum, the Athenian silver mines made an important contribution to the national wealth. In the years before 413 they seem to have been actively worked, for the state collected a lucrative tax from mine slaves. Moreover, in their surveys of Athenian resources, Alcibiades, Aristophanes and Xenophon's Socrates all include the mines.[17]

The Decelean War damaged the industry considerably, mainly by offering slaves the opportunity to desert. Lauffer has argued vigorously against the thesis that many mining slaves were among the 20,000 deserters: the fortifications which Athens erected in the mining district in 409 (Xen. 1.2.1, *Vect.* 4.43) prevented their flight.[18] But a considerable number could have escaped easily between 413 and 409. Nor, *contra* Lauffer, need deserters have been deterred by the discovery that they were not to gain their freedom at Decelea — better a Boeotian farm than an Attic mine.[19] A high proportion of the 20,000 deserters, therefore, were probably mine slaves.[20] One can agree with Lauffer that the mines continued to be worked in the Decelean War, but it is necessary to insist on a decline in manpower, until the final blow (as Lauffer notes) of a mass emancipation to fight at Arginusae in 406.[21]

When peace came, the slaves were not replaced quickly. Not that there was any shortage of candidates: wars in Asia Minor and Sicily would soon provide a market. But Athenian capital was in short supply, and investors probably preferred to put their money in maritime loans. Not only were these loans generally more lucrative than the mines, but they were easier to hide from the tax collector — no small consideration after 405, when there was no longer any imperial tribute to protect the affluent from *eisphora*.[22]

Moreover, since the mines were worked intensively before 413 (perhaps especially since the loss of Amphipolis in 424) it would now be necessary to dig new shafts, a costly and risky process. Finally, until Sparta's land power was broken in 371, mining might have seemed particularly risky. The industry did not recover until the mid-fourth century. The first known mining-lease inscription, from 367/6, lists only 17 concessions, while the leases of the 340s list over 100 in some years.[23]

Domestic Urban

Light Industry. There was no manufacturing on a large scale in ancient Athens: no workshop is known to have employed more than 120 persons (Lys. 12.19). But small-scale manufacturing (with an average shop comprising perhaps 20–30 workers) was big business, and Athens and Piraeus were busy with the making of pots, knives, lamps, beds, clothing, leather goods, weapons, ships, jewellery, etc. Citizens did not dominate light industry as they did agriculture, where non-citizens could not own land (although they could and did lease land or do seasonal agricultural work). In light industry, perhaps metics outnumbered citizens. Nevertheless, citizens played an important part.[24]

Several examples from the postwar period indicate the variety of roles citizens played in light industry by 403. The poor speaker of Lysias 24.19 was a craftsman. Socrates was a stone-cutter. Cephalus the politician was called a potter by Aristophanes; given the expense and leisure time needed to be a politician, he is more likely to have owned a slave workshop than to have sat at the wheel himself (*Eccl.* 248–53). His rival Anytus had inherited a tannery and shoemaker's business. Xenophon records four men who made big money from slave workshops: Nausicydes the miller, who rose to the liturgical class; Cyrebus the breadbaker; Demeas of Collytus, the capemaker; and Menon, the cloakmaker.[25]

Moreover, manufacturers and artisans were well represented in both the political elite and political community, probably in greater proportion than their numbers in society as a whole, thanks to their concentration in the city. When, for example, Xenophon's Socrates assesses (*Mem.* 3.7.6) the make-up of the assembly, he finds fullers, cobblers, builders and smiths (in addition to farmers and traders). That the owners of slave manufactories rose to prominence in the political elite in the last third of the fifth century has been well documented. In the postwar period, several names can be added to those of Cephalus and Anytus: Lysias (of great political importance, although a metic), whose family owned a slave-staffed weapons manufactory; Isocrates, whose father owned a workshop of slave flutemakers; perhaps Thrasybulus too — the vulnerability of his property to confiscation by the Thirty suggests slaves, perhaps in a workshop.[26]

Like farming and mining, light industry suffered during the Decelean War, although not as much. The buildings and tools were safe behind the walls of the Athens–Piraeus fortress. The 'animate tools' (Arist. *Pol.* 1253 b 32) however, the slaves, could escape to Decelea; according to Thucydides, a large part of the escapees were 'skilled workers' (*cheirotechnai*, Thuc. 17.7.5) and therefore mainly from urban workshops. The huge losses that Isocrates' father suffered in the Peloponnesian War may reflect the escape of slaves.[27] Moreover, the drain of Athenian wealth from 413 to 403 could only have decreased the domestic market for manufactured goods. Tools of war are a significant exception. The smithies, tanneries, woodshops and dockyards that produced weapons, armour, ships, ships' gear and wagons boomed with business from 431 to 405. In *Peace* 1255, Aristophanes gets a laugh by showing a weapons-maker in despair at the conclusion of hostilities, but one suspects that the joke has a basis in fact. A significant part of the manufacturing sector probably prospered in the Decelean War (and by the same token, languished in the postwar period).[28] The Decelean War struck a 'severe blow at Athenian industry'[29] but it also provided a stimulus. It has been suggested that Athenian manufactories generally increased production for export after 403 in order to fill the gap left by a decline in olive oil and silver production. This is unlikely, however, for there is little evidence of international trade in manufactured goods (rather than agricultural products).[30] Athens had never been primarily a manufacturing city, nor did it turn into one after 403 (despite Socrates' advice in 403 to one Aristarchus to turn his female dependents into wool-workers, Xen. *Mem.* 2.7.1–14). There was more money to be made in commerce and, as many admitted bluntly (see Xen. 3.5.10, And. 3.15) in an imperialist war.

Commerce, Culture, Real Estate and Finance. Commerce had been more important than manufacturing for fifth-century Athens and would continue to be so. Contemporaries sing the praises of the Piraeus and its trade, but they have little or nothing to say of Athenian manufacturing.[31] The Piraeus was the major commercial centre of the eastern Mediterranean. A study of the goods mentioned by Athenian sources, and of the merchants named in forensic speeches, shows that every major trading city between Carthage and the Crimea sent its ships to the Piraeus. They came not only to sell but to buy: Athens was a centre of re-export as well as of import and export.[32]

Athenian commerce comprised a great variety of professions and of economic groups, from humble men with booths in the marketplace (*kapeloi*), to dock-hands and ferrymen, to shipowners travelling with their goods (*naukleroi*), and to merchants who travelled on others' ships (*emporoi*). Wealthy Athenians who owned land or slave manufactories often also invested in lucrative commercial ventures, without ever getting near a wharf.[33]

Although metics and non-resident foreigners played a major role in trade, they were not uniformly predominant. For instance, while non-citizens were probably in the majority among *emporoi* and *naukleroi*, most of the known makers of nautical loans were citizens.[34] Several citizens are known to have taken part in foreign trade in the decade beginning in 403. The orator Andocides was a seagoing *naukleros* (Lys. 6.19). The relatives of the wealthy Eraton of Lysias 17 are described as *emporoi* (Lys. 17.5). One Diogeiton lent money to ships travelling to the Adriatic and Chersonese (Lys. 32.6, 15, 25). Mantitheus, though a knight who wore his hair long in the aristocratic style, came from a family involved in the grain trade: as a boy, his father had sent him to live at the court of King Satyrus of Pontus, Athens' trading partner (Lys. 16.4). Other citizens got into the business at the bottom. The father of the orator Demades (fl. 340–320), if ancient gossip is to be believed, was a mere sailor.[35] Xenophon's Socrates says the assembly was full of men who bought and sold in the agora (Xen. *Mem.* 2.7.6).

Other Athenians took part in trade in less direct ways, but their income was no less dependent on it. At the top of the trading pyramid were bankers and tax-farmers. The collection of major taxes was lucrative enough to be worth fighting for, as the quarrel between Andocides and Agyrrhius over the 2 per cent import tax shows.[36] Banking, too, was big business in Athens: trade required loans and the exchange of money. Almost all known bankers were non-citizens, some even slaves.[37] But not all citizens were indifferent to money-lending or finance. In addition to working at tax-farming, Agyrrhius was a confidential agent for the banker Pasion.[38]

In other ways, too, money that trade brought to Athens found its ways into citizens' pockets, some pockets of rather humble cloth. As they had a monopoly on the ownership of real property, citizens alone could lease rooms to foreign visitors and metics.[39] Foreigners needed food as well as shelter; they rented slaves, hired carriages and patronized tradesmen. They also visited prostitutes, an economic activity important enough to be taxed.[40]

By the same token, such citizens would have suffered if trade were hurt by the Peloponnesian War. As a result of Decelea, there was a small decline in the production of olive oil and a larger one in the production of silver, two of the main items of export. There may also have been small, localized disruptions throughout a Greek world at war.

Yet, balanced against these drops is the city's greatly increased dependence on importing necessities, thanks to Decelea (Thuc. 7.28.1). Someone made a nice profit in the carrying business, perhaps those whom Lysias 26.22 describes as making a fortune in the Peloponnesian War. Andocides of Kydathenaion, for example, although deprived of his property in 415, quickly made another fortune importing grain to Athens and timber, grain and bronze to Samos, an Athenian naval base.[41] Other examples might include one Diodotus, who had 7 tal. 4 min. invested in maritime loans in 410/409 (Lys. 32.5) and the extremely wealthy speaker of Lys. 21.[42] One should also recall the popular prejudice that everyone involved in the grain trade was rich.[43] But the facts speak for themselves: the Decelean War was by no means a disaster for Athenian commerce.

Peace brought bad news to Piraeus. Attica was no longer completely dependent on imports. Then, too, war and its disruptions continued in Asia Minor and Sicily. Furthermore, a rise of piracy accompanied the fall of the Athenian fleet. It was a sign of the times that when Lysander wanted to post news of Aegospotami to Sparta as quickly as possible, he sent one Theopompus, a Melian buccaneer.[44]

But the main problem was the loss of the empire. No longer did the allies have to come to Athens to plead and cajole — and spend money. No longer could the tyrant city use its power, as it had, to enforce the delivery of strategic materials to Piraeus: e.g., timber, wax, iron, bronze, dye and flax for warships and war material, and of course, the foodstuff, grain.[45] Now, market forces and Spartan power deflected these goods elsewhere. The new reality was, above all, that there was no longer an Athenian fleet to build.

To sum up, commerce prospered on balance during the Decelean War. Exports were down, but the rise in imports compensated. The more serious problems began after 405.

The total volume of imports and exports at Piraeus was 1,800 tal. in 402/401 and even more in 401/400 — a decline no doubt from the *status quo* of 413, when the total seaborne trade of the entire Athenian empire was over 18,000 tal., and, according to Hopper's reasonable guess, Piraeus' share was at least 25 per cent, or 4,500 tal.[46] Still, 1,800+ tal., which would have been *c.* 10 per cent of the trade of the Athenian empire in 413, is no mean sum. One is speaking, therefore, of a major decline but not of a collapse.

Just as Athens was an entrepot for goods, so was it a centre of culture, the 'school of Hellas' in Thucydides' famous phrase (2.41.1); the source of the 'sweetest pastimes,' according to Isocrates 4.41. Post-imperial Athens still attracted foreigners by its civilization, although with less Athenian money for the liberal arts, the number of attractions perhaps fell.[47] While Socrates was alive, for example, he drew foreign enthusiasts of philosophy to him. Three Thebans, two Megarians and an Elean were present at his deathbed. After his death, however, many Socratics quit Athens for a time.[48] Some foreigners still came to see the sights, though. Isocrates' client in the *Trapeziticus*, a young Bosporan, came to Athens in the mid-390s 'to trade and see the world' (17.4).

Empire

If one were surveying the Athenian economy in 431, the city and the country would tell a great deal of the story, but not all of it. Much of Athens' wealth consisted of foreign possessions, public and private. After the defeat of 404, Athenians lost virtually all of their property overseas. Strictly speaking, therefore, a survey of the postwar economy ought not to include foreign possessions. Ancient memories, however, were no shorter than modern ones. The loss of Amphipolis was still felt bitterly in Athens 80 years after the fact.[49] It is to be expected that when Athenians considered economic matters after 403, they thought of what they had lost, as well as what they had managed to keep. To understand them as they did themselves, it is therefore necessary to survey briefly the missing prizes of empire.

To the Athenian people, the empire had always been more than a political proposition; it had been an economic arrangement as well, and an extraordinarily profitable one. The annual tribute and other monies collected from the allies provided the state with 600 tal. in 431; 1,300 tal., after a series of increases, in 425; and *c.* 900 tal. in 413.[50] Combined with imposts on metics and foreign commerce, imperial income protected the potential payers of *eisphorai*.[51] Some of these same men might have profited from contracts for building and repairing the imperial war fleet.[52] They were the citizens most likely to have the education and ambition to serve in the magistracies abroad or in Piraeus which the imperial administration demanded.[53] Citizens in lower income categories, however, were not without opportunities. A pool of up to 6,000 jurors was eligible for a salary of 3 obols a day each for 150–200 days a year.⁵⁴ As sailors or hoplites they had the chance to earn regular pay and, if lucky, booty. In addition to the tremendous opportunities which the Piraeus dockyards offered to artisans and unskilled labourers (many of whom were metics) they provided employment for 500 citizen guards.⁵⁵ Building programmes were another important source of employment. Although activity had peaked under Pericles, even an Athens under siege could still afford to pay one drachma per day to construction workers on the Erechtheum in 409/408 and 408/407.⁵⁶ Athenian power compelled the allies to come to Athens for the delivery of tribute and certain court cases. Imperial income supported the many festivals which provided Athenians with recreation — and food: meat sacrificed to the gods generally ended up in the mouths of mortals.⁵⁷ Athenian power attracted windfall profits such as the grain the king of Egypt sent to the citizens of Athens in 445/44.⁵⁸

The most striking economic benefit of empire, however, was land. Most Greeks were, as Pericles said of the Peloponnesians, *autourgoi*, 'farmers of their own land' (Thuc. 1.142.1). The Athenians were different. 'We have much land both in the islands and on the mainland,' said Pericles, and there is every reason to take him literally.⁵⁹ In the years between the Persian and Peloponnesian Wars, Athens established a score of settlements abroad, and several others followed during the Peloponnesian War itself. In each settlement, Athenians were given land lots, some of which they worked themselves, others of which they let out to local tenants — an arrangement allowing the beneficiaries to remain in Athens.⁶⁰

How many Athenians became cleruchs or colonists under the empire is not known. Modern estimates range between 5,000 and 10,000 people,⁶¹ but the settlements benefited far more Athenians than even the highest figure would suggest. For not only those who received land, but even those who did not, saw their condition improved. If one's brother went off to Amphipolis, for example, one no longer had to share one's land in Attica with him.⁶²

Most settlers abroad were probably thetes, the men with the most to gain and least to lose in leaving Attica.⁶³ Wealthier Athenians, however, had nothing to complain of; they took part in the foreign land market too, by private purchase, rather than public allotment. 'Respectable Athenians,' the Old Oligarch writes, '. . . protect the interests of the respectable people in the allied cities' (Ps.–Xen. *Ath. Pol.* 1.17). Thucydides, a shrewder judge of character, knew that aristocratic solidarity broke down before the demands of self-interest.[64]

A few examples will illustrate his judgement. The men accused in 415 of mutilating the Herms or of profaning the Mysteries were all young aristocrats: just the sort of people likely to share the sympathy for the allies expressed by Thucydides son of Melesias or by Antiphon the orator.[65] Seven of them, nevertheless, owned land and property abroad. Adeimantus of Scambonidae, for instance, had farmland in the Troad and a house and farm in Thasos. Oionias of Atene owned various parcels of land in Euboea, including one farm that sold at a public auction for the considerable sum of 81 tal. 2,000 dr. Davies has collected three other cases (including the historian Thucydides himself) of Athenians who owned private property abroad before 404, and there is no reason to think these cases are exceptional.[66] The former holders of private property were vocal and numerous enough for Andocides to consider them a war tendency in 392/91 (And. 3.15). Moreover, if many Athenians had acquired private wealth in the empire before 404, it is easier to explain the manifest enthusiasm with which many members of the upper classes greeting the imperialist ventures of the 390s.[67]

Conclusions

The Iono-Decelean War cost the Athenian economy dearly. In Attica itself, the most obvious casualty was the number of slaves who fled: over 20,000. The average price per slave was 150–200 drachmas in the fourth century; even using the lower figure means a great loss — 500 tal., not to mention the opportunity cost if the slave was not replaced immediately. These defections probably hurt the mining industry most severely, but agriculture and manufacturing were also damaged.[68]

Peloponnesian raiders hurt agriculture considerably, mainly by plundering stock, furnishing and slaves; the damage to fruit trees, vines and grain was relatively small. Manufacturing was a mixed bag. It suffered from a loss of artisan slaves, from a depressed market, and from the general scarcity of capital. On the other hand, the production of armaments in all their various forms prospered. Imports prospered too, but the decline in mining and agricultural production hurt the export trade.

However great the economic costs to Athens of the enemy fort at Decelea, they pale before the staggering loss of the Athenian empire in 405: the loss of c. 1,000 tal. tribute annually; of employment in the army or navy, in building projects or in the shipyards; of the business generated by the people and products obliged to come to the imperial capital; of overseas property.

Meiggs argues that two statistics about *eisphora*, one from 428/27 and the other from 378/377, give us some sense of the magnitude of the loss of Athenian private property in the Peloponnesian War. In 378/77, the *timema* of Attica, the value of property liable to *eisphora*, was 5,750 or 6,000 tal. (Dem. 14.19; Philochorus, *FGrH* 328 F 46; Polyb. 2.62.7). In 428, the first *eisphora* of the Peloponnesian War produced 200 tal. (Thuc. 3.27). In the fourth century, a levy of 1 per cent for *eisphora* was normal and 2 per cent exceptional. Assuming the same was true in 428/27, the *timema* then was 20,000 tal. or 10,000 tal. Contrary to Meiggs (who prefers 20,000), there is no way of choosing between the two; an off-hand joke in *Eccl.* 823–29 about a yield of 500 tal. from a 2½ per cent levy (implying a *timema* of 20,000 tal.) is no basis for argument. If anything, it only raises the possibility of a 2½ per cent levy, or a *timema* of 8,000 tal. in 428. Hence, there was a drop of either 25 or 40 or even 70 per cent.[69]

It is a very rough guide, and one that assumes (a) the *timema* included the same items of property and was calculated with similar efficiency in 428/27 and 378/77,[70] (b) that the *timema* of Attica was roughly similar in 377 to what it was in 403, and (c) that repeated *eisphorai* after 428 did not drive more Athenians to hide their property in liquid assets (cf. n. 22). The only thing to be confident of, then, is a drop.

The Balance Sheet of Revolution

In addition to the foreign war, the civil war of 404/403 resulted in a transfer of wealth, this time within the propertied class. Although probably small in absolute terms, this transfer was large in its political significance. Damned as murderers, the Thirty were also bitterly remembered as thieves who confiscated the property of their enemies and then sold it to a willing public (i.e. the Three Thousand). As Lysias says (*Against Hippotherses*, frg. 5): 'the Thirty would not have been offering anything for sale unless there had been interested buyers'. According to Aristotle, no less than 1,500 citizens were killed, and the regime had designs on their property (Arist. *Ath. Pol.* 35.4; cf. Xen. 2.3.21; Lys. 12.6–7, 83). In addition, between 10 and 60 of the richest metics were victimized. Isocrates says that the estates of the rebels in Piraeus — several hundred citizens[71] — were declared public property. Even if one subtracts 50 per cent for exaggeration and for those citizens who, like one Nicias, mortgaged their houses, sent their slaves abroad and gave their money to a friend (who, in Nicias' case, allegedly kept one third, Isoc. 21.2–3), 800–1,000 victims of confiscation are left.[72]

The terms of the amnesty regarding confiscated property are relatively clear. It is certain that all property which had been confiscated but not sold reverted to the original owner. The buyers were able to keep 'invisible property,' i.e. slaves, money and furnishings, but had to return 'visible property,' i.e. land and houses. It has been suggested that the exiles had to pay something, perhaps the purchase price, in order to regain land or a house. This is unlikely, however, for in the two known roughly contemporary settlements of civil war — Selymbria in 407 and Phlius in 384 — there are similar provisions but no mention of a compensation fee to repossess 'visible property'. Therefore, Athenian oligarchs who had bought confiscated land or houses were probably left in the lurch.[73]

But so were the returnees and relatives of the executed who had lost invisible property, among them Thrasybulus, Anytus and the families of Leon of Salamis, of Lycurgus son of Lycomedes of Boutadai, of Alcibiades and of Niceratus son of Nicias.[74] It is uncertain just how much property these families lost, but one need not assume the sum was enormous. As the cases of Anytus and Thrasybulus show, the amounts were not necessarily so big as to remove the victims from the propertied class altogether.[75] Niceratus' children inherited 14 tal. from their father, a large sum, but much less than the 70 tal. they might have expected (Lys. 19.47). Presumably the Thirty failed to get hold of the family's whole fortune.[76] Even if the average victim only lost a small percentage of his total property to the oligarchs, that was more than enough to secure a legacy of bitterness, a dangerous political undercurrent.

Classes and Conflict

In 403, Athenians as a whole were considerably poorer than they had been ten years earlier. All classes suffered, but there was a major difference between the two ends of the social spectrum. The estate of

Ischomachus, for instance, had shrunk by 50 tal. during the Decelean War, but he still had 20 tal. to leave his sons.[77] Similarly, Niceratus son of Nicias, who was expected to bequeath 70 tal., 'only' left 14 tal. (Lys. 19.46–47). Callias of Alopece, cult official of Eleusis, was reduced to a 'begging priest' in the 390s, but he was still worth 2 tal.[78] Likewise, Isocrates and Lysias, forced by their financial losses to become speech writers, were not impoverished.[79] In other words, many of the rich were still rich, or at least still members of the propertied class.

As one moves down the social ladder, one finds Athenians who lost far less than 50 tal. but could hardly afford to lose 50 dr. A man like Socrates' acquaintance Eutheros seems to have made it into the hoplite class before 405 through his overseas property, probably a cleruchy. Back in Attica after Aegospotami, he was reduced to working as a hired labourer, and testy at Socrates' suggestion that he become a farm bailiff (why he considered the second occupation a slave's job but not the first, is unclear).[80] Nikarete daughter of Damostratos came from a family of small means, but she had to hire herself out as a wet nurse (normally a slave's job) while her husband was away with Thrasybulus in 390/89 (Dem. 57.42).[81] According to her son Euxitheos, speaking c. 345, 'in that time of the city's misfortune, all people were badly off' (Dem. 57.35) and citizen women sometimes had to take jobs usually reserved for slaves or men: nursing, working at the loom or working in the vineyards (Dem. 57.45). Of course, Euxitheos has a motive to exaggerate, in order to make his mother's case seem more acceptable, but the details are plausible. They fit the description of poverty in *Ecclesiazusae*: Athenians without cloaks, suffering from pneumonia, with no place to sleep (415–421). For that matter, they add a sobering note to Aristophanes' joke of Athenian women active in politics.[82]

What did Euxitheos or Nikarete think, one wonders, when they passed the sons of the leisured, in the palaestra as usual after 403,[83] or a fine woman decked out in Ionian luxury (*Eccl.* 883, 918)? Or the expensive funerary monument erected at the death of a knight in 394? What did the jurors think when four *philoi* of Socrates offered to pay a half talent fine at his trial in 399?[84] In other words, what did those who had been impoverished by the Decelean War or the defeat of 405 think of the rich who were still rich?

The likely answer is that they resented them. True, Athenian hoplites and thetes are well known for exhibiting tolerance toward the property of the upper classes. In spite of postwar economic pressure, there is no evidence of a fundamental change in that attitude. What there is, however, is a series of straws in the wind that add up to a significant increase of tension between have and have-not.[85] They are:

(1) In spite of the general identification of the orators with the interests of the propertied class, even they provide a few direct instances of this tension. For example, the cripple of Lys. 24.16–17 unfavourably compares the characteristic *hybris* of the *plousioi* with the moderation of the *penetes* — a theme repeated in *Ploutos* 563 in 388 (although not unique to the postwar era[86]). The speaker of Isocrates 20 *Against Lochites*, who is prosecuting Lochites for allegedly striking him, also complains of the general violence and arrogance of the *plousioi* (20.15) and property-owners (20.22: *tous ousias echontes*). Lysias also makes frequent reference (1.4; 27.9; 28.1,2,4) to the misuse of public funds in order to go from *penia* to *ploutos*. Here the emphasis, of course, is on the mode of acquisition, not on the wealth itself, but there is an element of status jealousy — or why not simply mention the theft of funds?

(2) According to And. 1.88, there was talk (or just scare talk?) of cancelling debts upon the revision of the laws in 403.

(3) The frequent and repeated attacks on the former Three Thousand (or City Men), attested to as late as 382, carry the connotation of an attack on the upper classes in general. Thrasybulus himself identifies the City Party with the *plousioi* and the *demos* with the *penetes*. (Xen. 2.4.40; on these attacks see pp. 3–4, 102).

(4) Aristophanes' last plays, *Ecclesiazusae* and *Ploutos*, evince great concern both about the gulf between have and have-not (esp. *Eccl.* 591–93) and the capricious and unjust distribution of wealth (a major theme of *Ploutos*). Moreover, Aristophanes' decision in *Ecclesiazusae* to parody the communism later attested to in Plato's *Republic* suggests a widespread concern about the distribution of wealth on the part of the Athenian intelligentsia *c*. 390.[87]

(5) On the other end of the scale, consider the resentment of the propertied classes against the *eisphorai* of the Corinthian War (Lys. 28.3–4) and the lack of enthusiasm of some for the reinstituted trierarchy (*Eccl.* 197–98).

The total, then, is a noticeable rise in tension between the two ends of the economic scale. In retrospect, the problem did not lead to revolution, but one should not underestimate its effects on contemporaries.

Ehrenberg has argued that the bulk of the citizenry of late fifth-century Athens was a unified middle class or petite bourgeoisie of farmers, tradesmen and artisans. After 403, the middle is likely to have dropped lower, the gulf between wealth and small property to have widened, and the median to have fallen well below the mean in a calculation of personal wealth. Funke's recent description of a broad consensus, even after 403, among Athenians of middling wealth is an underestimate of the divisions in postwar society.[88]

The tension between have and have-not after 403 might have been even greater than it was, if not for a demographic factor passed over by most earlier scholars. The Iono-Decelean war took a much greater toll on thetes than hoplites. There would, otherwise, have been even more thetes and *ptochoi* in postwar Athens, and politics might have taken on a more radical colour (*infra*, Chapter 3).

Class tension need not mean a thoroughgoing battle. To take one important and often-discussed point: war and empire. Several scholars have drawn a socioeconomic dividing line on these matters, arguing that in general 'the rich' were opposed to war because they would have to finance it and saw little to gain from empire, while 'the poor,' free from liturgies and *eisphorai*, and lured by pay and booty, dock-yard jobs and cleruchies, were quick to urge foreign adventures.[89]

The sources for this period contain a number of complaints about taxation. Lysias supplies three examples (Lys. 28.3–4, 29.4, 18.21) and Aristophanes *Eccl.* 197–98 is often cited: 'Ships must be launched; the *penes* approves, the *plousioi* and farmers disapprove' (for a full discussion, see *infra* 'Town and Country'). Moreover, in Xen. *Oec.* 2.6, with a dramatic date between 401 (5.4.18) and 399, Socrates commiserates with the wealthy Critobulus: 'If war breaks out, I know that the people will require you to maintain a ship and pay *eisphora* that will nearly crush you.'

Complaints about taxation are the common currency of political rhetoric, however, and must be taken with a grain of salt. If Ste Croix is right, the rate at which *eisphora* was generally levied cannot objectively be called 'crushing'.[90] If Jones is right, the burden of *eisphora* was shared by 6,000 men. Furthermore, one cannot assume that the tax-exempt were indifferent to the state's insolvency, or that they would cheerfully march off to war knowing that a soldier or rower was only paid half of what he had been (three obols per day instead of six) before 415.[91] War was not a free ride for the *penetes*.

On the other hand, both groups did have an enormous amount to regain from the war: the restoration of the Athenian empire. This was almost as great a *desideratum* for a liturgist as for a *ptochos*. When it came to war and empire, perhaps the greatest difference between the two ends of the socioeconomic scale was *political*. To the former Three Thousand, a rebuilt empire meant both (a) more power to the *demos* and (b) the eclipse of Sparta, protector of the former oligarchic sympathizers. Hence, although it promised economic gain, war also offered the risk of political loss, perhaps even an abrogation of the reconciliation agreement of 403. In foreign affairs, these last issues were probably the greatest point of division in the body politic.[92]

Town and Country

Just as several scholars have envisioned a foreign policy division between Athens' socioeconomic classes, so others (or sometimes the same scholars) have made the division a geographical one. The empire, it is argued, was good for townsmen, but of little benefit for the freeholders of the countryside.[93] It is also said that the city had little to fear from a foreign invasion, but for those outside the walls (as the farmers had learned in the Decelean War) war could be disastrous.[94] The result was a general political division, particularly on foreign policy, between town and country.

The country was underrepresented in the assembly, courts and council, both because of the distances involved (e.g., 42 km to Marathon, 61 km to Eleutherae, 70 km to Sunium) and because of the age-old mental distance between peasants and city slickers.[95] On the other hand, evidence from the classical period in general and the postwar period in particular makes it clear that peasants often *did* attend the assembly.[96] A peasant from Sunium was unlikely to be able to attend on a regular basis, but was likely to go to a meeting at which the question of war or peace was to be put to a vote. Moreover, many peasants lived within several miles of the city, on the Attic Plain, where the populous deme of Acharnae was only seven miles from the Pnyx.[97] Indeed, some farm owners, many no doubt affluent, lived inside the city. Hence, although the country was a minority in the assembly and not the majority it was in real life, it was a very significant minority.[98]

What did the country want? It may not have yearned for the lost empire as much as the city did (the prosperity of Piraeus was rather far removed from, say, Mesogeia) but it yearned for it nonetheless. *Contra* Aristotle (*Ath. Pol.* 24.1, *Pol.* 1319a) it was not necessary to live in town to row in the fleet. Athens was famous for the diffusion of rowing skills among the whole citizenry (Ps.-Xen. *Ath. Pol.* 1.19–20). During the summer, a slow time for olive cultivation, the peasant may have been happy to earn extra money as a rower. If Piraeus was rather far from Marathon or Salamis, these places had their own good harbours.[99] Furthermore, *contra* Ehrenberg, cleruchies were not restricted to city dwellers. Most farmers would probably have gladly sent a second son to an overseas cleruchy or colony rather than see him divide a paltry Attic patrimony with his brother. Finally, farmers, particularly those close to town, could be employed on a state building project during the slack season for agriculture.[100] Hence, the country had a considerable stake in the empire.

At the same time, it had a considerable stake in peace. The country was not likely to go back to war after 403 without a guarantee against a second Decelea, a new combination of material loss and physical uprooting. Yet, although the city had not suffered as much as the town between 413 and 403 (indeed some townsmen had prospered) on the whole, it too was likely to worry at the prospect of another invasion.

The modern perspective makes it easy to exaggerate the split between town and country. For all their differences, the two were intimately connected in classical Athens.[101] When the Spartans forced the state to import all food from abroad, the town as well as the country had to pay a price. The disruption of Attic agriculture hurt some townsmen, who had been among the labourers employed on Athenian farms during the harvest.[102]

Many wealthier inhabitants of the city invested in farms or mines outside the walls. When farming suffered, so did the urban craftsmen who supplied farming tools, no inconsiderable occupation in a country with as many farmers as Attica.[103] If farmers found the overcrowded city unpleasant during wartime, so did townsfolk. By the end of the war, both groups had known malnutrition, plague and famine.

The impression of an urban–rural split derives, to a large extent, from scholars' interpretations of the plays of Aristophanes. Dicaeopolis in *Acharnians* and Trygaeus and the chorus of farmers in *Peace* all attest to the longing of rural Attica for an end to war's sufferings. There is a note of hostility to the town when the chorus of *Peace* (1183–85) accuses the taxiarchs of favouring townsmen when it came to posting hoplite lists.[104]

To read an urban–rural split in Aristophanes, however, is to misread. For one thing, he does not consistently depict the country as pacifistic. The greatest hawks of his plays are the country chorus of *Acharnians* (e.g., 205–236). When Trygaeus asks for help in 'digging up' peace, he does not restrict his plea to farmers:

O all ye farmers, merchants, artisans,
O all ye craftsmen, aliens, sojourners,
O all ye islanders, all ye peoples.[105]

(*Peace* 296–98)

Moreover, a comic poet need not choose his themes according to strict standards of accuracy. Although Aristophanes was particularly concerned about the farmers, other groups may yet have suffered grievously in the war. Perhaps Aristophanes considered farmers, who made up a majority of the citizen population, to be the typical citizens of Attica.[106] Perhaps, like other thinkers of his own and succeeding ages, he believed that farmers uniquely exemplified the sturdy qualities he admired.[107]

One passage in particular, *Ecclesiazusae* 197–8, has often been cited as proof of a deep split between town and country regarding war and empire. Because they have drawn the attention of so many scholars, the lines deserve a close examination here. They read:

Ships must be launched; the poor man approves,
The wealthy men and farmers disapprove.[108]

In transliteration, they read:

Naus dei kathelkein: toi peneti men dokei,
Tois plousiois de kai georgois ou dokei.

Some scholars have interpreted these lines as proof of a political alliance between the rich and the peasants against the imperialism of the urban masses. In the words of one recent study, 'The "rich" (that is, the large landowners) and the farmers find themselves in opposition to the people, to the "poor".'[109] In other words, there was a return to the political configuration of the Archidamian War, as recorded by the Old Oligarch (Ps.-Xen. *Ath. Pol.* 2.14):

> In the present situation the farmers and the wealthy Athenians are more inclined to make up to the enemy, but the common people live without fear and do no such thing because they know that none of their property will be burnt or destroyed.

On both occasions, the result was 'a deep split in the structure of the Athenian citizenry'.[110] The urban poor wanted state-pay and empire; the rich and the farmers only peace.

This evidence, however, is not convincing. Aristophanes' exegetes have made insufficient allowance for comic exaggeration. The speech of Praxagora in *Ecclesiazusae* from which the lines in question come is cast in terms of black and white:

> This League again, when first we talked it over,
> It seemed the only thing to save the State.
> Yet when they got it, they hated it. (193–95)

or

> You used to hate the Corinthians, and they you (199)

or

> Argeius was a fool: Now Jerome's wise. (201)[111]

The contrast between 'the poor man' and the 'rich and farmers' is similarly overdrawn; it is valid mainly as caricature. As Ehrenberg has suggested, Aristophanes' comment can be understood as a joke about landlubbers' fear of the sea.[112]

The most important point, however, is that the usual translation of this passage is a mistranslation. Note that while 'the poor man' (*toi peneti*) and 'the wealthy men' (*tois plousiois*) have the usual generic article, 'farmers' (*georgois*) does not. A good poet does not omit an article *metri gratia*. Aristophanes is linking 'farmers' very closely to 'the wealthy men,' i.e., taking advantage of the trope of hendiadys, as he does elsewhere. This permits the poet to express a single complex idea through two words: not 'the wealthy and the farmers' but 'the wealthy, especially farmers'.[113] This translation not only makes good poetry but also good sense. If the *plousioi* had good reason to vote against a fleet and the consequent trierarchies, the wealthy farmers had the best reason of all, because their wealth, 'visible property,' was particularly hard to hide from the assessor. One does not have to go far for a contemporary appreciation of the problem: *Eccl.* 601–602 speaks to it:

> With regard to the land, I can quite understand,
> But how, if a man have his money in hand,
> Not farms, which you see, and he cannot withhold,
> But talents of silver and Darics of Gold?[114]

Hence, *Eccl.* 197–98 is no evidence of a deep split between town and country.

One further point calls this division into doubt. In postwar Athens, townsmen were just as vulnerable to invasion as countrymen, without either walls or fleet to protect them. Even when they began to rebuild the walls, it was a long project. The refortification of Piraeus, begun at the latest in summer 394, was not completed until the 380s.[115]

To sum up, tension between country and city played only a minor role in postwar Athenian politics. On the other hand, tension between the former Three Thousand and the rest of the population, based on both economic and political differences, was a serious political factor. A unified policy might be achieved, but the achievement would require a struggle. To put it in other terms, social (and hence political) divisions in postwar Athens were greater than such recent writers as Funke and de Ste Croix have allowed, but not so great as Mossé and Audring imagine.[116]

To understand these divisions, a close look at demographic changes in Athens as a result of the Peloponnesian War, especially its last phase, is necessary.

Notes

1. J. Hemelrijk, 'Penia en Ploutos' (Diss. Utrecht: 1925), 52–4, German summary 140–2; Davies, *WPW* 10–11; Finley *Politics in Ancient World* 10.
2. Davies, *WPW* 9–14, 22, 34.
3. Davies, *WPW* 28, 34–5.

4. Ste Croix, *CSAGW* 115.
5. Jones *AD* 9–10.
6. Jones, *AD* 31, 76, 79–80; Davies, *WPW* 34 ff.
7. The figure of 5,000 is provided by Dion. Halicarn. in the *hypothesis* to Lys. 34. For the other figures, *infra*, chap. 3.
8. Isocrates' father had both land and a factory of slave flutemakers. See *APF* 246. The sons of Nicias' brother Eucrates owned valuable land (Lys. 18.14), but the family was well known for its investments in the mines (*APF* 403). See also Euctemon of Cephisia (b. 460), *APF* 562.
9. Peasants in city: G. Glotz and R. Cohen, *Histoire Grecque*, vol. 3 (Paris: 1936) 5. *Contra*: Ehrenberg, *Aristophanes* 86; Gert Audring, 'Über Grundeigentum und Landwirtschaft in der Krise der athenischen Polis', in *Hellenische Poleis, Krise — Wandlung — Wirkung*, vol. 1, ed. Welskopf (Berlin: 1974), 116; A Andreev, 'Some Aspects of Agrarian Conditions in Attica in the Fifth to Third Centuries BC', *Eirene* 12 (1974).
10. Glotz, *Ancient Greece at Work*, tr. Dobie (London, 1926), 254; Jones, *AD* 10, 138 n. 61. Note too that the Thirty had encouraged movement out of the city: Krentz, *Thirty* 65–6.
11. Thuc. 7.27, Lys. 7.6–7, 20.33; W. G. Hardy, 'The *Hellenica Oxyrhynchia* and the Devastation of Attica', *CP* 21 (1926), 346–55; V. D. Hanson, *Warfare and Agriculture in Ancient Greece* (Pisa: 1983), 155–9. M. Jameson, 'Agriculture and Slavery in Classical Athens', *CJ* 73 (1977/78), 125, 136, 141, argues for large numbers of Athenian agricultural slaves, and hence a significant number of agricultural slaves among the 20,000 Decelean deserters. *Contra* Ober, *FA* 22–3, with the scholarly debate summarized on p. 22, n. 19.
12. *Hell. Oxy.* 12.4–5; Isoc. 16.13; Gomme *HCT ad* Thuc. 2.14.1. Cf. J. E. Jones, L. H. Sackett, and A. J. Graham, 'The Dema House in Attica', *BSA* 57 (1962), 100–1.
13. Hanson, *Warfare and Agriculture* 159–71.
14. There is no evidence for the proposition (Beloch GG^2 3.1, 316 n. 5; C. Mossé *La fin de la démocratie athénienne* (Paris: 1961), 48) that rich land speculators forced peasants off their farms in the years after 403. See Andreev, 'Agrarian Conditions', 18–19; M. I. Finley, 'Land, Debt, and the Man of Property in Classical Athens', *Poli. Sci. Qrtrly* 68 (1954) 250.
15. Replacements: Ehrenberg, *Aristophanes* 59–61; Michell, *Economics* 68, 72–3; Gomme, *HCT ad* 2.14.1; French, *Growth* 109. Olives: Michell, *Economics* 77; French, *Growth* 109; Finley, *The Ancient Economy* (Berkeley: 1973), 77.
16. Ischomachus: *APF* 266–8.
17. Tax: Xen. *Vect.* 4.25. Surveys of resources: Thuc. 6.97.1, Ar. *Wasps* 656–66, Xen. *Mem.* 3.6.
18. S. Lauffer, *Die Bergwerkssklaven von Laureion* vol. 2 (Wiesbaden: 1956), 220–2.
19. Lauffer, *Bergwerkssklaven* 227; *contra* A. Andreades, *Geschichte d. griech. Staatswirtschaft* vol. 1 (1931), 287.
20. According to Thucydides 17.17.5, more than 20,000 Athenian slaves escaped to Decelea, of whom 'the greater part' (τὸ πολὺ μέρος) were skilled workers (χειροτέχναι). But Jameson ('Agriculture', 136 n. 72), following the Budé editors, reads πολὺ μέρος: 'a large part'. In either case, it is difficult to tell how many of the deserters were mining slaves. Those slaves who dug for ore would not be described as 'skilled labourers', but others who worked in refineries might be. The 'skilled labourers' might also have been slaves employed as artisans in the city or Piraeus. As for the unskilled workers, they could have been employed in the mines, in manufacturing, as domestics, on trading vessels, or in agriculture. See Dover, *HCT ad loc*.
21. Xen. 1.6.24, *Vect.* 4.42; Lauffer, *Bergwerkssklaven* 224–5.

22. R. J. Hopper, *Trade and Industry in Classical Greece* (London: 1979), 179.
23. Hopper, *Trade and Industry* 176–7; M. Crosby, 'Greek Inscriptions', *Hesperia* (1941), 14–30.
24. Workshop size: Hopper, *Trade and Industry* 104. Non-citizens in agriculture: of the *c.* 50 non-citizens on the enfranchisement decree of 404/403 or 401/400 whose professions are recorded, 10 are listed as γεωργό(ς). Tod, *GHI* vol. 2, no. 100; D. Hereward, 'New Fragments of *IG II²*, 10', *BSA* 47 (1952), 102–17. General discussions: Michell, *Economics* 169–209; Ehrenberg, *Aristophanes* 120–46; H. Bolkestein, *Economic Life in Greece's Golden Age*, rev. Jonkers (Leiden: 1958), 17–18; A. French, *Growth of the Athenian Economy* (London: 1964), 123–4; S. Isager and M. H. Hansen, *Aspects of Athenian Society in the Fourth Century BC*., tr. Rosenmeier (Odense: 1975), 38–42; Hopper, *Trade and Industry* 93–107, 126–46.
25. Socrates: According to Lucian (*Somn.* 13), Socrates was originally a sculptor, but deserted the craft for education. His father was either a stonemason or sculptor. See W. K. C. Guthrie, *A History of Greek Philosophy*, vol. 3 (Cambridge: 1969), 378–9. Anytus: *APF* 41. Four men: Xen. *Mem.* 3.7.6; cf. on Nausicydes, Ar. *Eccl.* 426; *APF* 315.
26. Assembly makeup: cf. Ar. *Ploutos* 510ff., 532ff. Owners of slave manufactories: Connor, *NP* 151–3. Lysias: In general, see K. J. Dover, *Lysias* 28–46. Isocrates: *APF* 246. Thrasybulus: *APF* 41, 240.
27. Skilled workers: *supra*, n. 20. Isocrates: *APF* 246.
28. Cf. Ar. *Knights* 278 f., *Frogs* 362ff. Dem. 19.286, Plato *Laws* 847d; cf. Ehrenberg, *Aristophanes* 140–1.
29. Hopper, *Trade and Industry* 106.
30. Suggestion: Isager and Hansen, *Aspects* 42. International trade: Ehrenberg, *Aristophanes* 138–9; Michell, *Economics* 233–6.
31. Contemporaries: Thuc. 2.38.2; Ps.-Xen. *Ath. Pol.* 1.12, 2.7–8; Isoc. 4.42; Xen *Vect.* 3.1–2, cf. 5.4 (χειροτέχναι). Cf. French, *Growth* 174; Michell, *Economics* 23.
32. See Michell, *Economics* 252–5, 270–5, 279–98; Bolkestein, *Economic Life in Greece* 104–34; French, *Growth* 118–19; R. Meiggs, *The Athenian Empire* (Oxford: 1975), 265; Isager and Hansen, *Aspects* 19–52.
33. On the terminology, see Isager and Hansen, *Aspects* 64–6. On wealthy Athenian commercial investors, see E. Erxleben, 'Die Rolle der Bevölkerungsklassen im Aussenhandel Athens im 4. Jahrhundert v.u.z.', in *Hellenische Poleis* 477, 502; Casson, 'Athenian Upper Class', 43–5; Isager and Hansen, *Aspects* 72.
34. Erxleben, 'Aussenhandel Athens', 502; Casson, 'Athenian Upper Class', 45; Isager and Hansen, *Aspects* 72.
35. *APF* 99.
36. And. 1.133–5. See MacDowell, *Andokides, On the Mysteries* (Oxford: 1961), commentary *ad loc.*; French, *Growth* 125–6.
37. See Michell, *Economics* 335–8; R. Bogaert, *Banques et Banquiers dans Les Cités Grecques* (Leiden: 1968) 61–91; Casson, 'Athenian Upper Class', 47, has found only one certain instance of an Athenian citizen as banker.
38. *APF* 278. The father of the speaker of Lys. 17, a citizen, had lent two talents to Eraton (2). For a full discussion of hypothecary loans, see Finley, *Land and Credit* 29–31.
39. Ps.-Xen. *Ath. Pol.* 1.17; Xen. *Mem.* 3.11.4; cf. Casson 'Athenian Upper Class', 33–4. Cf. Davies, *WPW* 49–52. Other examples from the 390s: Lysimachus, Lys. 3.11; Aristarchus, Xen. *Mem.* 2.7.2.
40. Ps.-Xen. *Ath. Pol.* 1.17 says that Athenians let out rooms, carriages and slaves to the allies visiting on court cases.
  On the prostitution tax, see Busolt-Swoboda, *Griechische Staatskunde* (Munich: 1920–26), 1223.
41. MacDowell, *Andokides* 4–5.
42. *APF* 31.

43. Ehrenberg, *Aristophanes* 119, n. 6; Lys. 22.14–16; R. Seager, 'Lysias Against the Corn-Dealers', *Historia* 5 (1956), 172–84.
44. Xen 2.1.30 called Theopompus a Milesian, Pausanias 10.9.10 a Myndian, and Meiggs-Lewis *SGHI* no. 95 indicates he came from Melos. Perhaps one should take the confusion of the sources as a sign of Theopompus' travels as a pirate, and, therefore, of the unsettled conditions of the times. Cf. Isoc. 17.35; E. Ziebarth, *Beiträge zur Geschichte des Seeraubs und Seehandels im alten Griechenland* (Hamburg: 1929), 12–14; Michell, *Economics* 308–9. Mossé, *Athens in Decline, 404–86 BC,* trans. Stewart (London: 1976), 14, suggests that unsettled conditions in the Aegean made it difficult for Athens to procure grain.
45. See Ps.-Xen. *Ath. Pol.* 2.11–13. During the Archidamian War, Athens regulated the amount of grain Methone (Meiggs-Lewis *SGHI* no. 65) and Aphytis (*ATL* D. 21.1–6) could import through Byzantium. In the 350s, Athens enforced a monopoly on the export of the ruddle dye from the island of Ceos (Tod, *GHI* vol. 2, no. 162). The dye was used for painting triremes, according to the thesis of E. Hasebroek, *Trade and Politics in Ancient Greece*, trans. Fraser and MacGregor (London: 1933), 151; cf. Michell, *Economics* 103; Tod, *GHI* vol. 2, no. 185. For a general discussion, see French, *Growth* 119–22; M. I. Finley, 'Empire in the Greco-Roman World', *Greece and Rome* n.s. 25 (1978), 7–8.
46. And. 1.333, Thuc. 7.28 + Dover, *HCT ad loc*; Hopper, *Trade and Industry* 100.
47. Callias of Alopece was a leading patron of the sophists in the 430s and 420s, but his fortune, which rested on the silver mines, seems to have been destroyed by conspicuous consumption, Peloponnesian invaders and liturgies. See *APF* 261.
48. Deathbed scene: Plato, *Phaedo* 57a. On the other hand, Echecrates of Phlius was ignorant of the details of Socrates' death, because in 399, few Phliasians travelled to Athens: perhaps a sign of poverty in the Peloponnesus, the declining importance of Athens or both (ibid.).
49. Athens continued to claim Amphipolis until the Peace of Philocrates in 346.
50. For full discussion and citations of the ancient evidence, see Gomme, *HCT ad* 2.13.3 and 7.28; Meiggs, *Athenian Empire* 253, 325–32.
51. For the metic tax, see Hommel, 'Metoikoi', *RE* 30 (1932) col. 1448; Whitehead, *Athenian Metic* 75–82. Metics were also liable for *eisphorai, epidoseis,* and the encyclical liturgies, but not the trierarchy (ibid.). For taxes on foreign commerce, see Gilbert, *Greek Constitutional Antiquities,* trans. Brooks and Nicklin (London: 1895), 350; D. M. Lewis, *Hesperia* 28 (1954), 243.
52. On the construction and maintenance of Athens' triremes see *IG* II/III^2 1604–32; Michell *Economics* 200–1; French, *Growth* 155; Jordan, *Athenian Navy* 30–60.
53. In Piraeus there were, for instance, annually elected boards of ten curators of the dockyards (*epimeloumenoi tou neoriou*), supervisors of repairs (*architektones*), and dispatchers (*apostoleis*); Arist. *Ath. Pol.* 46.1, cf. Jordan, *Athenian Navy* 30–55. Arist. *Ath. Pol.* 24.3 mentions 700 magistracies abroad, but the figure is a copyist's mistake, see Hansen, 'Seven Hundred *Archai* in Classical Athens', *GRBS* 21 (1980), 151.
54. Jones, *AD* 5.
55. On a metic shipwright (*naupegos*) see *IG* I^2 428 + Jordan, *Athenian Navy* 53; on the 500 guards, Arist. *Ath. Pol.* 24.3.
56. On the Erechtheum, see *IG* I^2 372–4. As French, *Growth* 147 points out, of the 71 Erechtheum workers in the fragmentary records only 20 are Athenian citizens, which testifies to a shortage of citizen labourers.
57. Ps-Xen. *Ath. Pol.* 2.9; Plut. *Arist.* 24.3, *Praec. Ger. Reipub.* 818–d. Cf. J. Buchanan, *Theorika* (Locust Valley, N.Y.: 1962), 31–4.
58. Philochorus *ap* Schol. Ar. *Wasps* 718; Plut. *Per.* 37. Cf. Gomme, *Population* 16–17.

Society and Economy in Postwar Athens 67

59. Thuc. 1.142.3. Cf. Gomme, *HCT*, *ad loc.*; Ps.-Xen. *Ath. Pol.* 1.19. See too Jones, *AD* 167–77; P. A. Brunt, 'Athenian Settlements Abroad in the Fifth Century BC', *Ancient Society and Institutions* (Oxford: 1966), 71–92; P. Gauthier, 'A propos des clérouquies athéniennes du Ve siècle', *Problèmes de la terre en Grèce Ancienne* (Paris: 1973).

60. In some cases, e.g. Euboea, the cleruchs may have been absentee landlords (Brunt, 'Athenian Settlements', 87), but *contra* Jones *AD* 176, Athenian cleruchs were not normally absentee landlords; several sources state clearly that the cleruchs were *sent out* (see Gomme, *JHS* 79 [1959] 74; Calder, *CP* 54 [1959] 141; Graham, *Colony and Mother City in Greece* [Manchester: 1964] 181; Meiggs, *Athenian Empire* 261–2).

61. See *RE* 21 (1921) col 823; Glotz-Cohen *Histoire Grecque*, vol. 2, 203; Jones *AD* 173–4; Meiggs, *Athenian Empire* 260; Brunt, 'Athenian Settlements', 72.

62. Jones *AD* 169.

63. This, the generally accepted view (based on Plut. *Per.* 11; *hyp.* Dem. 8.), has recently been challenged by Brunt, 'Athenian Settlements', 71–2. He points out (a) that orthodoxy rests on the authority of late writers, and (b) that sound strategic reasons called for the admixture of men of standing, wealth and hoplite experience. Note too that late sources identify as cleruchs the fathers of Plato and Aristophanes, two men who were far from being thetes: Plato: Diog. Laert 3.3. Aristophanes: Schol. Plato *Ap.* 19c = *FGrH* 511 F 18.

64. Thuc. 8.48.5–6; cf. Gauthier 'Clérouquies', 177; M. I. Finley, 'The Athenian Empire: A balance sheet', in Finley *Economy and Society in Ancient Greece* (New York: 1983), 52–3.

65. On Thucydides, see Kagan, *Outbreak of the Peloponnesian War* (Ithaca: 1969), 134–8. On Antiphon, see K. J. Maidment, *Minor Attic Orators*, vol. 1 (Cambridge, Mass.: 1968), 4; Antiphon frgs. 1–2, ibid.

66. Adeimantus: Gauthier, 'Clérouquies', 158; Amyx, *Hesperia* 22 (1953) nos 6.55–6, 10.11; *Hesperia* 27 (1958) pp. 168–70. Oionias: *Hesperia* 22 (1953) no. 7 col. 2.78, no. 9 col. 1.314. In general, see Davies, *WPW* 56–60. He identifies (57–58 esp. n. 35) a fourth category of Athenian land ownership abroad in the fifth century, land owned by an Athenian god or goddesses (*temene*) and leased out to Athenians or locals.

67. Cf. Davies, *WPW* 60.

68. Cost of slaves: Lauffer, *Bergwerkssklaven* 63–5.

69. Meiggs, *Athenian Empire* 257.

70. Against this assumption, see Davies, *WPW* 146–50.

71. There were more than 100 citizens among the 700 men at Phyle (Aesch. 3. 187, 195; Whitehead, *Athenian Metic* 156–7). Thrasybulus' army had reached 1,000 men when he arrived at Piraeus (Krentz, *Thirty* 91) and continued to grow after Munychia (Xen. 2.4.25, Diod. 14.33.4, Arist. *Ath. Pol.* 38.3) including 900 foreigners on Krentz's restoration: Thirty 94; Krentz, 'Foreigners Against the *Thirty*: *IG* 2^2.10 Again', *Phoenix* 34 (1980), 305.

72. Executions: see also Isoc. 7.67; Aesch. 3.235; Dem. 59.112–13; Hyp. 1.13. cf. Krentz, *Thirty* 79.

73. Payment: J. H. Lipsius, *S. B. Akad. Sachs.* 71 (1919) 9ff.; cf. Krentz, *Thirty* 105. Selymbria: Meiggs-Lewis *SGHI* no. 87, pp. 267–9; Phlius: Xen. 5.2.10.

74. Thrasybulus and Anytus: Isoc. 18.23. Leon: Xen. 2.3.39, *Mem.* 4.4.3. Lycurgus: Plut. *Mor.* 843e, 852a. Alcibiades: Isoc. 16.46. Niceratus: Lys. 19.47. See Krentz, *Thirty* 79–81.

75. Krentz, 'The Thirty at Athens' (Diss. Yale: 1979), 95.

76. *Contra* Krentz, *Thirty* 80.

77. On Ischomachus, see *APF* 265–8.

78. Arist. *Rhet.* 1405a 19–20; Lys. 19–48. Cf. *APF* 261–2.

79. Lysias: See n. 26. Isocrates: F. Blass. *Die Attische Beredsamkeit*^{2} vol. 1 (Leipzig: 1887) 69f.

80. Xen. *Mem.* 2.8.1–5; Davies, *WPW* 58.

81. Cf. *APF* 94.
82. For poverty in Aristophanes *Ecclesiazusae* and *Ploutos*, *infra*, chap. 6 'The Testimony of Aristophanes'.
83. Lys. *Against Teisis*, frg. 2.2, Gernet and Bizos, *Lysias, Discours*, vol. 2 (Paris: 1962). The date of this speech is unknown, but like most of Lysias' speeches, it probably belongs after 404. See Dover, *Lysias* 44–5.
84. See the monument to the fallen knight Dexileus (b. 414/3, d. 394/3, Tod, *GHI* vol. 2, 105; photo in Bury and Meiggs, *A History of Greece*[4] (New York: 1975), 340). The elaborate, sculpted relief would have been considerably more expensive than one of the simple stelai also used at the time. See D. C. Kurtz and J. Boardman, *Greek Burial Customs* (Ithaca, NY.: 1971), 121–32. For Socrates, see Plato. *Ap.* 38a.
85. Tolerance: Dover, *GPM* 40; Jones, *AD* 35–7. Tension: Ehrenberg, *Aristophanes* 251; Lintott, *Civil Strife* 176–8.
86. Dover, *GPM* 110–11.
87. *Supra*, n. 82.
88. Ehrenberg, *Aristophanes* 145, 250–2, 361; Dover, *GPM* 38, for the phraseology; Funke, *HA* 6–7.
89. M. I. Finley, in 'Empire in Greco–Roman World', 1–15, argues that the wealthy classes got relatively little from the empire compared to the massive gains of the poor. Mossé, in *Athens in Decline* 12, 30, argues that 'the rich' in fourth century Athens were generally anti-imperialist, having little to gain and much to lose in the way of liturgies and *eisphora*. 'The poor', on the other hand, supported such ventures, in the hope of booty and wages. For similar arguments, see Ussher, *Ecclesiazusae* commentary *ad* 197–8.

Cloché, 'Conflits', 151–2; *Idem, La politique étrangère d'Athènes de 404 à 338 avant J.-C.* (Paris: 1934) chaps. 1 & 2 and D. Kagan, 'The Economic Origins of the Corinthian War', *La Parola del Passato* 80 (1961), 321–41, argue similarly, but they both recognize certain exceptions: the depredations of the Spartans and the Thirty, and the loss of imperial property induced some men of property to join the poor in their enthusiasm for war and empire.
90. G. E. M. de Ste Croix, 'Demosthenes' *timema* and the Athenian *eisphora* in the Fourth Century BC', *Classica et Mediaevalia* 14 (1953), 30–70.
91. Thuc. 8.45.2; cf. W. K. Pritchett, *The Greek State at War*, vol. 1 (Berkeley: 1971), 24, 28.
92. For an excellent assessment of the general popularity of the empire, see P. Harding, 'In Search of a Polypragmatist', *CC* 41–50.
93. According to Mossé, *Athens in Decline* 12, 30, the town favoured war in order to get cleruchies and cheap grain from abroad; the country did not need the grain and did not benefit from the cleruchies. Of the cleruchies, Ehrenberg (*Aristophanes* 62) has written that they

> were attempts, not to improve the conditions of Attic peasants, but to provide with land the surplus of Athenian citizens, and thus to relieve the overpopulated town. The Attic farmers were not much affected by such measures, at least those of them who remained at home.

94. Mossé, *Athens in Decline* 12–30; Mossé, 'Les classes sociales à Athenès au IVe siècle', *Ordres et classes, colloque d'histoire sociale* (Paris: 1973), 25–6; Ussher, *Ecclesiazusae* commentary *ad* 197–8; M. Croiset *Aristophanes and the Political Parties at Athens*, trans. J. Loeb (London: 1909), 25; Beloch, *Attische Politik* 27, 124–6; Audring, 'Grundeigentum und Landwirtschaft', 108–31.
95. The distances, by modern roads, come from S. Rossiter, *The Blue Guide to Greece* (London: 1973) *passim*. On peasants feeling out of place in the city, see: Ar. *Acharnians* 32–34; *Clouds* 41–55; *Eccl.* 291, 432–33; *Ploutos* 322–27; Theophrastus *Characters* 4.1; cf. G. Audring, 'Grundeigentum und Landwirtschaft', 116–17.

96. Xen. *Mem.* 3.7.6, *Oec.* 6.6; Ar. *Eccl.* 280–82, 300–310, 432ff.; Dem. 1.27.
97. Since the nineteenth century, most scholars have emphasized the exclusion of rural residents from the assembly. Forrest, *Emergence* 31, offers a valuable corrective. For the traditional view, see Beloch, *Attische Politik* 6–7; Croiset, *Aristophanes* 6–7; Finley, 'Demagogues', 11 (but see now Finley, *Politics in Ancient World* 11); Kluwe, 'Die soziale Zusammensetzung', 304, 312–13; *Idem*, 'Nochmals', 80; C. Mossé, 'Les classes sociales à Athènes au IVe siècle', in *Ordres et Classes, Colloque d'Histoire Sociale* (Paris: 1973), 26; G. Audring, 'Über die Stellung der Bauern in der athenischen Demokratie', *Klio* 57 (1975), 401. If a matter of public safety — 'national security'? — i.e., *peri tes soterias*, was to be discussed at an assembly, the fact was announced in advance. Such assemblies tended to draw large crowds. See Ar. *Eccl.* 394–402; P. J. Rhodes, *Athenian Boule* (Oxford: 1972), 23.
98. Xen. *Oec.* 1–4, Lys. 1–11; Ehrenberg, *Aristophanes* 64.
99. Kluwe 'Soziale Zusammensetzung', 312.
100. See Humphreys, 'Economy and Society', 14.
101. See Ehrenberg, *Aristophanes* 64–5; P. Lévêque, 'Les différenciations sociales au sein de la démocratie athénienne du Ve siècle', in *Orders et classes* 20.
102. See Ar. *Wasps* 712; Ehrenberg, *Aristophanes* 61.
103. Ar. *Peace* 547–49, 1198–1206, show a pitchfork-seller and sickle-maker welcoming the end of the war.
104. See e.g., W. E. Heitland, *Agricola* (Cambridge: 1921), 41; C. Mossé, 'Le Statut des Paysans en Attique', in M. I. Finley, ed., *Problèmes de la terre en Grèce ancienne* (Paris: 1973), 179–80; Ussher, *Ecclesiazusae* commentary *ad* 300.; Audring (see n. 109).
105. Trans. B. B. Rogers, *The Comedies of Aristophanes* vol. 3 (London: 1913), 41. Cf. Ar. *Lys.* 506–86.
106. Even Athenian townsmen used expressions drawn from agriculture. Ehrenberg, *Aristophanes*, 64–5.
107. For examples of the sturdy ideal in Aristophanes and of its connection with the countryside, see *Acharnians* 692–700, *Clouds* 985–86, *Eccl.* 304–10. Cf. Xen. *Oec.* 6.6–10; Eur. *Orest.* 917–29.
108. Rogers, *The Comedies of Aristophanes* vol. 5 (London: 1902), 33. I have changed his 'the poor men' to 'the poor man', to follow the Greek:

Ναῦς δεῖ καθέλκειν· τῷ πένητι μὲν δοκεῖ,
τοῖς πλουσίοις δὲ καὶ γεωργοῖς οὐ δοκεῖ.

109. Audring, 'Grundeigentum', 130 n. 11. My translation from the German. Similar views: *supra* n. 89.
110. Audring, 'Grundeigentum', 119.
111. All trans. Rogers, *Aristophanes* vol. 5, 31–5.
112. Ehrenberg, *Aristophanes* 62.
113. For examples from tragedy, see H. W. Smythe and G. Messing, *Greek Grammar* (Cambridge, Mass.: 1956), section 3025. For Aristophanes, see *Peace* 556, 639.
114. Ar. *Eccl.* 601–2, trans. Rogers, *Aristophanes* vol. 5, 01:

πῶς οὖν ὅστις μὴ κέκτηται γῆν ἡμῶν, ἀργύριον δὲ
καὶ Δαρεικούς, ἀφανῆ πλοῦτον;

Cf. Jones, *AD* 6, 84–5.
115. Rebuilding walls: *infra*, chap. 5, nn. 25–6. The 380s: Ober. *FA* 56 n. 11.
116. *Supra*, Introduction.

3 Athenian Manpower After the Peloponnesian War

Who were the Athenians in 403? What was their numerical distribution among social and economic classes? No one can answer these questions precisely. As A. W. Gomme wrote in 1933, 'We cannot even attempt (and perhaps never shall be able to attempt) a tithe of a true *Social Structure* of Athens, such as is done for modern countries.'[1]

If precise answers are impossible, however, estimates are not. It has long been established that the number of Athenian citizens in 403 had dropped dramatically since the beginning of the Peloponnesian War: there were less than half as many Athenians in 403 than in 431.

It is important, however, to consider the full consequences of this disastrous decline: both the factors that contributed to decline and the serious impact on politics. Battle casualties and morbidity (the great plague of the 420s) are relatively well-documented and have received some attention. Both these and other possible checks on population, however, contraception, abortion, infanticide and malnutrition, as well as emigration and immigration, require further examination and, where possible, statistical elaboration.

The subject of Athens' population decline in the Peloponnesian War and the years immediately following it, therefore, must be reopened. Statistical precision is beyond reach, but it should be possible, at least, to expand Gomme's 'tithe of a true *Social Structure*' to a fifth.

Population Trends, 431–395

One might begin a demographic essay about a modern country by listing population statistics; interpretation of the figures would follow. Here, however, the order must be reversed because of the controversial nature of ancient Athenian population figures.[2] The figures refer only to hoplites, not to the whole adult male population — to say nothing of women, children and slaves (or,

Athenian Manpower After the Peloponnesian War 71

for that matter, accuracy).[3] Moreover, statistics which seem to refer to the same group in succeeding years may, in fact, each be based on different criteria. Before interpreting the figures, therefore, one must first have some idea of the general trends influencing the make-up of the population.

The most significant factor in Athenian demography for many years after 431 was the Peloponnesian War. A great war checks population growth by increasing mortality and often also entails, as a by-product, a decrease in fertility. The greatest agent of increased mortality in wartime is generally death in battle. If the Athenians ever tallied up their total battle losses in the Peloponnesian War, no extant ancient source has recorded the fact. Still, it is possible to estimate the numbers. If one adds up the casualty figures for hoplites in Thucydides, Xenophon and Diodorus, a total of 5,470 is reached.[4] Remembering that some metics are included in this figure, and also remembering that the sources mention other battle casualties for which they provide no figures, this total may stand as roughly accurate.[5]

Rough as this casualty figure is, it is hard to reach one nearly as reliable for the thetes, who were rowers, archers and petty officers in Athenian warships, and who served as light-armed troops on land. Indeed, the dearth of evidence about the thetic population is a well-known problem in Athenian demographic history.[6] The sources are vague as to the percentage of personnel on an average trireme that was Athenian citizen. Not only did metics serve in great numbers as rowers, petty officers and archers, but foreigners from the allied cities also served as rowers and archers. Moreover, although there is fairly good information about the number of ships lost in specific engagements, it is rarely stated how many men were killed.[7]

Nevertheless, we are not totally in the dark. It is certain that from 407 on, when Persia subsidized a raise in the Spartan pay rate for rowers, and when the metic population of Athens had declined, the percentage of citizen rowers on Athenian ships was high. M. Amit has argued persuasively that at the outbreak of the Peloponnesian War, as again in Samos in 411 (and presumably in between), 'the core of the crews' was made up of Athenian citizens and metics. Unless a sizable percentage of the rowers was composed of citizens, whence the power of the 'naval mob' (Arist. *Pol.* 1304 a 22) that was so important in fifth-century politics?[8]

We can be even more specific. At the beginning of the war,

Pericles assured the Athenians that even if they lost all their foreign rowers to a higher bidder, Athenian citizens and metics could man a fleet equal to their enemy's (Thuc. 1.143.1). Judging by Plutarch's information, Pericles had reason to be so confident, for in the years before the war, Athens regularly sent out 60 ships each year in which 'many citizens earned eight months' pay' (Plut. *Per.* 11.4). Although the Peloponnesians could muster a total fleet of at least 150 ships in 431, only once before 413 did they send out as many as 100 ships at a time; around 50 was the more usual number. Hence, if Pericles knew his citizens could man 60 ships themselves, he had reason to be confident.[9]

Plutarch of course does not say these 60 ships were manned exclusively by citizens, and although a smart politician would want to restrict so lucrative a job to the voters, it was militarily necessary to give the metics some practice. If, at a guess, about two thirds of the thetic crewmen (*infra*) on these annual ships were citizens and one third metics, the result is one group of 7,500 citizens and one of 3,700 metics. These figures should stand as minima. First of all, the Athenian budget was not unlimited, and had he been able to pay for them, Pericles might have been able to fill more than 60 ships a year. Second, if one is to take Pericles at his word about matching the enemy, he might have had as many as 100 ships in mind: that is, 19,000 thetic crewmen, of which two thirds is 12,500.

Using the age distribution model described below, and assuming the 12,500 thetic crewmen represent the age groups 18–39, the thetes age 18–59 would be *c.* 18,500. This is close both to the figure of 20,000 thetes which the ancient testimonia supply (*infra*) and to the figure of 18,000 thetes which, by a different set of calculations, Gomme proposes as the minimum number of thetes in 431. Since Pericles might have sent out more than even 100 ships, and since more than two thirds of the crewmen might have been citizens, it is fair enough to regard 18,500 as a minimum. Ruschenbusch indeed argues for a higher figure, 26,500 thetes in 432; although this figure is somewhat too high, the general line of his argument is sound.[10]

As Ruschenbusch points out, Athens had enough thetes to man 143 triremes in 413. Since there had been few thetic battle casualties since 431, aside from the perhaps 1,000 fallen at Delium, the thetic population of 413 represents roughly 66–75 per cent of the thetic population before the plague (*infra*), that is, the thetic population in 431. We may calculate 10,300 thetes on 143 triremes (i.e. 36 per cent, *infra*), which would imply 14,000–15,000 thetes in 431. These would, however, only represent the thetes of battle age, i.e. 18–39; if one includes those aged 40–59, the totals would be roughly 21–23,000 in 431 and 15,000 in 413.[11] Hence, a figure on the order of 20,000 thetes in 431 (the traditional figure) may be accepted.

Ruschenbusch also provides an attractive criterion for calculating the number of citizen thetes per ship. He argues that the citizen contingent among the rowers was roughly equivalent to the *thranitai*, the 62 men on each ship who sat on the highest tier of benches; that is, 36 per cent of the rowers. Assuming that, say, half of the 6–8 petty officers, 4 archers and 10 seamen on each ship were also citizen thetes, the total citizen thetic contingent per ship was normally 72 men out of 200, or 36 per cent. The marines, on the average about 10 men per ship, were usually citizen hoplites.[12]

These figures are of course rough estimates, but plausible ones, and grounded in the facts. On their basis, at least 12,600 thetes died while fighting in the Peloponnesian War.[13]

For a country with an adult male citizen population of over 40,000, the loss of *c.* 18,000 men (hoplites and thetes) over almost 30 years would be a serious blow but not a fatal one. If, as is likely, there was heavy population pressure on available resources in 431, there would have been candidates on hand to replace the fallen. Besides, in the 27 years of war, a whole new generation could have grown up.[14]

Unfortunately for Athens, battle losses were only the beginning of demographic woes during the Peloponnesian War. The death in battle of an unmarried young man in the 420s also represented the loss of a soldier or parent 20 years later. In that latter period, as a result of the Spartan occupation of Decelea, Athens was subject to considerable economic privation, possibly including malnutrition.[15] An improper diet is not generally fatal to adults, but it can be devastating to the old and to children — an ominous sign for the next generation of Athenians. During the last months of the war, of course, when Athens was under siege by Lysander, the population strove not for proper nutrition, but for any nutrition at all: according to Xenophon 2.2.22, 'a mass' of people died because of the severing of the city's food supply line.[16]

Did the birth rate decline? Severe malnutrition may reduce female fertility.[17] Moreover, under the pressure of want, Athenians may have decreased the number of children they raised. Contraceptive methods as efficient as those used today were not available, of course, but partially-effective means of birth-control were well-known in antiquity — as were abortion and infanticide.[18]

Whether Athenians could have reduced the number of children they bore, and whether they wanted to, however, are two different questions. Athenian parents did not have the luxury of assuming their children would survive until adulthood. A leading scientist who has tried to implement family planning programmes in the underdeveloped world today has noted: 'A basic dictum is that parents will not stop having children until they believe that those they already have are going to survive.'[19] On the same principle, some Athenian parents during the Peloponnesian War may have tried to increase their number of children.

If one is to believe the stories of Diogenes Laertius 2.26 and Aulus Gellius 15.20 (doubted by Athenaeus 555d–556), during the lifetimes of Socrates and Euripides the assembly recognized a shortage of husbands and so allowed citizens to have more than one wife at a time. The decree has been reasonably dated to the Ionian War era, and it may reflect a desire for more Athenian children. Perhaps at about the same time Pericles' citizenship law of 451, which disenfranchised the offspring of unions between male citizens and foreign wives, was abrogated, only to be reimposed in 403 (Ath. 577 B-C).[20]

The Peloponnesian War was followed by a civil war which, demographically speaking, did great damage. According to ancient sources, the oligarchs killed 1,500 men to bolster their regime, although some consider the figure exaggerated.[21]

Another factor in Athenian manpower during and after the war was the number of metics and resident aliens. Periclean Athens attracted foreigners because of its economic opportunities. As these opportunities decreased during the war, so may the number of foreigners. Moreover, it was one thing to make one's living on foreign soil, another to die for it. Metics served as hoplites, and both metics and resident aliens served in the fleet (*supra*). Metics were not subject to trierarchies, but they were responsible for the encyclical liturgies (a burden made heavier by the exemption of trierarchs) and for *eisphora*. Aristophanes' Trygaeus included metics among those at Athens who had been hurt by the Archidamian War: a scholiast explains that they had been required to pay a special tax.[22] There were other hardships to bear, among them, the confiscations of the Thirty and the famine during Lysander's siege.

Half a century after the end of the Peloponnesian War, Isocrates

(8.21) complained that during the Social War of 357–55, Athens was 'deserted by its merchants and foreigners and metics'. *Mutatis mutandis* and allowing for hyperbole, one may imagine some emigration, if not 'desertion' in the Peloponnesian War. Moreover, there might have been other metics who would have come to Athens in peacetime, but who stayed at home during the war.[23] Metics and other foreigners may have begun to return to Athens after the peace in 403, but given the city's economic troubles and political instability, the process was probably a trickle rather than a flood.

A number of factors damaging to Athens' manpower has been discussed. None of them, however, and perhaps not even the combination of all of them, was as serious as the epidemic that struck the city in 430–27. 'Nothing did the Athenians so much harm as this or so reduced their strength for war,' Thucydides writes (3.87.2). The disease not only crippled Athens' hoplite strength in the 420s, but it held Athens hostage for the future, since most likely children as well as grown men were victims.[24] Not until 406 would children born after the disease reach the age of active military service; nor would even an increase in fertility easily make up for at least a 25 per cent decline in the number of parents in 426. In 396, the Athenians were able to excuse themselves from participating in Agesilaus' latter-day Trojan expedition on the grounds that they were still recovering from both the war and the epidemic, the latter event now 30 years in the past.[25]

Thucydides 3.87.3 gives some indication of the number of Athenians who died: at least 4,400 hoplites, 300 cavalry and 'an incalculable number' of the rest of the population.[26] There has, however, been much disagreement about the interpretation of these figures.[27] One obvious difficulty is Thucydides' failure to provide casualty figures for the entire population. Another stumbling block is deciding precisely what is meant by 'the rest of the population'. According to Thucydides 3.87.3, his casualty figures for hoplites refer only to hoplites *ek ton taxeon*; modern scholars have crossed swords over the meaning of the three words.

Beloch and Gomme are in essential agreement about the problem. Thucydides provides careful figures for Athens' hoplite strength at the beginning of the war. When doing so, he draws a distinction between one group of 13,000 hoplites — whom Gomme has conveniently labelled as those fit for 'active service'[28] — and a second group of 16,000 more in garrisons and on guard duty on the city's walls. The latter group was made up of the youngest and oldest classes of citizens and all the metic hoplites; the former, presumably, was restricted to citizens of an age to be sent into battle (*infra*).[29] Both Beloch and Gomme refer Thucydides' figures for hoplite plague casualties to only those 13,000 hoplites who normally went into battle: Beloch translates *ek ton taxeon* as 'aus den taktischen Verbände,' and Gomme renders the expression as 'from the regiments'.[30] By this interpretation, Athens would have lost far more than 4,400 hoplites because of the plague. Thucydides' figures would then mean that 34 per cent of the active-service hoplites died in the plague. This compares to 30 per cent of the cavalry (300 out of 1,000) and 29 per cent of Hagnon's troops (1,150 out of 4,000, Thuc. 2.58.3) lost to the epidemic in 40 days at Potidaea in 430. With these figures as guidelines, and assuming a consistent casualty rate, between 8,410 and 9,860 hoplites *in toto* were carried away by the plague. Moreover, not all of the survivors continued to fight, because the disease left many maimed (Thuc. 2.49.8).

Such an estimate, however, is far too great, according to Jones' translation of *ek ton taxeon*: he renders it simply as 'from the tribal regiments'.[31] That is, Jones argues that Thucydides was referring not to the battle ranks (*taxeis*) in which some hoplites fought, but to all hoplites. Since Thucydides was manifestly able to obtain fairly precise figures for the size of both hoplite classes in 431, but none for the rest of the population, it seems likely that in his casualty figures, he would divide hoplites in general from the rest of the population.[32]

Jones' case is strong, but it falls down before a philological study of Thucydides. Although other authors may use the expression in question to refer to the total number of registered hoplites, Thucydides does not. He employs it to refer to the line of battle, or to fighting men in the field, as opposed to those on guard duty.[33] The older interpretation of Thucydides' language, therefore, with the staggering, plague-inflicted losses which it implies, is to be preferred to Jones': i.e., one fourth to one third of the Athenians were killed (again, assuming a consistent casualty rate).[34]

Its population was large enough that, in spite of the plague, Athens continued the war for another 20 years. It could not do so, however, without paying a great price. The social and political fabric was rent: to polygamy and the temporary repeal of Pericles' citizenship law (*supra*) one might add the growing popularity of oligarchy, of demagogy and of religious extremism, and also the cycle of arrogance and over-confidence which was bred by the growing need after the plague to squeeze the allies until the pips squeaked. After the plague, Athens might have retrenched; instead, it overextended itself and lost the war.

To look ahead to the years after 403, although it is evident that Athenian manpower could not return to its prewar level, there was some recovery. Economic privation was not as serious as during the war, although the situation had not returned to normal. Military manpower was boosted by the maturation of the cohort born 421–415, which was probably fairly large since those had been years of peace and prosperity, perhaps even of a postwar (i.e., between the Peace of Nicias and the Sicilian Expedition) baby boom.[35]

The return of cleruchs and owners of private property overseas tended to increase the citizen population of Attica. The victor of Aegospotami restored Aegina, Melos and other states to their original inhabitants, and sent home to Attica any Athenian he found in the Aegean.[36] It has become customary to speak of a massive movement of population back to Attica after 405, but the numbers were probably not great. Athens had sent out 5–10,000 cleruchs and colonists under Pericles and during the Archidamian War.[37] Many of these, however, had probably returned to Athens well before Aegospotami in order to fill manpower needs. The cleruchs sent to Mytilene in 427, for instance, were certainly gone by 412, and possibly as early as 424.[38] Moreover, some of those usually considered emigrants may have rather enjoyed their foreign property as stay-at-home rentiers. So although Athens may have sent out as many as 10,000 cleruchs, they did not all wait for the end of the war to come home; Beloch estimates an influx of only 3–4,000.[39]

Moreover, if immigration increased in 405, so may have emigration, at least on a small scale. Some men of oligarchic sentiment, like Xenophon and the 300 knights whom the Athenians sent to Thibron in 399, preferred serving the Spartans to staying in the hated democracy.[40] Democrats, too, sought foreign service, but from different employers. After Aegospotami, Conon and some of his friends preferred exile in Cyprus to a bleak political future (if any) at home.[41] Even before Demaenetus' mission in 395, the Athenians had frequently sent seamen to

Conon.[42] In the economic doldrums of the 390s, some Athenians may have found business opportunities abroad.[43] Some Athenians certainly left Attica after 403, although I doubt that we should accept Jones' estimate of 'many thousands of citizens'.[44]

Hoplites and Thetes, 431–394

Let us consider the statistics of Athens' changing hoplite strength from 431 to 394 in light of the previous, more general discussion. Thucydides' appraisal (2.13.6) of Athens' hoplite force in 431 has been mentioned: 13,000 citizens were of age for active service, while 16,000 men, including (a) the youngest and oldest hoplite citizens and (b) all the metic hoplites, stood on guard duty. As Jones argues, the status of active-service hoplite was normally restricted to citizens between 20 and 39.[45] With this in mind, it is possible to make an informed estimate of the total numbers of citizen and metic hoplites in 431.

Jones, following A. R. Burn, argues that age distribution of the population in Periclean Athens (as in better-documented Roman Africa) was close to an underdeveloped, pre-industrial population such as early twentieth-century Egypt or India. In the five Indian censuses between 1891 and 1931, the cohorts of males 20–39 average 62 per cent of the male population between 18 and 59. In the late-nineteenth-century Greek censuses of 1870, 1879 and 1889 (a model put forward by Rhodes), these cohorts average 63 per cent of the male population between 18 and 59.[46]

If one applies these percentages to Athens in 431, then Athens' total citizen hoplite strength was c. 21,000 of whom c. 8,000 were either aged 18–19 or 40–59. There were c. 8,000 metic hoplites of whom c. 5,000 were aged 20–39 and c. 3,000 aged 18–19 or 40–59. The necessities of the Peloponnesian War compelled Athens to use metics in active service: in the first year of war, 3,000 metics were sent to join 10,000 citizen hoplites in a 'full-force' invasion of the Megarid. They seem to have continued in these raids and served again at Delium in 424, and perhaps on other occasions (Thuc. 2.31.3, 4.90.1).[47] Athens therefore had c. 18,000 battle-aged hoplites, citizen and metic, at its disposal and c. 11,000 citizen and metic hoplites for guard duty at home. Add the 1,000 cavalrymen (Thuc. 2.13.8) and a total is reached of some 22,000 citizens of hoplite census in 431.[48]

Athenian Manpower After the Peloponnesian War 79

Athens next sent out a hoplite invasion with a 'full complement' seven years later in 424 to Delium.[49] This time, however, only 7,000 hoplites were counted (Thuc. 4.93.4). The drop from the 16,000 hoplites deployed in 431 (13,000 in the Megarid and 3,000 at Potidaea, Thuc. 2.31) is 56 per cent (not to mention a drop of 61 per cent from the potential total of 18,000 active-service hoplites). One may account for most of the decline by battle losses (*c.* 600 men since 431), plague losses (one third of 16,000 is 5,280), and the deployment of *c.* 1,000 hoplites in other theatres of action, and 500–1,000 hoplites on service in the new cleruchies of Aegina, Potidaea and Lesbos.[50] The remaining *c.* 1,000–1,500 men are perhaps to be accounted for in several ways: by the incapacitation of men maimed by the plague; by the inability, or unwillingness, of some of the eager hoplites of 431 to furnish battle armour and join the muster after seven years of war; by the rise in emigration, and decline in immigration of metics.[51] In short, the decline in hoplite numbers was considerable.

A glimpse of Athens' hoplite manpower is next afforded for the year 411. In that year, after the fall of the radical oligarchy of the Four Hundred, Athens established the more moderate regime of the Five Thousand. Thucydides 8.97.1 describes the members of this latter regime as 'those men who bore arms' — that is to say, by the simplest interpretation, the hoplites. Scholars have long debated the political consequence of this statement, but the demographic consequences have not received the same attention.[52] If Thucydides was right, the hoplite class had undergone a shocking decline since 431 and 424.

Even considering the plague, the hoplite battle losses of *c.* 4,500 men since 431, and the likelihood that Spartan raiders at Decelea had driven many hoplites into the thetic class, so great a decline is hard to credit. The revelation at Lysias 20.13 that the registrar of the Five Thousand found 9,000 arms-bearing men for his regime is more palatable, although it is somewhat vitiated by the suggestion that he included some unqualified men in order to please the *demos* (Lys. 20.13). Further help comes from those passages in Thucydides and Aristotle in which the Five Thousand are described as a far more select group than the hoplites: e.g., 'those most able to carry out liturgies with their money and body' (Arist. *Ath. Pol.* 29.5, cf. 33.1, Thuc. 8.65.3). The suggestion, again, is of far more than 5,000 hoplites *in toto*.

In 394, Athens had at least 6,000 active-service hoplites, the number sent with 600 knights to the battle of the Nemea River (Xen. 4.2.17). Presumably some of them were metics, although probably not so high a percentage as the 23 per cent metic army of the Megarid in the exceptional case of 431. Presuming only 10 per cent metics, the total number of citizen hoplites, including men aged 18–19 or 40–59, would be a minimum of 8,500, plus the cavalry, this perhaps reduced by losses in population, wealth and morale since 431 to perhaps 750 men; thus a total of c. 9,250. This figure is in line with the 9,000 men of 411, with subtractions made for subsequent battle casualties and the addition of young men born after the plague.

The sources are not nearly as informative about the thetes as about the hoplites. Aristotle states (*Ath. Pol.* 24.3) that the empire supported 20,000 men, and likewise there is the remark of Aristophanes' character Bdelycleon (*Wasps* 709) that, if honestly run, the empire could nourish 20,000 'demesmen' (*demotai*). These are at best conventional figures, but a scholarly estimate of 20,000 thetes in 431 is in order (*supra*).

That total had dropped dramatically by 403. By 425, the plague had killed about a fourth to a third of the thetes, leaving c. 15,000. Only c. 150 thetes (vs. c. 600 hoplites) had died in battle by 425. About 1,000 fell in 424 at Delium; between 415 and 405 there were a minimum of 11,450 thetic casualties — for a total of at least 12,600 thetic casualties in the Peloponnesian War. In addition, the thetes had to cope with malnutrition and famine, and perhaps had to resort to contraception, abortion and infanticide. So did more affluent Athenians, but historically, these problems have always cost the poor more dearly than the affluent.

Conclusions

As much as the hoplites suffered in the Peloponnesian War, the thetes suffered even more so. Hoplites incurred at least 5,470 casualties, thetes over twice as many, at least 12,600. Moreover, the hoplites had 2,210 casualties by 421 and 4,490 by 413; they only incurred 980 casualties in the Ionian War. The thetes, on the other hand, had only 1,150 casualties by 421 and 6,600 by 413; they had another 4,850 casualties in the Ionian War, almost five times as many as the hoplites. Therefore, while the hoplites had a chance to replenish their numbers between 413 and 405, the thetes had been bled, especially the cohorts born between 452 and 425.

The political consequences were considerable. By 405, a good part of the political power of the thetic class was at the bottom of the Aegean. It is small wonder then that *hoi polloi* were no more assertive after the restoration of democracy in 403.

Hoplite numbers were cut by 50 per cent or more between 431 and 394, from some 22,000 to *c.* 9,250. There were *c.* 15,000 thetes in 415 and some 11,000 thetic battle casualties in the next ten years. Many hoplites, including former cleruchs, dropped into the thetic class, as one must assume to explain why the drop in hoplite numbers was even greater than the plague and battle casualties would suggest. Moreover, the cohorts born after the plague began to raise the size of the population at the end of the fifth century. Even so, it is difficult to imagine more than 5,000–7,000 thetes in 394.[53] Hence, the adult male citizen population of Athens after the Peloponnesian War was 14,000–16,250. It had been over 40,000 in 434, so the cost of the Peloponnesian War to Athens in citizen population loss was some 60 per cent.[54] In political terms, while the numbers of hoplites and thetes were roughly equal in 431, by the end of the century hoplites outnumbered thetes by at least 20 per cent.

In the case of the metics, the evidence is so scanty that one must be content with a general impression of a great decline in numbers, comparable to if not greater than that of the citizens.[55]

Taken as a whole, therefore, the demographic costs of the Peloponnesian War were staggering, and except for the small grace that there were now fewer mouths to feed, immensely deleterious to Athens. The new demography was, however, not without value to those members of the Athenian upper classes who feared a more radical democracy.

Notes

1. Gomme, *Population* 48.
2. The main works on classical Athens' population are K. J. Beloch, *Bevölkerung*; Beloch, *GG*² vol. 3.2, 386ff.; E. Meyer, *Forschungen zur Alten Geschichte* vol. 2 (Halle: 1899), 149ff.; Gomme, *Population*; Jones, *AD* 8–10, 76–9, 161–80; E. Ruschenbusch, *Innenpolitik*; Ruschenbusch, 'Die soziale Herkunft der Epheben um 330', *ZPE* 35 (1979), 173–6; Rhodes, 'Ephebi, Bouletae, and the Population of Athens', *ZPE* 38 (1980), 191–201; Ruschenbusch's replies in *ZPE* 41 (1981), 103–5 and *ZPE* 44 (1981), 110–12; M. H. Hansen, *AJAH* 7 (1982) 172–89; J. M. Williams, 'Solon's Class System, the Manning of Athens' Fleet, and the Number of Athenian Thetes in the Late Fourth Century', *ZPE* 52 (1983), 241–5.
3. There are no figures for the number of women and children in this period. The customary procedure is to multiply the number of free adult males by four (Gomme,

Population 75–83). Since women were not liable to battle casualties, there may have been an unusual excess of women, compared to the number of men, at the end of the Peloponnesian War (Sarah B. Pomeroy, *Goddesses, Whores, Wives and Slaves: Women in Antiquity* (New York: 1975), 69, where the adoption of a niece by the wealthy Hagnias in 395 is cited as a possible indication of this trend. See Isaeus 11, *passim*; Dem. 43, *passim*). The number of slaves declined dramatically, thanks to the plague and the Spartans at Decelea (*supra*, chap. 2).

4. See Appendix.

5. See Hommel, 'Metoikoi', cols. 1446–7; D. Whitehead, *Ideology of the Athenian Metic* (Cambridge: 1977), 82–3, n. 107. In the Megarid campaign of 431, 23 per cent of the army was metic (Thuc. 2.31.2) and we know of several other occasions on which metics perhaps served in the field. See *infra*, p.78.

6. As Meiggs puts it, the evidence is 'almost negligible' (J. B. Bury and R. Meiggs, *A History of Greece*[4] (New York: 1975), 535, n. 8). Gomme's uncertainty about the subject is admirable (*Population* 12–16); Beloch's confidence, unfounded (*Bevölkerung*, 72–4). Cf. n. 10.

7. In most cases, a fair number of men were probably saved. Note that in the extraordinary case of Arginusae, Xenophon took pains to say that Athens lost 25 ships, 'crews and all' (αὐτοῖς ἀνδράσιν), 1.6.34. In this battle, at any rate, it was assumed that there would be survivors of damaged ships, and that the generals were to rescue them.

8. M. Amit, *Athens and the Sea* (Brussels: 1958), 29–48. For the Persian pay-raise, see Xen. 1.5.4–9, 20; Gomme, *Population* 13. Another vexing question is that of the number of sailors on a troop-transport. I have followed the argument of Dover, *HCT ad* 6.43.

9. Sixty ships: *contra*, S. K. Eddy, 'Athens' Peacetime Navy in the Age of Perikles', *GRBS* 9 (1968), 141–56, criticized by Jordan, *Athenian Navy* 113 n. 71. Total fleet: Thuc. 1.46, 2.93.2; cf. B. Henderson, *The Great War Between Athens and Sparta* (London: 1927), 31; T. Kelly, 'Thucydides and Spartan Strategy in the Archidamian War', *AHR* 87 (1982), 32. One hundred ships: Thuc. 2.66 (430 BC). Usual number: Henderson, *Great War* 31.

10. Gomme, *Population* 14. Estimates close to 20,000 are also to be found in Beloch, *Bevölkerung* 73 and Jones, *AD* 9; 30,000 in French, *Growth* 137–8. Ruschenbusch, *Innenpolitik* 141–7; see next note.

11. Ruschenbusch *Innenpolitik* 142 erroneously assumes that all the petty officers and archers as well as the marines were citizen thetes and that all of the thetes sent to Sicily died there (*infra*, n. 13).

12. Ruschenbusch, 'Zur Besatzung Athenischer Trieren', *Historia* 28 (1979) 106–10. Ship's crew: see Appendix. Marines: Jordan, *Athenian Navy* 195–8, Dover *HCT ad* 6.43.

13. See Appendix.

14. On the length of a generation, see T. H. Hollingsworth, *Historical Demography* (Ithaca, NY: 1969), 376. Population pressure: Periclean Athens was renowned for its abundant population, Thuc. 1.80.3.

15. Even before the occupation of Decelea, Athens brought much of its food in from Euboea. After the Spartans took the fort, supplies had to be shipped in around Sunium, which was more expensive than the previous overland route (Thuc. 7.28.1). After the revolt of Euboea in 411 (8.95.7), essential foodstuffs had to be brought in from even further away, at, presumably, a greater expense. How many thetes could afford to maintain the quality of their diets under such conditions?

16. Malnutrition and child mortality: B. Winikoff, 'Nutrition, Population and Health: Some Implications for Policy', *Science* 200 (May, 1978), 895–901. In French's opinion (*Growth*, 140), Periclean Athens' success in reducing infant mortality from malnutrition was 'the most significant factor in [its] population

movement'. Famine of 405: see Andocides F 3.1, Loeb, with the commentary of Ober, *FA* 53–4.

17. Many scientists believe that acute or chronic malnutrition may reduce a woman's fecundability, lead to serious complications of pregnancy or delivery, and significantly reduce the chance of survival of offspring. These conclusions have, however, been challenged. See R. K. Anderson, 'Nutrition, Fertility and Reproduction', in *Prognosis for the Undernourished Surviving Child*, ed. by A. Chavez, *et al* (Basel: 1975), 7–10.

For a recent study of a wartime famine's demographic effects — a famine with certain similarities to the Athenian one of 405 — see Z. Stein, M. Susser *et al.*, *Famine and Human Development: The Dutch Hunger Winter of 1944–1945* (New York: 1975).

18. If individuals wanted to raise fewer children, they certainly had the ability to do so. One method was the exposure of unwanted infants, well known in classical Greece. For further discussion, see Gomme, *Population* 79–82; A. Zimern, *The Greek Commonwealth* (Oxford: 1931), 330f.; Pomeroy, *Women* 69–70; W. K. Lacy, *The Family in Classical Greece* (Ithaca: 1968), 165–6; A. Cameron, 'The Exposure of Infants and Greek Ethics', *CR* 46 (1932), 105–14; M. Golden, 'Demography and the Exposure of Girls at Athens', *Phoenix* 35 (1981), 316–30 and W. V. Harris, 'The Theoretical Possibility of Extensive Infanticide in the Graeco-Roman World', *CQ* 32 (1982), 114–16, both convincing replies to D. Engels, 'The Problem of Female Infanticide in the Greco–Roman World', *CP* 75 (1980), 112–20 and now 'The Use of Historical Demography in Ancient History', *CQ* 34 (1984), 386–93.

Abortion: W. A. Krenkel, 'Erotica 1: Der Abortus in der Antike', *Wiss. Zeitschrift Rostock* 20 (1971), 443–50.

There were also means of preventing conception. By Aristotle's day, some Greeks did so by filling the vagina with olive or cedar oil, lead ointment or frankincense, contraceptive methods which modern scientists consider partially effective (*Hist. An.* 583a; cf. N. E. Himes, *Medical History of Contraception* (New York: 1963), 80; K. Hopkins, 'Contraception in the Roman Empire', *Comparative Studies in Society and History* 8 (1965), 134. No Greek source refers to the practice of *coitus interruptus*, but the Hebrews knew of it (*Genesis* 38.7–10), and it is likely enough that the Athenians did too (*contra* Hopkins, 'Contraception', 143–8). Another expedient was anal intercourse (K. J. Dover, 'Eros and Nomos', *Bull. Inst. Classical Studies* 11 (1964), 36–7).

19. J. D. Wray, 'Will Better Nutrition Decrease Fertility?', in *Undernourished Surviving Child*, 30.

20. Cf. Ar. *Lys.* 591–97 and Pomeroy, *Women* 66–7, plus bibliography in n. 34.

21. See chap. 2, n. 72.

22. Ar. *Peace* 296–8, and scholion *ad loc*. Liturgies and *eisphora*: Whitehead, *Athenian Metic* 77–82.

23. See Gome, *Population* 19–20. Perhaps the general anti-Athenian sentiment in Greece around the start of the Archidamian War dissuaded some men from coming to Athens. (Thuc. 2.8.4).

In the late fourth century, an Athenian law forbade metics from leaving the city in wartime (Hyp. 5.33, cf. 3.29). The law may have been old, perhaps even from the fifth century; if so, Isocrates suggests that it was honoured mainly in the breach.

24. Children influenza, smallpox, tularaemia, typhus can be fatal, see J. O. Forfar and C.C. Arneil, *Textbook of Pediatrics* 2nd ed (New York: 1978) s. v.; J. Longrigg, 'The Great Plague of Athens', *Hist. Sci* 18 (1980), 222n. 5. *contra*: J. A. H. Wylie and H. W. Stubbs, 'The Plague of Athens: 430–428 BC Epidemic and Epizootic', *CQ* 33 (1983), 11. The nature of the disease has long been debated. The most recent suggestions are smallpox (R. J. and M. L. Littman, 'The Athenian

Plague: Smallpox', *TAPA* 100 [1969] 261–75), typhus (J. Scarborough 'Thucydides, Greek Medicine and the Plague at Athens: A Summary of the Evidence', *Episteme* 4 [1970] 77–90), glanders (C. H. Eby and H. D. Evjen, 'The Plague of Athens: A New Oar in Muddied Waters', *Jrnl Hist of Med and Allied Sci* 17 [1962] 258–63; contra J. C. F. Poole and A. J. Holladay, 'Thucydides and the Plague: A footnote', *CQ* 32 [1982] 235–6) tularaemia (Wylie and Stubbs, 'Plague', 6–11) and influenza virus complicated by a toxin-producing strain of noninvasive staphylococcus (A. D. Langmuir, T. D. Worthen, *et al.*, 'The Thucydides Syndrome, A New Hypothesis for the Cause of the Plague of Athens', *The New England Journal of Medicine* 313.16 [Oct. 17, 1985] 1027–30). As McNeill argues, however, it may be impossible to identify the disease since (a) today's diseases probably exhibited different symptoms when they first appeared and (b) the Athenian disease may not have a contemporary descendant. W. H. McNeill, *Plagues and Peoples* (Garden City: 1976), p. 318 nn. 34, p. 36; Poole and Holladay, 'Thucydides and the Plague of Athens', *CQ* 29 (1979), 282–300.

25. Paus. 3.9.2. Pausanias implies that the Athenians were exaggerating, for their real motive was a desire to help Conon. On the other hand, the Spartans accepted the excuse.

26. Cf. Diodorus (Ephorus?), who counts 4,000 *stratiotai*, 400 cavalry and 10,000 others, free and slave, among the dead (12.58.1). I prefer Thucydides' agnosticism about the total number of victims, for he was extremely careful about his figures and terms.

27. See Beloch, *Bevölkerung* 66; *GG*^{2} vol. 3.2.393; Gomme *Population* 7; Jones, *AD* 165–6.

28. Gomme, *HCT ad* 2.13.6.

29. Thuc. 2.13.6. For an argument (unpersuasive) that fifth-century generals used a selective call-up of the best men rather than the fourth-century method of call-up by age groups, see A. Andrewes, 'The Hoplite *Katalogos*', in *CC* 1–3. Gomme (*Population* 5) is not persuasive when he posits an additional 500–1,000 men in the forts.

30. Beloch, *Bevölkerung* 66; Gomme, *Population* 7.

31. Jones, *AD* 165.

32. Jones, *AD* 165–6.

33. E.-A. Be'tant lists 20 occasions on which τάξις appears in Thucydides, but on none of them does it mean 'tribal regiment'. In one case, Thucydides uses τάξις to distinguish between men in the field and those on guard duty: a usage which neatly parallels the distinction in the discussion of 431 (8.69.1). The argument is clinched by Thucydides' use of another word to describe the official Athenian register of hoplites: κατάλογος (6.26,31, 43). If he meant to say that the plague killed 4,400 hoplites from among those on the official register, he would have used this word and not τάξις. See Bétant *Lexicon Thucydideum*. Geneva: 1843, 1847, s.v. τάξις.

34. Consistent casualty rate: civilian thetes suffered more crowded living conditions than did civilian hoplites, but hoplite soldiers lived in crowded camps (Thuc. 2.58.3; Jones, *AD* 166). Staggering losses: mortality as great as 25 to 33 per cent has frequently been observed when an infection strikes a previously unaffected population. See McNeill, *Plagues and Peoples* p. 116 and n. 56.

35. Thuc. 6.12.1; Beloch, *GG*^{2} vol. 3.2.396.

36. Xen. 2.2; Plut. *Lys.* 13.2. The sources preserve the stories of two such men, Socrates' friends Eutherus (Xen. *Mem.* 2.8.1) and Euthyphro (Plato *Euthyphro* 4c). Jones (*AD* 176), thinks both men were private landowners, because they both seem to have lost rather large estates. Gauthier ('Clérouquies' 167), believes Eutherus was either a cleruch or colonist, on the grounds that his father had left him no property in Attica: a private landowner would surely have had an inheritance. See Davies, *WPW* 58; *supra*, chap. 2, n. 65.

37. *Supra*, chap. 2, n. 61.

38. See Brunt, 'Settlements', 81–4.
39. Beloch, GG^2 3.2, 394. The settlers on Lemnos, Imbros and in the Black Sea cities may have escaped Lysander's wrath. See Brunt, 'Settlements', 79–80; contra, Graham, *Colony* 185. Rentiers: *supra*, chap. 2, n. 59.
40. Xen. 3.1.4. In addition to Xenophon, seven Athenian soldiers are known to have served in the Ten Thousand (and there may have been more, as Xenophon only identifies 61 soldiers by name). See H. W. Parke, *Greek Mercenary Soldiers* (Oxford: 1933), 28.
41. Isoc. 9.51; cf. E. Meyer, *Geschichte des Altertums*, vol. 5 (Stuttgart: 1958), 192.
42. *H. Oxy.* 2.1; Isoc. 4.142.
43. Aeschines' father, who served in Asia (2.147) might have been a mercenary. See *APF* 545.
Athenian know-how was held in high regard by contemporaries, if the Corinthian speech in Thucydides is any indication (Thuc. 1.68–71). Athenian connections were vast, and some citizens may have parlayed these connections into jobs abroad. In a later period, the 360s, for example, Callistratus of Aphidna left Athens and became economic adviser to the king of Macedon (Arist. *Oec.* 1350a16).
44. Jones, *AD* 9.
45. Beloch (*Bevölkerung* 62), Gomme (Population 5; *HCT ad* 2.13.6) and Jones (*AD* 163–5) all agree that the age of 20 was the lower limit; the men between 18 and 20 — the ephebes — being reserved for guard duty (Aesch. 2.167). Beloch (ibid.) and Gomme (ibid.) set 49 as the upper age-limit. Jones, however, makes a persuasive argument that although men up to 49 might be called in a dire emergency (e.g., Delium or Chaeronea), the active-service hoplites were normally meant to include only men between 20 and 39 (*AD* 163–5).
46. A. R. Burn, 'Hic Breve Vivitur', *Past and Present* 4 (1953), 1–31; Jones, *AD* 82–3; J. H. Hutton, *Census of India*, 1931, vol. 1 — *India*, part 1 — *Report* (Delhi: 1933) 98; B. R. Mitchell, *European Historical Statistics 1750–1970* (London: 1975), 39; Rhodes, 'Population', 194 n. 13. Following Rhodes and *faute de mieux*, I mechanically estimate 18–19-year-olds as 20 per cent of the 15–24-year-olds.
47. See Jones *AD*, 164. As he points out, Thuc. 2.31.2 does not mean that there were only 3,000 metic hoplites in the active-service age groups: 'It is hardly a coincidence that 3,000 metics were called up at the time when 3,000 Athenians were detained at Potidaea (Thuc. ibid.): only so many metics were levied for the Megarid campaign as would bring the invading army up to full strength.'
48. The corresponding figure in Beloch, *Bevölkerung* 71, is 15–16,000; in Gomme, *Population* 5, 25,000; in Ruschenbusch, *Innenpolitik* 137–40, 24,000 (tromabore) in Duncan-Jones (*Chiron* (1981) 103), 17,000; in Hansen (*Symb Oslo* (1981) 23), max. 18,000.
49. The army that invaded the Megarid in 431 was sent out πανστρατιᾷ, the army sent to Delium, πανδημεί (2.31.2, 4.90.1). The latter word is more appropriate in the second case, since the Athenians sent out not only all their hoplites, but also all the thetes, citizen, metic and other foreigners (4.90.1).
50. Plague: Since Thucydides does not consider metics to be a normal part of the active-service army (e.g., 2.31.2), his figures for the plague casualties presumably do not include metics. Other theaters, cleruchies: The calculation is Gomme's, 'The Athenian Hoplite Force in 431', *CQ* 21 (1927), 149. Beloch's estimate (*Bevölkerung* 67) of at least 7–8,000 troops in the empire is not supported with evidence, and seems exaggerated to me. Hoplite cleruchs: Usually, most cleruchs were thetes (Jones, *AD* 168). The three cleruchies founded since 431, however, served a military purpose as well as a socioeconomic one, and needed trained infantrymen. Potidaea had 1,000 cleruchs, Lesbos 2,700, and Aegina an unknown number (Jones, *AD* 169–71). Of these, say, *c.* 4,000 men, perhaps one fourth were hoplites.

86 *Athenian Manpower After the Peloponnesian War*

51. Hoplites becoming thetes: Jones, *AD* 180.
52. Hignett, *Constitution*, 356–77, with a full discussion of earlier bibliography; G. E. M. de Ste Croix, 'The Constitution of the Five Thousand', *Historia* 5 (1956); Jones, *AD* 178–9.
53. Throwing away one's shield (ῥιψάσπις) was a crime to which contemporaries often referred. See And. 1.74; Ar. *Clouds* 353–54, *Knights* 1372, *Wasps* 19, 822; *Peace* 446, 673ff., 1295ff.; *Birds* 290, 1473ff.; Lys. 1.10.
Number of hoplites: Beloch, *Bevölkerung* 74 estimates 8,000 hoplites in 394; Gomme, *Population* 26, ?11,000; Ruschenbusch, *Innenpolitik* 146, 8,000.
Number of thetes: Beloch, *Bevölkerung* 74, estimates c. 10,000 thetes in 403; Gomme, *Population* 26, ?11,000; Ruschenbusch, *Innenpolitik* 135–6, 5,000, i.e., those whom Phormisius would have disenfranchised (*infra*, chap. 4).
54. Beloch (GG^2 vol. 3.2. 410) and Gomme (*Population* 26) each estimates about 40,000 citizens in 431 and about 22,000 in 400: about a 45 per cent drop. Ruschenbusch (*Innenpolitik* 146) estimates 50,500 in 432 and 13,000 in 403, a 75 per cent drop.
55. On this problem, see Gomme, *Population* 20; Jones, *AD* 165.

PART TWO
POLITICS AND POLICY

4 Reconciliation and Recrimination, 403–395 BC

In September 403, after swearing oaths of reconciliation with the men of the City, the victorious army of the Piraeus marched in solemn procession toward the Athenian Acropolis to celebrate the restoration of democracy. The procession had reached the gates of the city, and had stopped to ground arms before entering, when a commotion broke out. The commander, Aesimus, had discovered an impostor in the ranks of the hoplites: Agoratus, a notorious informer under the Thirty who later tried to change sides but was refused admission to Phyle. When he discovered Agoratus, Aesimus went up to him, seized his shield, and threw it away, crying, 'Go to hell! No place for a murderer like you in the procession to Athena!' (Lys. 13.81). On this note, the parade continued.

It was an unfortunate, but appropriate omen, for disunity was to be one of the major themes of Athenian politics in the next generation. This in spite of the amnesty, and in spite of the signal solidarity of the democrats who fought the Thirty. The leadership at Phyle and Piraeus had represented a diverse combination of backgrounds and opinions. In addition to Thrasybulus of Steiria, who had consistently fought oligarchy, and Epicrates of Cephisia, a leader of the Many after 403, there were three followers of the moderate oligarch Theramenes: Archinus of Coele, Anytus of Euonymon, and Phormisius. Aesimus and Anytus would later be *philoi* of Thrasybulus, as would Ergocles, but another Thrasybulus at Phyle — Thrasybulus of Collytus — would not, as his vociferous enmity to Alcibiades, the political patron of Thrasybulus of Steiria, seems to indicate.[1]

The unity of Phyle was not to survive the crisis of 404–403. This truth, hinted at in the Aesimus–Agoratus incident, became clear shortly afterwards. Thrasybulus of Steiria and Archinus of Coele, both of whom had been at Phyle, were considered the leaders of the *demos*. Nevertheless, soon after the restoration of democracy, Archinus indicted and convicted Thrasybulus for illegally proposing, without consulting the *boule*, to enfranchise slaves who had helped the democrats. That the two men were prominent, and the action a hostile gesture, underlines the significance of the incident.[2]

Postwar domestic politics saw serious strife. It is true, of course, that the Athenians did a commendable job of maintaining the amnesty. There were, however, attempts to violate it, and at least until 382 an oratorical chorus rehashing the crimes of the Thirty and their supporters. Moreover, while there were few dramatic ideological struggles in postwar politics, the years 403–387 were not marked by concord and unanimity. Nor does the failure of an oligarchic tendency to emerge in public mean that no one sympathized with oligarchy in private; indeed, in 403, Phormisius went so far as publicly to advocate limiting the citizenship to landowners (Lys. 34 *hypoth.*).

The following pages present a reappraisal of Athenian poitics from 403 to 387. They first discuss the general political tendencies in the years after 403, and then proceed to reconstruct the specific existing factions — a study limited, of course, by lacunary evidence, but one whose conclusions are substantially different from previous reconstructions. Domestic issues will be the focus when the early postwar years are considered, but with the outbreak of war again in 395 (the Corinthian War), foreign policy receives greater attention.

Domestic Politics in the Immediate Postwar Years

A well-known passage in which the Oxyrhynchus historian (P) describes Athenian politics in 395 (*Hell. Oxy.* 1.3) sets the stage. The writer discerns two political tendencies: the 'populist many' (*hoi polloi kai demotikoi*) and the 'men of breeding and property' (*hoi epieikeis kai tas ousias echontes*). Earlier, P speaks approvingly of 'all the notables and gentlemen' (*hosoi gnorimoi kai charientes esan*), a phrase which, considering the usual political implications of these terms, is probably a synonym for *epieikeis kai tas ousias echontes*. P therefore identifies the faction of Epicrates and Cephalus (1.2) with *hoi polloi kai demotikoi* and the faction of Thrasybulus, Aesimus and Anytus (1.2) with *hoi epieikeis kai tas ousias echontes*: a division, so common in classical writers, between the Many and the Few.[3]

If there is any truth in this division, it is only very rough. First of all, another fault line runs through postwar politics: that between the Piraeus men and the City men. If, for example, Thrasybulus, Anytus and Aesimus could be called *epieikeis kai ousias echontes*, so could Rhinon of Paeania, member of the two oligarchic Boards of Ten; his fellow demesman Cephisophon, a respected private citizen among the Three Thousand; and Epichares, member of the oligarchic *boule*.[4] The rebellion led by the first group of *epieikeis* against the regime in which the second participated prefigured a division that would mark postwar politics.

Second, I question the classification of Thrasybulus as *epieikes kai ousias echon*. Compared to a Cleon or a Cleophon, Thrasybulus might have seemed like a spokesman of the Few, but he was no more so than Pericles had been. As a working hypothesis, let us assume that by *hoi polloi kai demotikoi*, P means politicians in the tradition of Cleon, Hyperbolus, and Cleophon, who offered the *demos* fiery rhetoric (probably often attacking the Three Thousand), state pay, and promises of speedily restoring the empire: in short, men whose style and sometimes substance were more populist (for want of a better word) than Thrasybulus.[5]

Third, the question of parties again. One must resist the temptation to talk of Left, Right and Centre: nothing so formal or self-conscious existed. There were considerable differences between Thrasybulus of Collytus bandying the charge of oligarch as late as 382 and Archinus moving heaven and earth to make people forget the Thirty even in 403; or between Agyrrhius introducing ecclesiastic pay and Aristophanes' opposition to it. On the other hand, the differences between Archinus and Thrasybulus are much less clear. Moreover, as the careers of Phormisius or Epicrates demonstrate, it was sometimes possible to switch from one extreme to the other. Hence, while Athenian politicians did tend to champion the interests of either the Many or the Few, and while there were differences between 'populist' and 'patrician' champions of the Many, the faction was the elite political building block, and at times faction demanded the sacrifice of principle.[6]

The terms Left and Right are plausible approximations of the Many and the Few, and are less clumsy. They are, however, anachronistic, denoting ideological concepts not present in Athenian thought. I will refer to the Many and the Few.

To turn to narrative, the defeat of oligarchy in 403 did not mean a radicalization of democracy. A commission to revise the laws was constituted (or rather reconstituted, since it had begun work in 410 and been interrupted by the Thirty) but did not make any radical changes. Thrasybulus failed to win approval for the almost one thousand new citizens he wished to induct. Cries of vengeance against the men of the city were stifled by Archinus.[7]

The ranks of the men of the City were not small, for Archinus had limited the number who could emigrate to Eleusis. They included a general and secretary of the Council for 403/402. Three leaders of Phyle and Piraeus were former Theramenists: Anytus, Archinus and Phormisius. Add to this the population problems of the thetes and the watchful eyes of Sparta, and it is no surprise that the restored democracy avoided radicalism.[8]

Thrasybulus

The men of Phyle were the natural leaders of the restored democracy, none of whom had a greater claim to glory than their chief general, Thrasybulus. With Thrasybulus, therefore, a survey of postwar politicians should begin.[9]

With only two short and rather conventional speeches of his preserved in Xenophon (what Xenophon would have said had *he* been Thrasybulus), Thrasybulus must be judged by his deeds and his associates.[10]

He first appears in the historical record in 411, when, as a trierarch with the fleet at Samos, he was a leading opponent of the oligarchy of the Four Hundred (Thuc. 8.73–75). He was then about 35 and, since he was a trierarch, he was a man of means. But he does not appear to have come from an important family; the lack of information about his ancestors may show that he came from the newly important class of manufacturers or merchants.[11] This apparently unimportant trierarch decided in 411 to attach himself to one of the most important men in Athens, Alcibiades, whose recall he championed (Thuc. 8.81). What does this say of Thrasybulus?

According to his own statement at the time, his main reason for recalling Alcibiades was the desire to obtain Persian help for Athens' war effort (Thuc. 8.81.2). In other words, Thrasybulus claimed to be a patriot, interested above all in winning the war and preserving the empire. His actions in the remaining years of the Ionian War uphold this view, for he played important roles in the battles of Cynossema, Abydus and Cyzicus, and reconquered Thasos and Abdera. In the Corinthian War as well, Thrasybulus showed himself an able general and 'full blooded' imperialist, winning over the cities of Thrace, the Hellespont and Lesbos, and imposing a 10 per cent duty on ships that sailed past Byzantium.[12] In supporting Alcibiades, Thrasybulus may also have had a more selfish motive. By placing one of the most famous Athenians of the day in his debt, a rather young man gave himself the chance to rise from obscurity to political prominence. The lack of his own power base may help explain why Thrasybulus supported Alcibiades tenaciously and loyally until the latter's death.[13] For four years after 411, he served with Alcibiades in the Hellespont. When Alcibiades' star rose in 407, Thrasybulus, like his friend, was elected general. When Alcibiades failed to secure re-election the next year, after the fiasco at Notium, his faithful lieutenant was also dropped from the board of generals.[14] In 406, when Thrasybulus had to fight for his life after the battle of Arginusae, one of his leading opponents was the general Thrasyllus, an enemy of Alcibiades; one of his supporters was the orator Archedemus, who was associated with Alcibiades' son.[15]

Finally, in 404, when Theramenes accused Critias before the council of oligarchs of exiling 'capable leaders of the common people,' he mentioned Thrasybulus and Alcibiades in the same breath (Xen. 2.3.42). The reference to Theramenes points to another side of Thrasybulus. For, excepting Alcibiades, there is no other politician with whom the liberator of 403 was so closely attached. Fellow demesmen of Steiria, both men favoured the recall of Alcibiades in 411, both were generals in Alcibiades' Hellespontine fleet in the following years, and both accompanied him on his triumphal return to Athens in 407. Theramenes was Thrasybulus' codefendant in the Arginusae trials of the next year. During the civil war and after Theramenes' death, the oligarchs offered Thrasybulus his seat on the Thirty.[16]

Thrasybulus did not share his fellow demesman's preference for oligarchy, however, as his actions in 411 and 404 make clear. Even so, their views of the Athenian constitution were not light years apart. Thrasybulus was a democrat, but not of the stamp of Cleon or Cleophon, not a man to stoke the fires of class antagonism, to promise to exalt the man in the street and lay low the mighty. He seems to have been devoted to upholding the reconciliation agreement of 403, and to avoiding unnecessary recriminations. If one believes Isocrates 18.23, although Thrasybulus knew who turned a list of his property in to the Thirty, he did not bring suit.

The Oxyrhynchus historian distinguishes Thrasybulus from the representatives of 'the populist many,' and even Xenophon, no friend of democracy, eulogizes Thrasybulus on his death: 'So died Thrasybulus, who was a very good man' (Xen. 4.8.31).[17]

Nor is style irrelevant. The more a politician relied on *hoi polloi kai demotikoi*, the more he depended on oratory. He had to master the techniques of rhetoric, as Cephalus had, or to adopt an undignified and theatrical style, like Cleon's. Thrasybulus was not an outstanding orator, however, nor did he have the common touch. He was reproached for being 'haughty' (*semnos*), 'honoured and arrogant' (*axiomatikos kai authades*), and 'because, contemptuous of the *demos*, he wanted to be the one to do everything' (*hyperoptes tou demou, ebouleto di'autou panta prattesthai*). Thrasybulus' model, as Saur argues, was more likely Pericles than Cleon.[18]

To sum up, Thrasybulus was a patriot, an imperialist, a man loyal to the ancestral constitution and thus an enemy to oligarchy, but at the same time a defender of the interests of his own propertied class, and no populist. His Athens would be unified at home and, when the time was right, resurgent abroad.

Anytus and Socrates

Anytus of Euonymon was associated with Thrasybulus in 395; they were probably *philoi*, members of the same faction, and not just allies of the moment. Anytus too had been close to Alcibiades; indeed, gossip made him Alcibiades' lover. Inheritor of a fortune in tanning and shoe-making, and habitué of the highest society, Anytus had already been a general, perhaps a councillor, and had stood accused of bribing an entire jury before he turned up in Theramenes' faction in 404. In short order, under the Thirty, he fled to Phyle and lost much of his property to confiscation. Like Thrasybulus, Anytus wins Isocrates' praise (18.23) for not prosecuting those who had denounced him.[19]

But Anytus was not so devoted to reconciliation as to shrink from prosecuting Socrates in 399. Xenophon makes his motive anger at Socrates' rebuke that Anytus had raised his son solely for the tanning business (*Apology* 29). But Plato supplies more credible motives: Anytus' general hostility to sophists (with whose brush Socrates could be tarred) and his specific belief that Socrates was an excessive and slanderous critic of Athenian politicians (*Meno* 91C–92B, 93A–94B).[20]

Anytus is likely to have had a third motive as well: to attack a symbol of the threat to democracy. The trial of Socrates was a matter of religion, philosophy and pedagogy, but its political and social aspects must not be overlooked. Socrates was not the most egregious anti-democrat in Athens in 399, and as the *Crito* indicates, he respected Athens' laws. Nevertheless, his slate was not clean. Openly opposed both to the lot and to popular election, Socrates opposed democracy in theory if not in practice. As far as his record under the Thirty goes, Plato takes pains to point out that Socrates refused to dirty his hands by arresting the general Leon on the Thirty's orders. What Plato does not say is that Socrates made no effort to warn or help Leon; in fact, Socrates' very presence in the *asty* under the Thirty is indicative.[21]

A more vivid and powerful symbol, though, was the degree to which Socrates was associated with 'them' — with Critias, Alcibiades and a wide circle of aristocrats that looked down on the common person. This association gives substance to the charge made in a pamphlet of the 390s that Socrates had been a 'hater of the people' (*misodemos*). Although the indictment of 399 makes no reference to such an association (its charges are impiety and religious innovation), the pamphlets and counter-pamphlets of later years indicate that it would have, had not the amnesty of 403 prevented any such overt accusation. One must remember, in any case, that in Athens, religion *was* political; the *demos* believed that the enemies of Athens' gods were also the enemies of its laws. One need only consider the Affair of the Herms of 415 or the views of Andocides' accuser just the year before, in 400 (Lysias 6). The Athenian jury was likely to extrapolate Socrates' politics from his religion, and his misdeeds from his assoicates'. For Xenophon and Plato, for the Socratics Aeschines and Antisthenes, for Aeschines the orator, and for Polycrates, author of a much-read *Accusation of Socrates*, Socrates' connection to Critias and Alcibiades, and hence to their crimes, was a central point.[22]

Hence Anytus' prosecution of Socrates, four years after the fall of the oligarchy, was a way to focus the ever-smouldering anger of the *demos* against a symbol of their enemies. It was also, of course, a way of building up his own reputation as a popular champion (*prostates tou demou*). Anytus won the battle but not the war. He probably expected Socrates to accept banishment, not martyrdom. Although Anytus was still prominent in 395, tradition says that he was eventually exiled by a repentant *demos* for his role in the prosecution of Socrates (D.L. 2.43).

Anytus was supposedly stoned to death at Heraclea-ad-Pontus, and Roman tourists could see his ostensible grave (D.L. 2.43, Themist. 20.239C). The story smacks of moralizing ('Socrates' persecutor persecuted') but it might just explain Anytus' disappearance from the historical sources after 395 — the one possible but unlikely exception being Anytus, a grain official in Piraeus in 388/87 (Lys. 22.8), not a position to which a former general would aspire.

To return to 395, Anytus and Thrasybulus had personal connections in common (Alcibiades and Theramenes), came from the same class, and were united in a faction that stood for the democratic constitution without the 'excesses' of the populists. One does not hear of them in connection with the creation of ecclesiastic pay or with attacks on the aristocratic cavalry corps (*infra*).

Little is known of their associate (and the third member of the faction?), Aesimus, besides his anger in 403, his 'reeling' in *Ecclesiazusae* 208 (a political eclipse like Thrasybulus'?), and his embassies after the King's Peace.[23] It may be possible to add other *philoi* of Alcibiades to the faction: Adeimantus of Scambonidae and Alcibiades' son Alcibiades. Ergocles and Philocrates, Thrasybulus' lieutenants on his naval campaign in 390, may conceivably have played an earlier, political role.[24] One must shrink, however, from adding another name: Archinus.

Archinus and the Factions of the Few

Philoi do not engage in lawsuits with each other; hence Archinus' indictment of Thrasybulus for an illegal motion constitutes evidence of political enmity, even if they had co-operated in the war against the Thirty.[25] To what extent Archinus' motive was principle (abhorrence of metics and slaves or a fear of tilting the political balance toward the Many), to what extent profit (Thrasybulus stood to gain around 1,000 new supporters from his enfranchisements), one cannot say. A man as ambitious as Archinus would take both factors into account.[26]

Archinus has sometimes been underrated as a political leader, but Funke has recently granted him the prominence he manifestly had in the first year or so of the restored democracy.[27] He played the most important role of all in making the amnesty work; it evidently had enemies and needed protection. Aristotle praises Archinus for three measures in particular. First, Archinus cut short the period of registration for the oligarchic stronghold of

Eleusis, a move which strengthened the former Three Thousand in the assembly at Athens. Soon afterwards, he procured the execution of a returned democrat who sought to violate the amnesty. In between, he had Thrasybulus' citizenship law quashed (Arist. *Ath. Pol.* 40.1).[28]

Other sources also attest to Archinus' special concern for the amnesty. A speech of Isocrates relates that Archinus developed a special judicial procedure, a *paragraphe* by which anyone attacked contrary to the amnesty could attempt to halt his opponent's case.[29] Furthermore, in the year of democracy's restoration, Archinus blocked efforts to give the men of Phyle extravagant rewards. He succeeded in limiting the prize to a small sum of money and an olive wreath for each man (Aesch. 3.187). Tight finances alone may explain Archinus' parsimony, but there may have been a political motive as well. By de-emphasizing the achievement of the men of Phyle, Archinus also de-emphasized the villainy of their opponents, thus reducing tension between democrats and the former Three Thousand.

Funke argues that Archinus steered a middle course between Many and Few, and that his guiding principle was reconciliation, which both strengthened the state and deprived Sparta of an excuse for intervening.[30] The evidence shows that Archinus indeed strove to avoid civil strife, but his sympathies were closer to the Few than Funke allows. Like Anytus, Archinus had originally been a supporter of Theramenes in 404, before joining the rebels (Arist. *Ath. Pol.* 34.3). After the return from Piraeus, he protected and strengthened the presence of former oligarchs in politics, without trying like Phormisius to limit the size of the citizen body.

He was a politician of wide interests and, evidently, of liberal education. Even in late antiquity, he was still celebrated for his funeral oration. Before 405, he moved the decree restricting the pay of the comic poets. In 403 he moved the decree changing Athenian documents from the Attic to the Ionic alphabet. He was several times a general.[31]

Despite this impressive record, no reference to Archinus can be securely dated after *c*. 402, which suggests that he died shortly after 403.[32]

One cannot be certain who was in his faction while he was alive, but it would not be surprising if it included some of the more moderate former City Men. Quite a few of them played a role in postwar politics. Rhinon of Paeania, for instance, a leader of the two boards of Ten under the oligarchy, and an advocate of reconciliation with the men of Piraeus, was elected general on the democracy's return. He was still prominent enough the next year to be chosen treasurer of Athena. His fellow demesman, Cephisophon, also stood for reconciliation with the men of Piraeus in 403. After the restoration, Cephisophon proposed a motion to reaffirm an earlier decree of Athenian citizenship to the Samians. In 398, he too was a treasurer of Athena.³³

The prosecutors of Andocides in autumn 400 included Epichares, who had served on the oligarchic *boule*, and Meletus, who had arrested the general Leon of Salamis on order of the Thirty. This may have been the same Meletus who went with Cephisophon on a mission from the City Men to Sparta in 403 to arrange terms with the Piraeus Men.³⁴

Another case is Teisis, a *bouleutes* under the Thirty, who in the early 390s prosecuted Alcibiades' son over a private quarrel (Isoc. 16.42–44, 50). Finally, there is the cavalryman Mantitheus, who, at his scrutiny for the *boule* in the late 390s, was accused of having been an oligarch. He seems to have been abroad in 404–403, but his silence about his family's activities then and earlier makes one suspicious (Lys. 16.3–8).

Both of these last two men opposed Thrasybulus' faction. Mantitheus attacked Thrasybulus outright (Lys. 16.15); Teisis prosecuted the son of Thrasybulus' greatest *philos*. They therefore shared an enemy with Archinus, and since all three of them (sc. Mantitheus, Teisis, Archinus) were on the same end of the political spectrum, they might have been *philoi*.

To sum up, Archinus was not a *philos* of Thrasybulus after 403. For as long as he lived, he belonged to (and probably led) a separate faction, one more receptive to former oligarchs. Nevertheless, the ideological gulf between Thrasybulus and Archinus was not enormous.

At least two factions in postwar politics have been identified. Those former oligarchs who were not members of Archinus' faction may have formed another faction or factions or they may have dropped out of politics altogether. Some certainly never reconciled themselves to democracy, men such as the 300 knights whom the Athenians sent to aid the Spartans in Asia in 399 (Xen. 3.1.4). But the contempt with which they were sent abroad by the democracy is a measure of their political impotence.

A Theramenean who joined the men of Piraeus, Phormisius proposed upon the return of the demos to limit the citizenship to landowners. The proposal would have disenfranchised about 5,000 Athenians and had the blessing of the Spartans, but the assembly refused it (Dion. Hal. *hypoth.* Lys. 34). Ruschenbusch makes the attractive suggestion that Phormisius' proposal was an attack on the thetes (who may, however, have numbered more than 5,000, just as the hoplites in 411 had).[35]

His plan for oligarchy rebuffed, Phormisius changed course. He did not drop out of politics, or if so only temporarily. Aristophanes pokes fun at Phormisius' long beard and rough manners, but he fails to appreciate Phormisius' political suppleness. When next heard of after 403, Phormisius is a colleague of Epicrates, with whom he served on an embassy to Persia during the Corinthian War. As the Oxyrhynchus historian states (1.2), Epicrates' politics were the opposite of oligarchic. Phormisius' association with such a man does not demonstrate a political conversion, for each man might have been chosen to counterbalance the other (although both men shared a charge of bribery).[36] Phormisius' action in 378, however, when the one-time proponent of an oligarchy dear to the Spartans was a leader of the movement to help democratic Thebes, bespeaks a sea change (Dein. 1.38). Others of his former colleagues probably followed.

Andocides of Kydathenaion is an interesting example. On his return from exile in 403, he had to live down not only his membership in the oligarchic *hetairia* that had mutilated the Herms in 415, but also the bad name of having turned in his friends for the crime. It is not surprising that, in order to win public favour, he spared no expense of the fortune he had won as a merchant-in-exile. His deliveries to the fleet at Samos in 411 backfired by angering the newly-installed Four Hundred and his promises of Cypriot grain left the post-411 democracy unmoved. After 403, he had better luck as an officer at the Hephaistia festival and at the Isthmian and Olympic Games, and as a choregos at the Dionysia. He also took pains to attack the oligarchy of 404, during which he had fortunately been abroad (And. 1.80, 94–95, 99, 101–102).[37]

Andocides was a vigorous and active politician, an excellent speaker, rich and well-connected. He boasts of his numerous *philoi* and *xenoi* abroad (1.145), and presumably had others at home. The speaker of Lysias 6 *Against Andocides* of 400 complains that Andocides is preparing for a political career, and already speaks before the people, makes accusations, and is for disqualifying some of our magistrates; he attends meetings of the Council, and takes part in debates on sacrifices, processions, prayers and oracles (Lys. 6.33, Loeb tr. modified).

Unless this is a total fabrication, Andocides was at least moderately active in politics. He certainly left a mark his enemies could feel: one of his first acts upon returning in 403 was to prosecute one Archippus for mutilating a Herm dedicated by Andocides' family — in other words, Andocides found a scapegoat for his own alleged crimes (Lys. 6.11).

In short, Andocides was a political leader in his own right, perhaps head of a small faction. Without acquiring a reputation as especially *demotikos* he cleansed himself of the stain of oligarchy. He was influential enough to bring both Cephalus and Anytus on to his defense team in 400 (And. 1.150).[38]

There was no common ideology among the factions of the Few, or even any common name besides such generalities as 'the men of property and breeding' (*Hell. Oxy.* 1.3). Still, certain propositions would have united most men of this stripe. First, of course, was strict support of the amnesty. Any measures such as Theozotides' decrees to support democratic orphans financially and to reduce the pay of the knights were to be opposed — and the orphan decree did indeed attract a *graphe paranomon* (unsuccessful). Second, assembly pay was repugnant both in principle and practice. As Aristophanes complains, the *ekklesiastikon* corrupted politics with money, making each man seek his private rather than the public good — so unlike the good old days. Moreover, it opened up the assembly to the wrong sort of people, 'the multitude of the poor' (*to ton aporon plethos*), as Aristotle notes. Finally, it gave power to 'wicked leaders' (*prostataisi ponerois*, Ar. *Eccl.* 176) such as Agyrrhius.[39]

A third proposition was less unanimous: support for Sparta. Philolaconism may have had to go underground in the restored democracy, but one suspects that the many places it surfaces are mere tips of the iceberg. Support for Sparta had a practical value for those former members of the Three Thousand who distrusted the sincerity of the democratic commitment to the amnesty. Nevertheless, as we shall see, at least a few 'men of property and breeding' preferred the risk of renewed Athenian imperialism and its profits to the safety (and impecunity) of obedience to Sparta.[40]

The Factions of the Many

What of the Many? Shortly after 403 two leaders of this tendency emerged, apparently in competition with each other: Agyrrhius of Collytus, who introduced ecclesiastic (assembly) pay of one obol and then raised it to three obols after Heracleides of Clazomenae had raised it to two (Arist. *Ath. Pol.* 41.3). According to Aristotle, ecclesiastic pay was introduced because it was difficult to get the masses (*to plethos*) to attend the assembly. A return to the countryside after Spartan withdrawal and the pettiness of the problems of post-imperial Athens are two likely reasons for nonattendance. Population decline was probably even more important. As far as results, one may speculate that the sponsors meant ecclesiastic pay to serve as political and poor relief. Perhaps they also hoped to increase the ranks of the Many in the assembly. Whatever their motives, their proposal was controversial. Aristotle writes that ecclesiastic pay was rejected the first time it was proposed; Aristophanes could still raise vehement objection in *c.* 391.[41]

Of Heracleides little is known except that he had been granted Athenian citizenship, perhaps for his services as a diplomatic go-between with the Persians (*PA* 6489).[42] Agyrrhius, on the other hand, plays an active role in postwar politics as an orator and general; Sealey is probably right to make him the leader of one of Athens' most important postwar political groups. Like other populists, Agyrrhius seems to have come from a family with more interests in business than landholding. Aristophanes sneers (*Eccl.* 102), but Agyrrhius certainly had an active political career. Although his first known public activity, a move before 405 to restrict the pay of comic poets, was made in concert with Archinus, they probably soon parted company: Agyrrhius' advocacy of ecclesiastic pay is not likely to have appealed to a former Theramenean. The reticence of his opponent Andocides (And. 1.133) indicates that Agyrrhius supported the *demos* in 404–403. He was rewarded with the secretaryship of the first restored Council in 403/402. In the next two years he was active as the leader of a group of tax-farmers and joined the prosecution against Andocides in 400 (And. 1.133).[43]

But financial affairs continued to consume Agyrrhius' time in the 390s, which may explain his failure to appear in public again until chosen general in 390. The sources are, however, quite fragmentary; yet another possibility is a temporary eclipse during the success of Thrasybulus, for there is some likelihood of enmity between the two. The circumstances in which Agyrrhius replaced Thrasybulus as general in 389 raise this possibility, as does the possible co-operation in 393–392 between Agyrrhius and Thrasybulus' worst enemy, Conon. So does the certain co-operation in 400 of Agyrrhius and an enemy of Thrasybulus' *philos* Alcibiades: Alcibiades' estranged former brother-in-law, Callias of Alopece (see Ps.-And. 4. 13–15, And. 1. 132–136). Not that Callias, a leading priest of Eleusis, a frequenter of the sophists and Spartan *proxenos*, would himself support such populist policies as ecclesiastic pay. But he was not an oligarch either: again, Andocides' silence is virtual proof of Callias' support for the *demos* in 404–403.[44]

There are traces of other voices of the Many shortly after 403, men who may or may not have belonged to Agyrrhius' faction. The attacker of Agoratus, for example, urges that his opponent be executed, a sentence which, if carried out, would have violated the amnesty. Both this speaker and the prosecutor of one Nicomachus, another collaborator with the Thirty, refer favourably to Cleophon, a populist in whose company Thrasybulus would not have felt comfortable. The speaker of Isocrates' *Against Lochites* is also more an advocate of vengeance than was Thrasybulus. In his speech, probably delivered between 400 and 396, he urges the judges to punish potential oligarchs before they destroy the city again. Another case is that of Theozotides, son of Nicostratus, who, shortly after the restoration, proposed a decree granting state support for orphans of Athenian citizens who died fighting oligarchy. In another (related?) decree, he reduced the pay of the cavalry (known for its oligarch sympathies).[45]

Whatever the affiliation of these men, another populist faction, quite independent of Agyrrhius, had emerged by the early 390s if not before. Led by Epicrates of Cephisia and Cephalus of Collytus, this group probably employed vigorous and powerful oratory and lambasted the villains of oligarchy. Judging by the *hoi polloi kai demotikoi* of *Hell. Oxy.* 1.3, the two men were leaders in the manner of Cleon and Cleophon. Aeschines 3.194 calls Cephalus *demotikotatos*, literally 'very populist,' but the term is so common in fourth-century rhetoric that it may mean no more than 'a good patriot' or some such phrase.

Epicrates had been one of the men of Piraeus in 403. Like Phormisus, he was the butt of jokes about his long beard, but

Epicrates also knew how to turn humour to his advantage. According to tradition, he once freely confessed to an indictment of bribe-taking, and then joked his way out of punishment. It is indicative of Epicrates' populism that the joke is about poor relief. Instead of sending nine ambassadors to Persia, he says Athens should send nine poor men of the people (*ton demotikon kai peneton*) to get rich on the king's gifts.[46]

Cephalus would die with fame as an orator, as a supporter of the *demos*, and as a shrewd politician: he boasted that although he had proposed more decrees in the assembly than anyone else, he had never been prosecuted under a *graphe paranomon* (proposing an illegal decree).[47] In his defence in 400, Andocides accused as many of his opponents as he credibly could of supporting the oligarchy, and Cephalus was one of Andocides' supporters (And. 1. 150). In 400, Cephalus was a councillor (And 1.115); by 395, he and Epicrates were prominent enough to be accused of accepting Persian money (*Hell. Oxy.* 1.2; Paus. 3.9.8).

To judge from the *Hellenica Oxyrhynchia* 1–2, the cause of their political advancement and the hallmark of their oratory was their agitation for the rapid restoration of the empire. As Epicrates' joke about poor relief sugests, he made an explicit issue of the economic plight of the common man, and presumably promised to find relief in a revived empire. Beginning in 397, Epicrates and Cephalus called for co-operation with Conon and the Persian fleet. In 395, at the time of the Demaenetus affair, they had won enough political power to challenge Thrasybulus seriously (if not successfully). Demaenetus himself made common cause with Epicrates and Cephalus, whether his primary loyalty lay with them, with Conon, or elsewhere.[48]

Among the partisans of the Many, one would probably also find Thrasybulus son of Thrason of Collytus, a prominent orator and general (Dem. 18. 219, Xen. 5.1. 26–27). He had never been associated with oligarchy, and showed his support of the *demos* at Phyle (Dem 24. 134). Unlike his leader there, Thrasybulus of Steiria, the Collytan was an arch enemy of Alcibiades: in 407 he left the fleet for Athens to accuse Alcibiades after Notium (Plut. *Alc.* 36). Moreover, he was more willing than the Steirian to bring up the charge of oligarchy against his opponents: even as late as 382 he blocked one Leodamas from the archonship by tying him to the Thirty (Lys. 26. 13, 21–24; Arist. *Rhet.* 1400 a 25). Hence the Collytan was a political rival of the Steirian, perhaps a particularly bitter one, both because of Alcibiades and because the two Thrasybuli each vied for the support of Boeotia (Aesch. 3.138, Xen. 3.5.16, Paus. 9.11.6). A factional leader in his own right, the Collytan no doubt often collaborated with other enemies of the Steirian.[49]

To sum up, sympathy for the economic problems of the *penetes*, advocacy of state pay, and hostility to the men of the City were the domestic political hallmarks of the leaders of the Many after 403. Their foreign policy (*infra*) consisted of vigorous hostility to Sparta and the revival of Athenian imperialism.[50]

We have now traced a minimum of six leading factions (those of the two Thrasybuli, and of Agyrrhius, Andocides, Archinus and Epicrates-Cephalus) in the immediate postwar years, which can each be assigned a rough and tentative position in the political spectrum. Given the state of the evidence, this list cannot be exhaustive. It omits, for example, several men who are little more than names: e.g. Philon of Acharnae, a councillor-elect challenged at his scrutiny not long after the restoration of democracy (Lys. 31). It leaves out one Sostratus, a man of the greatest influence in Athens, at least according to his *philos* Polyaenus (Lys. 9.14). It leaves out Archestratides, the prosecutor in 395 of Alcibiades' son Alcibiades (Lys. 14.3, 15.12). It is enough, however, to demonstrate the inadequacy of the binary division of the *Hellenica Oxyrhynchia* or of Sealey's schema of three 'leading political groups,' those of Thrasybulus, Cephalus and Agyrrhius.[51] Moreover, it is indeed possible to distinguish Athenian groups according to constitutional or socioeconomic categories, though not all groups on all occasions: some differences were a matter of faction. Finally, for all the support for reconciliation, there was a substantial amount of disunity in Athens, more than has been allowed.[52]

Athenian domestic politics after 403 cannot be understood in isolation from foreign policy.[53] Let us therefore add foreign affairs to the analysis.

Foreign Politics: Decision for War

403–397

From fall 403 to fall 397, Athens was a faithful ally of Sparta. One may imagine a foreign policy debate at Athens, but in practical terms, there were no options. In 397, however, the Persian King began to build a fleet to fight Sparta, and chose as admiral an Athenian general living in Cyprus, Conon. There was now a chance to oppose Sparta, so the next two years witnessed a great debate between advocates of action and counsellors of caution, a debate which was settled only by the rebellion of Boeotia.[54]

However much the Athenians wanted to regain their lost empire, in 403 there was little they could do about it. The walls of the city and its arsenals had been destroyed; the fleet was reduced to 12 triremes, and a Spartan harmost stood guard in Aegina. To the ravages of the Decelean War, the human and material destruction of the civil war had recently been added. The oligarchs had to repay the considerable sum of 100 tal. to Sparta, which the democrats agreed to accept as a public debt, perhaps with an *eisphora*. Until 401, Attica was divided into two states (an independent one at Athens and another, dependent on Sparta, at Eleusis) which effectively neutralized Athens' ability to conduct a foreign policy.[55]

Neither Boeotia or Corinth was happy with the Spartan settlement of the Peloponnesian War, but they were far from open rebellion. One index of Boeotia's lack of concern about Athens is its annexation in 402 of Oropus, a part of Attica until 411. Another index is Boeotia's reaction when, at some point between 403 and 401, the Athenians were unable to pay Boeotia two talents they owed: Boeotia seized Athenian goods to take payment. These were not the gestures of men eager to win allies.[56]

It is not surprising, therefore, to find the Athenians taking part in the Peloponnesian army sent to punish Elis in 399, even though the Boeotians and Corinthians refused to help. Nor is it surprising that in the same year Athens sent 300 knights to help the Spartan army in Asia.[57]

Yet, according to Xenophon 3.1.4, the knights were sent not so much to help Sparta as to rid Athens of oligarchs. Hence, even in this period of subservience, Athens managed to maintain some independence. First, although they were no doubt impeccably courteous to the Spartans with whom they dealt, among themselves, the Athenians were more frank about their new hegemon: 'You are incensed with any other Greeks who value the Lacedaemonians more than you,' said a speaker in the early 390s.[58] After the battle with the Spartans in 403, the restored democracy built an elaborate tomb in the Ceramicus for the fallen

Lacedaemonians. The monument was presumably presented to the Spartans as a gesture of good will. Athenian orators, on the other hand, intepreted it as a sign of Athenian valour, and a witness of Spartan defeat.[59]

Nor did Sparta's ally neglect the former empire. In the very year democracy was restored, the Athenians renewed a decree of 405 granting citizenship to their most loyal allies, the Samians. Within a few years, they also reinscribed the record of a Thasian proxeny which the Thirty had destroyed. Perhaps also at this time they granted honours to Heracleides of Clazomenae. Only the proposer of the decree concerning the Samians is known: Cephisophon. It is tempting to make him Cephisphon of Paeania, for the identification would confirm Chapter 2's conclusion about the popularity of imperialism after 403. Not merely the leaders of the Many wanted to restore the empire; in 403, a moderate oligarch was in the forefront of the movement. Indeed, these decrees probably enjoyed widespread support.[60]

Athens took its most independent action of all in 401, when a plot against the democracy by the oligarchs at Eleusis was discovered (or fabricated). The democrats took the field against their opponents, defeated them, and put down the Eleusis regime for good. Attica was reunited, but the Spartan settlement of 403 was a dead letter. Athens had bent the rules of loyalty but not broken them: so it might have seemed in 401.[61]

397–95

Before 397, therefore, Athens was loyal to Sparta in form, if not in spirit. In summer 397, the king of Persia began a programme of naval rearmament against Sparta, with the Athenian Conon as his admiral.[62] How was the news received in Athens? For a small but significant group of former oligarchs and their sympathizers, the news was bad, because Spartan power guaranteed the amnesty of 403. But most Athenians were probably enthused over Persia's action. In particular, the faction around Epicrates and Cephalus — which crystallized now, if it had not existed earlier — favoured a policy of active help to Conon. At the time of the revolt of Rhodes in summer 396, if not earlier, these men sponsored private missions of arms and sailors to Conon's fleet (*Hell. Oxy.* 2.1). In late 397 or early 396, they sent ambassadors to the Persian king, ambassadors whom, however, the Spartans intercepted and executed.[63] According to Pausanias, the news of

Conon's appointment emboldened Athens to deny Agesilaus' request for troops at the time that he was forming his expedition against Persia in early 396 (Paus. 3.9.2).

Perhaps so, but one must not overestimate the effect of Conon's appointment. Even after his fleet had won a major success by inspiring the revolt of Rhodes in summer 396, Athens was unwilling to send a state trireme to him (in the Demaenetus affair) because of the risk of Spartan retaliation. Athenian leaders were probably carefully watching another rival to Spartan power, Boeotia, and one leader above all: Thrasybulus.[64]

In 404, Thrasybulus had spent his exile in Thebes, whence he set out for Phyle (Paus. 9.11.6). He apparently kept up the connection in the following years, since *he* presented the Athenian offer of alliance to the Boeotians in 395 (Xen. 3.5.16). Sometime after the restoration of democracy, Thrasybulus sponsored a dedication in the temple of Heracles at Thebes: two colossal statues, one of Heracles and the other of Athena, symbolic of the ties between Boeotia and Athens (Paus. 9.11.6). It is likely that Thrasybulus had ties of *philia* with leading Boeotians, and that in 395 his eyes were directed more to the north than the east.

Moreover, Thrasybulus had two possible reasons for not merely underemphasizing the creation of a Persian fleet led by Conon, but for downright ignoring it. One was ideological. Many Athenians would remember Persia's role in defeating Athens in the Peloponnesian War. Although panhellenism was more a dream than a reality, some still hesitated to support Persia against Sparta. According to one reading of *Hellenica Oxyrhynchia* 1.2, the opponents of Demaenetus' mission to Conon in 395 were afraid lest, by aiding the barbarian, he give the city a bad name. The speaker of Lysias' *Funeral Oration* 2.60 later referred to Conon's triumph at the battle of Cnidos as a Persian victory, and other contemporary voices echo the charge.[65]

How important was anti-Persian sentiment to a man as pragmatic as Thrasybulus? Not enough in itself to keep him from applauding the creation of Conon's fleet. His fellow generals in the Hellespont had been willing to negotiate with Persia when necessary during the Ionian War, and he would do the same in 390. Hatred for the barbarian probably did not determine Thrasybulus' stand in 395. But personal alliances came into play. Upon the return of Conon to Athens in 393, Thrasybulus' career went into an eclipse. Moreover, Thrasybulus might have foreseen this result, because the antagonism had existed for years.[66]

Thrasybulus had supported Alcibiades during the Ionian War, but Conon was an opponent. While Thrasybulus served with Alcibiades in the Hellespont 411–407, Conon stayed in the city. In 407, the year of Alcibiades' return to Athens, Conon was elected general 'from among the men in the city' (Xen. 1.4.10). The next year, in the wake of Notium, Alcibiades and his *philoi* failed to return to the generalship. Conon, however, was not only re-elected, but sent to Samos to replace Alcibiades as head of the fleet: a sign of Conon's distance from and probably enmity toward the disgraced leader.[67] Conon and Thrasybulus, therefore, were not likely to have been *philoi* in the late fifth century.

If in 395 Thrasybulus now had reason to trust Conon, it is lost. Upon Conon's return to Athens in 393, the two men were enemies, as three pieces of evidence indicate.

First is Thrasybulus' eclipse in the sources for 393–392, although he is frequently mentioned in the years immediately preceding and following. Even the one possible exception, a reference in Aristophanes *Ecclesiazusae* 202–203, which may date from 393 or 392, testifies to Thrasybulus' weakness: 'Thrasybulus is angry because he is not called upon'.[68]

Second is a remark in Aristotle's *Rhetoric* 1400 b 20: 'Conon used to call Thrasybulus a man of bold [or rash] counsel [*thrasus boulei*]'.[69] The remark was presumably made on repeated occasions, perhaps in public. Since *thrasus* usually has a negative connotation (s.v. *LSJ*), Conon seems to have charged Thrasybulus with rash judgement. He could have made the remark at any time in his career, but probably did so after Cnidos (394) when he was important enough to have his witticisms remembered.[70]

Third is Conon's prosecution of Adeimantus in 393, immediately after Conon's return to Athens (Dem. 19.161). Like Conon, Adeimantus had been a general at Aegospotami (Xen. 2.1.30–32; Diod. 13.106.6). But unlike Conon, Adeimantus was an old and close *philos* of Alcibiades, and may have been a *philos* of Thrasybulus too, for the two men have a suggestive link in common: Alcibiades' son. In 395–94 the man who prosecuted Alcibiades' son for military misconduct also attacked Adeimantus and the board of generals — its most prominent member went unnamed, but was the well-known Thrasybulus. If the prosecutor of Alcibiades' son in 395/94 was hostile to Adeimantus and Thrasybulus, then the prosecutor of Adeimantus in 393/92 was probably no friend of Thrasybulus either. We may presume enmity between Thrasybulus and Conon.[71]

To return to the main subject, factional considerations were one of several reasons why Thrasybulus did not support Conon and the Persian fleet in 395. First, as a prudent man, he could not minimize the danger of Spartan retaliation. Secondly, as a general and diplomat, he had reason to prefer the Boeotians as allies to the Persians. Thirdly, as an Athenian imperialist, he had reason to hesitate before co-operating with Persia, a power that blocked Athens' future expansion. Finally, as a politician, he had to question the wisdom of aiding a past enemy and future rival.

Conon is sure to have had his supporters (*infra*, Chapter 5), but as the Demaenetus affair shows, he met considerable opposition. Anti-Persian sentiment accounts for some of it and prudence even more, but the fears of the former Three Thousand were also significant.

The Oxyrhynchus historian identifies the supporters of the *status quo* at the time of the Demaenetus affair as 'the men of breeding and property' and 'the notables and gentlemen' (*Hell. Oxy.* 1.3). This is somewhat better than a crude assertion that 'the rich' were content with Spartan domination — but not much. If, however, P is referring here to the kind of Athenians whose property and social standing had led them to support oligarchy, then one may salvage something from his analysis, for many former oligarchs did have something to fear from a resurgent and unrestrained *demos*. By the same token, such warhawks as Epicrates and Cephalus were champions of the common man.

P's analysis both clarifies and obscures. There was some correlation between wealth, 'breeding' and an opposition to war in 395, but only some. There were Athenians both of wealth and of good breeding in Conon's faction.

Demaenetus, for example, emissary of the warhawks in 395, was of the Bouzygid clan (Aesch. 2.78). Hagnias, ambassador to Persia in 396 when he was caught by the Spartans and executed, left an estate worth at least 2 tal. The father of the speaker of Lysias' nineteenth oration, an old friend of Conon, had, like a proper aristocrat, raced his horses at the Isthmus and Nemea (Lys. 19.63). He was connected by marriage to Socrates' aristocratic pupil, Phaedrus of Myrrhinus, and to one Critodemus of Alopece, perhaps a relative of Socrates' wealthy friend Crito of Alopece (Lys. 19.16).[72]

By winter 395, Conon had numerous, vocal and well-heeled supporters: shortly after Agesilaus reached Asia in 396, the

Persians sent Epicrates and Cephalus a payment of 50 silver tal. (*Hell. Oxy.* 2.2, Paus. 3.9.8). They were influential enough to persuade the *boule* to send Demaenetus secretly on a trireme to Conon. If the thetic population, their natural supporters, had not been so depleted by the Peloponnesian War, Epicrates and Cephalus might have carried the day. As it was, they were not strong enough to procure open support for Demaenetus. When news of his mission leaked out, there was an uproar. Thrasybulus led the movement to disavow him. The assembly had to give in before the danger of Spartan retaliation, and reported Demaenetus to the harmost on Aegina.[73]

395

Yet, within a year, Athens went to war, led by the main opponent of Demaenetus' mission: Thrasybulus. According to Xenophon (3.5.16), the decision to ally with Boeotia was made by a unanimous vote. How had the Athenians, so divided in the winter of 395, and so opposed to a dangerous policy, overcome their differences and decided upon war in such a short period of time?

Xenophon, it is argued below, is a misleading or badly-informed guide, because he leaves out the silent opposition to the alliance that is likely to have existed. Before elaborating this point, let us first review previous explanations of the alliance, which emphasize foreign policy, and then consider domestic politics.

The explanation most often cited, and indeed the most important, is the change in the military balance, the revolt of Boeotia from Sparta. By supporting Locris in its border dispute with Phocis, the anti-Spartan faction in Boeotia incited Sparta to invade Boeotia in retaliation (Xen. 3.5.3–5, *Hell. Oxy.* 11.1, 13.1–5). As a result, this faction rallied the country against Sparta. With Boeotian support and the possibility of help from Corinth and Argos, Athens was now able to follow suit, reversing its previous caution (Xen. 3.5.11–12). Moreover, a far-sighted leader might realize that unless Athens acted now, she might never get a second chance for such help. As Beloch put it, Boeotia's request was, in effect, an ultimatum: 'now or never'.[74]

Boeotia's change, therefore, is crucial. Yet is is not sufficient to explain Athenian behaviour. The alliance with Boeotia, in spite of its defensive form, was an open break with Sparta. Since one Spartan army was in Boeotia at the time of the negotiations for the pact and another was poised to invade, even a defensive alliance clearly meant that Athenian soldiers would fight Spartans. Nor was victory assured. Boeotia had a strong army, but not so strong that Lysander and Pausanias, had they combined forces as planned, could not have beaten it. Then, with the Piraeus unwalled, Athens would have been effectively defenceless. The problem remains: why were the Athenians, particularly Thrasybulus, so cautious in the winter of 395 and so bold in the summer?[75]

Sparta forced Athens' hand. In recent years, Sparta had intervened several times in central Greece. These actions seemed to threaten the independence of Boeotia. When Sparta invaded Boeotia in summer 395, it might have seemed that Attica itself would soon be threatened. Some scholars go so far as to make Athens' alliance with Boeotia strictly defensive — an exaggeration, but there was an important defensive element.[76]

A third explanation of Athens' turnabout emphasizes Persia's financial support, suggesting that the King's gold reassured potential Athenian liturgists and *eisphora*-payers. Chronology disallows this explanation, though, because Persian gold arrived in Athens *before* the Demaenetus affair. Chronology also disallows a fourth suggestion, that Conon's first victories at Rhodes emboldened the Athenians between the time of Demaenetus' mission and the Boeotian alliance: Demaenetus' mission took place after the defection of Rhodes from Sparta, and not before.[77]

Domestic political considerations, however, do help us explain Athens' change more fully. The previous winter a rebellious Athens would have been the handmaiden of Conon and the Persians, neither of whom Thrasybulus had any reason to trust. A Persian victory at sea might have improved the position of Athens, but it would have done nothing for Thrasybulus: in the event, the battle of Cnidos greatly damaged his political career. How much better it must have seemed to tie Athens' revolt to Thebes, a state whose leaders Thrasybulus had learned to trust in 404. The support of the Boeotian army meant that Athens might be able to fight Sparta on the Greek mainland. As a general, Thrasybulus could look forward to leading Athens' army. If victorious, he could hope to win lasting glory and to strengthen his political position at home. Finally, the gratitude which Thrasybulus owed Boeotia for its help against the Thirty may have played some part in his considerations. A man who so appealed to the taste of a simple Roman such as Nepos would not have taken the duties of *gratia* lightly.[78]

A second consideration was propaganda. In winter 395, Athens was asked to join the Persians in a war against the heroes of Thermopylae and Plataea. In summer 395, it was asked to help a fellow Greek state against a power-hungry invader. Objectively, little had changed. On both occasions, Athenian action would probably sabotage Sparta's attempt to free the Asia Minor Greeks. Nevertheless, the second enterprise was much more palatable than the first. Judging by Plato *Menexenus* 244e, a nearly contemporary source, Athens' rallying cry in 395 was to 'stop Sparta from enslaving the Hellenes'. A fragmentary inscription of 393, if correctly restored, puts it more simply: to fight 'for Hellas'.[79] How much easier to apply such slogans to a war for Boeotia than a war for Persia!

Cephalus, Epicrates, Agyrrhius and Thrasybulus of Collytus all disliked Thrasybulus of Steiria and at least some preferred Conon. But in summer 395, they had no choice but to follow Thrasybulus into war. At least they had the consolation, however, that while supporting the war effort abroad, they could continue their political campaign against Thrasybulus at home. If the defendant, like his father, was an ally of Thrasybulus, it may be more than an accident that the prosecution of Alcibiades' son, with its veiled attack on Thrasybulus, followed hard on the battle of Haliartus in autumn 395.[80]

What of 'the men of breeding and property' (*Hell. Oxy.* 1.3) who had opposed Demaenetus' expedition? If, as Xenophon 3.5.16 reports, the vote for the Boeotian alliance was unanimous, they too must have dropped their opposition to an open break with Sparta. Perhaps many of them weighed the situation and considered a renewed empire worth taking risks. Nevertheless, others, those whose wealth depended on landed property, feared Boeotian defeat and Spartan invasion. Moreover, the threat remained that, spurred by victory, the *demos* would seek vengeance yet for the actions of the Thirty.

Contra Xenophon, some of the former oligarchic Three Thousand are likely to have opposed the Boeotian alliance. Two pieces of evidence strengthen this presumption. First, in his speech requesting Athenian help, the Boeotian ambassador separated the men of Piraeus from the men of the City. He assumes that the first group were enthusiasts of the alliance, but the second needed to be persuaded (Xen. 3.5.8–10).[81]

Second, on the eve of accepting the Boeotian alliance, Athens sent a mission to Sparta, requesting that the Spartans submit their differences with Boeotia to arbitration (Paus. 3.9.11). So undiplomatic a mission cannot have been meant seriously. As might have been foreseen, Sparta rejected the request in anger; hegemons do not submit disputes with one subject to the arbitration of another subject. Might the Athenian mission be attributed to a desire to mollify the fears of the men of the City and to show them that Athens had made every effort to avoid a conflict?[82]

What then of Xenophon's report of a unanimous vote in favour of the Boeotian alliance? It ought not to be dismissed as a fabrication. Nor do I want to deprive the Athenians of the credit for uniting behind a decision for war, only eight years after the end of a terrible civil war.[83] Yet this is not the whole story. As Xenophon well knew, the lack of dissent on a particular measure in the assembly did not mean that there was no private opposition. When, for example, Alcibiades returned to Athens in 407, no one dared to speak against him in the assembly, although he had many enemies (Xen. 4.4.17, 20). Similarly in 415, the opponents of the Sicilian expedition had not dared to raise their voices openly (Thuc. 6.24.4). Given the past attitudes of many members of the Three Thousand, it would not be surprising if they were in silent opposition in 395. The lack of enthusiasm shown by many Athenians in the campaigns of 395-4 should also be taken into account.[84]

Between the winter and summer of 395, then, Athenian opinion shifted its position on war with Sparta. The main reason was strategic: a powerful ally, Boeotia, was suddenly but only temporarily available, while a dangerous enemy, Sparta, was on the warpath again, this time against a neighbour and fellow Hellene.

Conclusions

First, a minimum of six leading factions competed for political power. In no case could a faction win the support of the *demos* without a capable and attractive leader; in most cases, that leader had to offer not only his own personality, but the advocacy of positions of interest to a segment of the *demos*, e.g. revenge against oligarchs, or reconciliation, or state pay, or aggressive imperialist bellicosity.

Second, the lot of the men of the City was a mixed bag. On the one hand, the amnesty was a model of political moderation, admired by later generations. Some of the former Three Thousand served as hipparchs, members of the Council, ambassadors, even generals (Lys. 16.8, 26.16–20). On the other hand, other members of the Three Thousand were challenged or rejected at their scrutinies (Lys. 16.1–3, 26.9–10). Popular prejudice against both the men of the City and against *plousoi* continued, and sometimes led to calls for vengeance. The representatives of the Few had the right to speak their minds in the assembly, but did not always feel free to do so. On balance, and by the standards of ancient Greece, the men of the City were lucky. This was partly a function of Athenian moderation and good sense, but also a function of the exhaustion and decimation of the thetes.

The weakness of the thetes is the third point. Had they not been so devastated by the last phase of the Peloponnesian War, they might have changed the course of postwar history: by pressing demands for revenge or by forcing the revolt against Sparta at the time of the Demaenetus affair. Even in their weakened state, however, they were important in politics. A politician could still build a career after 403 as a champion of the thetes and poorer hoplites.

Fourth, the Athenian imperative to find scapegoats added poison to the political atmosphere. The record mentions two prosecutions of Alcibiades' son, Andocides' prosecution of Archippus for the desecration of a Herm, and the trial of Socrates as a surrogate for Critias and Alcibiades.

In short, postwar Athens was not a unified body politic. It was divided by class disputes (e.g., over ecclesiastic pay or Phormisius' proposal for oligarchy), by disputes over personal power with little reference to principle (e.g., Conon and Thrasybulus), by disputes over personal finance or gain (e.g., the heiress between Callias and Andocides or the tax-farming between Andocides and Agyrrhius) and finally by the very matter which some scholars would remove from factional politics — principles (e.g., Athenian citizenship, ecclesiastic pay, alliance with Persia).

Whether Athenians could close ranks behind the war effort now remained to be seen.

Notes

1. Thrasybulus of Steiria: *infra*, n. 10 Epicrates: Dem. 19.277. Followers of Theramenes: Arist. *Ath. Pol.* 34.4. Ergocles: Lys. 28.12. Thrasybulus of Collytus: *infra*, p. 103.
2. Aesch. 3.194–95, Arist. *Ath. Pol.* 40.2, Ps. Plut. 835F–836A (= Lys. frg. 46), *Pap. Ox.* 1,800 frg. 6–7. Cf. M. H. Hansen, *The Sovereignty of the Peoples' Court in Athens in the Fourth Century BC and the Public Action Against Unconstitutional Proposals* (Odense: 1974), 29; *infra*, n. 26.
3. Synonym: Bruce, *HCHO* 52–3; *contra* Seager, 'TCAI', 95. Critique of P's categories: see Funke, *HA* 6–7.
4. Rhinon: Arist. *Ath. Pol.* 38.3–4. Cephisophon: Xen. 2.4.36. Epichares: And. 1.95, 99.
5. Cf. Cleon in Thuc. 3.36.3–4. On 'the demagogues', 'new politicians', 'populists', see Connor, *NP* 87–175.
6. These politicians, *infra*, chaps. 4–5.
7. Revision of laws: Lys. 30.2–5; And 1.83–4. Cf. A. R. W. Harrison, 'Law-Making at Athens at the End of the Fifth Century BC', *JHS* 75 (1955), 26–35; P. J. Rhodes, *Athenian Boule* (Oxford: 1972), 49–50. M. H. Hansen, 'Did the Athenian *Ecclesia* Legislate After 403/2 BC?', *GRBS* 20 (1979), 27–53; P. J. Rhodes, 'Athenian Democracy After 403 BC, *CJ* 75 (1980), 305–23; K. Clinton, 'The Late Fifth-Century Revision of the Athenian Law Code', *Hesperia* Suppl. 19 (1982), 26–37. Thrasybulus: *infra*, n. 26. Archinus: *infra*, p. 96.
8. Archinus: Arist. *Ath. Pol.* 40.1. General and secretary: *infra*, n. 33. Theramenists: *supra*, n. 1.
9. Aesch. 2.176 makes Archinus co-leader at Phyle, and Dem. 24.135 neglects Thrasybulus in favour of Archinus, but most sources emphasize Thrasybulus (e.g. Xen. *passim*, Diod. 14.32–33, Paus. 1.29.3).
10. Xen. 2.4.13–17, 4.40–2, cf. 3.5.16. On the accuracy of Xenophon's speeches, see J. Buckler, 'Xenophon's Speeches and the Theban Hegemony', *Athenaeum* 60 (1982), 180–204.
11. *Supra*, p. 47; cf. *APF* 240.
12. Ionian War: See W. Schwahn, 'Thrasybulos', *RE* 6A (1936) cols. 569–70. Corinthian War: Xen. 4.8.25, Diod. 14.94, Lys. 28 *passim*. 'Full blooded' is a phrase of G. M. Cawkwell, 'The Imperialism of Thrasybulus', *CQ* 26 (1976), 270.
13. This support is emphasized by J. Hatzfeld, *Alcibiade* (Paris: 1940), 293, 316, 327; A. Andrewes, 'The Generals in the Hellespont, 411–407 BC', *JHS* 73 (1953), 3–4. See also my 'Thrasybulus and Conon', 42–3.
14. C. W. Fornara, *The Athenian Board of Generals from 501 to 404* (Wiesbaden: 1971), 70.
15. Thrasyllus was one of the generals who wanted to blame the trierarchs Thrasybulus and Theramenes for failing to save the shipwrecked and recover the dead. Xen. 1.7.16–17. See Andrewes, 'Arginousai', 116; W. McCoy, 'Thrasyllus', *AJP* 98 (1977), 264–89. Previously, in 409, when Thrasyllus brought troops from Athens to the Hellespont, there was hostility between his forces and Alcibiades'. Shortly before, in Ionia, he had ordered the execution of the exiled cousin of Alcibiades, Alcibiades of Phegus, which could not have improved relations between the two generals. See Xen. 1.2.12–13; Andrewes, 'Generals in Hellespont', 4. Archedemus: Xen. 1.7.2; Ar. *Frogs* 416ff.; Lys. 14.25; Eupolis frg. 71, Kock, *CAF*.
16. Theramenes' deme: Scholion on Ar. *Frogs* 541. Thrasybulus' deme: Xen. 4.8.25. Alcibiades' recall: Thuc. 8.81.1; Diod. 13.38.2, 42.2; cf. Plut. *Alc.* 33. Cf. Andrewes, 'Generals', 3, n. 7. Generalships together: Diod. 13.68.2–69.3; Nepos. *Alc.* 5.4–6.5; Plut. *Alc.* 32–35.1; *contra*, Xen. 1.4.8. Seat on the Thirty: Diod.

14.32.5; Justin 5.9.13. In general: W. J. McCoy 'Theramenes, Thrasybulus and the Athenian Moderates' (Diss. Yale: 1970).
17. On the translation: *supra*, chap. 1, p. 32 and n. 84.
18. Cephalus: Dem 18.219, *Suda* s.v. κέφαλος. Cleon: Arist. *Ath. Pol.* 28.3. Thrasybulus no orator: L. Saur, 'Thrasybule de Stiria: Une Certaine Idée d'Athènes' (Diss. Liège: 1978), 276–77. Σεμνός: Lys. 16.15. 'ὁ ἀξιωματικὸς καὶ αὐθάδης: Strattis frg.
17, Kock, *CAF ad.* Ar. *Ploutos* 550. ὑπερόπτης τοῦ δήμου, ἠβούλετο δι 'αὐτοῦ πάντα πράττεσθαι: Schol. *ad* Ar. *Eccl.* 202–203. Pericles: Saur 'Thrasybule' 280, 288.
19. Alcibiades' lover: Plut. *Alc.* 4.4–5, *Mor.* 762c; Athen. 534 e–f. In general: *APF* 40–41.
20. See J. Burnet, *Plato's Euthyphro, Apology of Socrates, and Crito* (Oxford: 1924), 74.
21. Socrates' political views: W. K. C. Guthrie, *A History of Greek Philosophy*, vol. 3: *The Fifth-Century Enlightenment* (Cambridge: 1969), 409–16. Theory and practice: T. H. Irwin, 'Socrates' Inquiry and Politics', *Ethics* 96 (1986); cf. R. Kraut, *Socrates and the State* (Princeton: 1984), chap. 6. *Contra* G. Vlastos, 'The Historical Socrates and Athenian Democracy', *Political Theory* II (1983), 495–516. Arrest of Leon: Plato *Ap.* 32c; Krentz, *Thirty* 82–3.
22. *Misodemos*: Polycrates *ad* Libanius *Ap. Soc.* 34.16; cf. A.-H. Chroust, *Socrates, Man and Myth* (London: 1957), 90. Religion: Guthrie, *Greek Philosophy* 381. Hidden charges: Guthrie, *Greek Philosophy* 381–3. Polycrates: Chroust, *Socrates* 69–100. Others: Guthrie, *Greek Philosophy* 383, n. 1.
23. On Thrasybulus' eclipse, *infra*, p. 108 and Strauss, 'Thrasybulus and Conon', 40–1. Aesimus' embassies: *infra*, chap. 6, p. 162.
24. Adeimantus: And. 1.16, Xen. 1.4–21; Strauss, 'Thrasybulus and Conon', 43. Alcibiades' son Alcibiades: Lys. 14.38, 22; 15.1–2; 16.15; Strauss, 'Thrasybulus and Conon', 43. Ergocles and Philocrates: Lys. 28–29. Ergocles fought with Thrasybulus in 403; Lys. 28.12.
25. I am unpersuaded by the assertion of Aeschines 3.194–95 that Archinus and Thrasybulus were *philoi* at the time of the indictment. Aeschines is biased. He needs to respond to the charge that his own indictment of Ctesiphon is mere political enmity, so he produces a precedent of legal action between *philoi*. The Attic orators did not scruple at distortion, however, and Aeschines' sole evidence of *philia* between Archinus and Thrasybulus is their common presence at Phyle.
26. Number of new supporters: Krentz, *Thirty* 110–12. In Krentz's convincing interpretation of *IG* II² 10, these men received *isoteleia* instead of citizenship: Krentz, 'Foreigners Against Thirty', 298–306; Idem, 'The Rewards for Thrasyboulos' Supporters', *ZPE* (1986); *contra* D. Whitehead, 'A Thousand New Athenians', *LCM* 9 (1984), 8–10; M. J. Osborne, *Naturalization in Athens* (Brussels: 1981–2), vol. 1, 37–42, vol. 2, 26–43; cf. D. F. Middleton, 'Thrasyboulos' Thracian Support', *CQ* 32 (1982), 298–303. Principle: E. Meyer, *Forschungen Zur alten Geschichte* vol. 2 (Halle: 1899), 175–6. Profit: Cloché, *Restauration*, 452–8.
27. Funke, *HA* 17, n. 3, Beloch, *Attische Politik* 111, makes Archinus a subordinate of Thrasybulus, and Sealey, 'Callistratos', 136 calls Archinus 'comparatively unimportant'.
28. Cf. Cloché, *Restauration* 279.
29. *Paragraphe*: Isoc. 18.2–3. Cf. G. M. Calhoun, 'Archinus and the παραγραφή,' *CP* 13 (1918), 169–85.
30. Funke, *HA* 17–18.
31. Funeral Oration: Plato *Menex.* 234b; Dion. Hal. *Dem.* 23; Photius *Bibl. Codd.* 260, p. 487; Clem. Alex. *Strom.* 6. 749. Comic poets: Scholion on Ar. *Frogs* 367 = Plato Comicus frg. 133, Kock, *CAF*. Alphabet: *Suda*, s.v. Σαμίων: ὁ δήμος General: Dem 24.135.
32. As Funke notes (*HA* 17, n. 3.), the Funeral Oration may date from the last phase of the Peloponnesian War.

33. Rhinon: *supra*, n. 4 and *IG* II² 1370–71, Addenda, p. 797; *SEG* 23 (1968), no. 81; *APF* 67. Cephisophon: *supra*, n. 4 and *IG* II² 1399; Tod *GHI* vol. 2 no. 97; *APF* 148.
34. Epichares: *supra*, n. 4. Meletus (Andocides and Leon): And. 1.94. Meletus (Cephisophon): Xen. 2.4.36. On the complicated question of the various Meleti in Athens in this period, see MacDowell, *Andokides* 280–10.
35. Ruschenbusch, *Innenpolitik* 135–6. R. calculates 5,000 thetes; there may have been considerably more.
36. Beard and manners: Ar. *Eccl.* 97, *Frogs* 956–66 + schol. and Rogers *Aristophanes* commentary *ad loc*. Embassy to Persia: Plato frg. 119–27, I. 632 Kock, *CAF*; Athen.. 6.251 a–b; Plut. *Pelop.* 30.12; *APF* 181.
37. On Andocides' political and liturgical career, see And. 1–2 *passim* and MacDowell, *Andokides* 4–5; *APF* 31.
38. See Sealey, 'Callistratos', 182.
39. Theozotides: *infra*, n. 45. Ecclesiastic pay: Ar. *Eccl.* 176–88, 206–207, 289–310, 375–93; *Ploutos* 171, 329. Agyrrhius: *Eccl.* 184–85.
40. Support for Sparta: Kounas, 'Prelude to Hegemony' 45–52. Underground: Kounas, *Prelude to Hegemony* 36, 54–6. Preferred imperialism: Thuc. 8.48.5–6, *infra* p. 109.
41. Sealey, 'Callistratos', 182. Funke, *HA* 117, n. 46, doubts the rivalry between Agyrrhius and Heracleides, but offers no reason.
42. Arist. *Ath. Pol.* 41.3; O. Schulthess, 'Misthos', *RE* 15A (1932), 2087. Date: P. J. Rhodes, *A Commentary on the Aristotelian Athenaion Politeia* (Oxford: 1981), 490–3. The theoric fund, which Harpocration (s.v. θεωρικόν) attributes to Agyrrhius, is best put off until Eubulus and mid-century: Rhodes, *Commentary* 492, 514.
43. Sealey, 'Callistratos', 182–5; *APF* 278; Rhodes, *Commentary* 492. Effeminate: Ar. *Eccl.* 102 + schol. Comic poets: *supra*, n. 31. Secretaryship of Council: Tod, *GHI* vol. 2 no. 97.
44. Agyrrhius' finances in 390s: Isoc. 17.31–32; *APF* 278. Thrasybulus and Agyrrhius in 389: Lys. 28.5, 29.2. Xen.: 4.8.31, 34; Diod. 14.99.5; *infra*, p. 155. Conon: *infra*, p. 135. Callias: *APF* 259–62.
45. Agoratus: Lys. 13.92–7; Cloché, *Restauration* 338. Cleophon: Lys. 13.12, 30.12. Cleophon, apparently, had been no friend of Alcibiades: Himerius 36.16; Photius *Bibl.* 337. Cf. Beloch, *Attische Politik* 84; Andrewes, 'Generals', 3. Lochites: Isoc. 20.12–13. The orator attacks the oligarchic way of life of his young opponent, using language reminiscent of the Athenians' fears of the mutilators of the Herms in 415. See Isoc. 20.4, 10, 12, 21–2; Thuc. 6.28.60. For the date, see G. Mathieu and E. Bremond, eds, *Isocrate*, vol. 1 (Paris: 1928), 37. Theozotides: See the fragments of Lysias *Against Theozotides* in Greenfell and Hunt, eds, *The Hibeh Papyri*, vol. 1 (London: 1906), 49–55, no. 14. On Theozotides and his decrees, see R. S. Stroud, 'Theozotides and the Athenian Orphans', *Hesperia* 40 (1971), 297–301; Hansen, *Sovereignty* 30; Krentz, *Thirty* 112–13.
46. Piraeus: Dem. 19.277. Beard: schol. *ad* Ar. *Eccl.* 71 and Rogers, *Aristophanes* note *ad loc*. Humour: Plut. *Pelop.* 30.7, Hegesander *ad* Ath. 6.58. The occasion was Epicrates' embassy (with the long-bearded Phormisius!) to Persia *c* 39 p4: *supra*, n. 36; *infra*, chap. 5, p. 126. In general: *APF* 181.
47. *Supra*, n. 18.
48. In general, see Bruce, *HCHO* 56–7; Sealey, 'Callistratos', 181–5. Co-operation with Conon: *Hell. Oxy.* 2.1; cf. Bruce, *HCHO* 55; Seager, 'TCAI' 96, n. 6. Funke advances salutary scepticism about the continued co-operation of Epicrates and Cephalus after 395, see Funke, *HA* 115.
49. Collytus was among the first postwar Athenian amphictyons in Delos (*IG* II² 1634), perhaps in 393/92, Conon's *annus mirabilis* — although this only suggests rather than proves competition between the two Thrasybuli. See Funke, *HA* 126, n. 67; *infra*, chap. 5, n. 29.

50. Kounas, 'Prelude to Hegemony' 155–7.

51. Evidence: Hansens's catalogue ('*Rhetores* and *Strategoi* in Fourth-Century Athens', *GRBS* 24 [1983], 151–80) is another reminder of the many Athenians in public life 403–386 of whom little is known. In addition to the famous *rhetor* Aristophon of Azenia in his early career (*PA* 2108) and to the generals Thoucleides of the Aiantid tribe in 394/93 (*IG* II² 5221.2–4) and Ctesicles, perhaps in 393/92 (Lys. 9.6), one might cite nine other men who are little more than names. They are Athenodorus (*IG* II² 26.6–7), Diocles (*PA* 3987), Lysitheus (Lys. 10.1), Monippides (*IG* II² 6.7, 7.3–4), Nicomenes (schol. Aesch. 1.39; cf. *GRBS* 20 [1979] 38), Phanias (Lys. frg. 143), Philagros (*IG* II² 2.8–9), Philepsius of Lamptrae (*PA* 14256), and Philon of Coele (Isoc. 18.22). Sealey: 'Callistratos', 183–4. Sealey is also criticized by Funke, *HA* 109ff.

52. *Contra* Funke, *HA* 22–5.
53. Funke, *HA* 25–6.
54. Cf. Hamilton, *SBV* 175ff.
55. Xen. 2.20, *Hell. Oxy.* 1.3; Arist. *Ath. Pol.* 40.3–4; Dem. 20.12, Isoc. 7.68. cf. R. Thomsen, *Eisphora* (Copenhagen: 1964), 176–9.
56. Corinth and Boeotia dissatisfied: Xen. 3.5.11–12. Oropus: Diod. 14.17.3; Thuc. 8.60. Boeotian raid: Lys. 30. 21–22.
57. Xen. 3.1.4, 2.25; Diod. 14.17.1, 4.
58. Lys. 18.15. The date is before the outbreak of war with Sparta in 395 (18.15), but not much, since the speaker was still young in 403 (18.10).
59. Lys. 2.63. For this interpretation, see L. Van Hook, 'On the Lacedaemonians Buried in the Kerameikos', *AJA* 36 (1932), 291–2.
60. Samians: Tod, *GHI* vol. 2, no. 97. Thasians: Tod. *GHI* vol. 2, no. 98. Heracleides: *SIG*³, 118; cf. 'Herakleides', *RE* 8 (1913) col. 458. Perlman, 'Revival Imperialist Expansion', 259, suggests that the Heracleides degree aimed at establishing a tie with the Persian King. His speculations about the various supporters of these proposals are intelligent guesses, if unverifiable.
61. Arist. *Ath. Pol.* 40.4; Xen. 2.4.43; And 1.90. Cf. Bengtson, *Staatsverträge* no. 215, p. 159; Hamilton, *SBV* 176; Krentz, *Thirty* 120–2.
62. On the date, see D. M. Lewis, *Sparta and Persia* (Leiden: 1978), p. 141 and n. 41. For a discussion of the complicated manoeuvres by which Conon got the job, see G. Barbieri, *Conone* (Roma: 1955), 79–89.
63. *Hell. Oxy.* 2.1. On the date, see Bruce, *HCHO* 55; Seager, 'TCAI', p. 96, n. 6.
64. On the date of the revolt of Rhodes, see Bruce, 'The Democratic Revolution at Rhodes', *CQ* n. s. 11 (1961), 166–70; Barbieri, *Conone*, 116; Swoboda, 'Konon', *RE* 11 (1922), col. 1323; Perlman, 'The Causes and Outbreak of the Corinthian War', *CQ* n. s. 14 (1964), 79.
65. *Hell. Oxy.* 1.2, reading δια] βᾶ [λου] σι for κατα] βα [λοῦ] σι with Bruce, *HCHO*, 51–2. Cf. Hamilton, *SBV* 181–2. On Lys. 2.60, see Seager, 'TCAI', 100.
66. Ionian War: Treaty of Chalcedon, 408/407, Xen. 1.3.8–9, Diod. 13.66.3, Plut. *Alc.* 31.1. See M. Amit, 'Le traité de Chalcédoine entre Pharnabaze et les stratèges athéniens', *Ant Cl* 42 (1973), 436–57. Amit ('Chalcédoine', 444–5) believes Thrasybulus was possibly one of the negotiators of this treaty, but Andrewes places him in the Thraceward region ('Generals in Hellespont', 7). For Thrasybulus' policy toward Persia in 390, see *infra*, chap. 6. Conon and Thrasybulus: see my 'Thrasybulus and Conon', 37–48.
67. Xen. 1.5.16–18; Diod. 13.74.1; Justin 5.5.4. See Beloch, *Attische Politik* 84.
68. Eclipse in the sources: Beloch, *Attische Politik* 118–19; Sealey, 'Callistratos', 182–83; Perlman, 'Revival Imperialistic Expansion', 263. Ar. *Eccl.* 202–03:

Σωτηρία παρέκυψεν, ἀλλ' ὀργίζεται
Θρασύβουλος αὐτὸς οὐχὶ παρακαλούμενος.

Salvation peeked out, but Thrasybulus
Is angry because he is not called upon.

For the text see P. Moraux, 'Trois Vers d'Aristophane (*Assemblée des Femmes*, 201–203)', *Mélanges Henri Grégoire* 12 (1952), p. 328, n. 2; Ussher, *Ecclesiazusae* 103. For a different interpretation, based on textual emendation, see R. Seager 'TCAI', p. 107, n. 111. It is difficult to date the play precisely. The best estimates place it at the Dionysia or Lenaea in one of the years from 393 to 390. See V. Coulon and H. Van Daele, *Aristophane*, vol. 5 (Paris: 1930), 5; Ussher, *Ecclesiazusae* xxi, nn. 2–3, xxv; Seager, 'TCAI', 106–7; Funke, *HA* 168–71.

69. Arist. *Rhet.* 1400 b 20: Κόνων Θρασύβουλον θρασ ύβουλον ἐκάλει.

70. Moraux, 'Trois Vers d'Aristophane', 341, n. 4, suggests that the remark refers to the charge of Thrasybulus' cowardice at Nemea (cf. Lys. 16.15). Funke, *IIA* p. 126 n.67, also cites this remark as evidence of hostility.

71. For Adeimantus' friendship with Alcibiades, see And. 1.16, Xen. 1.4.21. The two were fellow demesmen of Scambonidae (*PA* 202, 600). For the prosecution of 395–394, see Lys. 14.38, 22; 15.1–2; 16.15; Plut. *Lysander* 29; Paus. 3.5.4. Lys. 14.15 supplies the date of the prosecution. Its reference to a military expedition that saw no fighting fits the Athenian campaign of Haliartus. See R. C. Jebb, *The Attic Orators from Antiphon to Isaeus*, vol. 1 (London 1876), 257–8; F. Blass, *Attische Beredsamkeit*, vol. 1, 488–9; L. Gernet and M. Bizos, *Lysias, Discours*, vol. 1 (Paris: 1955), 221.

72. Father of the speaker of Lys. 19: *APF* 200. Crito: *APF* 336. Hagnias: *APF* 82, 87.

73. I follow Seager's chronology, dating the Demaenetus affair to winter 395 ('TCAI', 95, n. 2). Bruce's discussion is clear and thorough, but his date of spring 396 is in error (*HCHO* 66–72).

To judge from the language of *Hell. Oxy.* 1–2, P had already discussed, in a section now lost, the distribution of Persian gold by Timocrates of Rhodes. Presumably, therefore, Timocrates arrived in Greece before the time of Demaenetus' mission (*Hell. Oxy.* 2.2; Bruce, *HCHO* 58). Timocrates was sent by the Persian satrap Pharnabazus (Bruce, *HCHO* 59–60). According to Polyaenus 1.48.3, Pharnabazus only sent Timocrates after Agesilaus' arrival in Asia Minor in summer 396. Polyaenus deserves respect, for he seems to have relied heavily on *Hell. Oxy.* as (Jacoby (*FGrH* vol. IIC, 8). If Timocrates came to Athens before Demaenetus left, and if Timocrates did not arrive before summer 396, then Demaenetus' mission could hardly pre-date autumn 396. As Bruce (*HCHO* 66–72) shows, the mission must therefore be dated to winter 396/95.

Xen. 3.5.1 has the satrap Tithraustes, not Pharnabazus, send Timocrates, and dates the mission to late 395, but Polyaenus is preferable because he frequently consulted *Hell. Oxy.* Hamilton, *SBV* 182–3, 204, argues for *two* missions of Timocrates, one sent by each satrap.

74. Beloch, GG^2 3:1, 69.

75. Xen. 3.5.6–7; Tod, *GHI* vol. 2, no. 101. Cf. Seager, 'TCAI', p. 98, n. 21; Cawkwell, 'Imperialism', 275.

76. Spartan intervention: Andrewes, 'Two Notes on Lysander', 224–25. Defensive alliance: Perlman, 'Causes', 70; Bruce, *HCHO* 53.

77. Persian gold: Kagan, 'Economic Origins', 327–8. Rhodes: Perlman, 'Causes', 70. Chronology: *supra*, n. 73.

78. Nepos *Thras.* 1.1: *neminem huic praefero fide, constantia, magnitudine animi in patriam amore.*

79. For the date of *Menexenus* see C. Kahn, 'Plato's Funeral Oration: the Motive of the *Menexenus*', *CP* 58 (1963), 220–34. Inscription: see new frg. a, 1.17 of *IG* II^2 20 in D. M. Lewis and R. Stroud, 'Athens Honors King Evagoras of Salamis', *Hesperia* 48 (1979), 180–93.

80. *Supra*, n. 71; *infra*, chap. 5, p. 122 and n. 3.
81. Cf. Seager, 'TCAI', 97–8.
82. Hamilton, *SBV*, 204–5.
83. On Athens' remarkable unity, see G. Grote, *A History of Greece*[4], vol. 9 (London: 1869), 293. Funke, *HA* 102.
84. Cloché, 'Conflicts', 165–6.

5 The Politics of War, 395–391 BC

By late summer, the year 395 had seen a remarkable pair of achievements for Thrasybulus. Not only had he been able to keep Athens out of one war, but he had led it into another. Rare is the politician so successful in the choice of the time and place of a conflict, of opponents, and of allies.

If Thrasybulus did not know the fragility of his achievement, however, he was soon to find out. The following months would test the Athenian will to fight, the enemies they fought, the allies they chose, and the aims they set. In short, time would determine whether Athens' war would remain Thrasybulus' war.

The Troubled Phoenix

For future generations, Athens' march to Haliartus in late summer 395 was a symbol of courage, a triumph of the national will.[1] The dangers of the enterprise are clear, and not only in retrospect: Thrasybulus admitted at the time that the Piraeus was without walls, and knew what that implied (Xen. 3.5.16). Yet he and his countrymen marched out, and according to tradition, they did so without flinching. Several years later, in 392/91, Andocides used these words to describe the mood of Athens on the eve of Haliartus:

> Do you remember, Athenians, that day when we made the alliance with the Boeotians? Did we not think that Boeotia's power, combined with ours, would be able to defend us against all men?
>
> (And. 3.25; cf. Diod. 14.82.2)

Stirring words: neither they, however, nor those of other patriotic writers reflect the uncertainty of 395. Hoplites at either end of the socioeconomic scale feared service. Many of the poorest wanted to stay home because they could not afford the cost of provisions or because they did not want to neglect their farms or shops (Lys. 14.14).

Some of the wealthiest hoplites, on the other hand, insinuated themselves into the cavalry, which was considered safer than the infantry; so a popular accusation went (Lys. 14.7, 16.13). If the charge is true, the culprits may have been moved not merely by physical cowardice, but by political calculation. Some of them, believing in the greater safety of the cavalry, may have been unwilling to die on behalf of the *demos* they had fought against eight years before. Others may have preferred to fight in an aristocratic corps rather than in a common body. At any rate, knights and *demos* had not put aside mutual suspicion with the call to arms. The actions of one Mantitheus show the lengths an aristocrat had to go to combat popular hostility. This knight found it expedient not only to enlist voluntarily in the infrantry, but to subsidize two hoplites of his deme who could not afford provisions for the campaign (Lys. 16.14).

The Thebans defeated the Spartans at Haliartus, a victory that may have eased Athenian fears somewhat. So may have other events of the fall of 395 and the winter and spring of 394: the addition of Corinth, Argos and many other states to the Atheno–Boeotian alliance, and the first victories of this league in north-central Greece.[2] Athenian doubts, however, persisted. On the eve of the battle by the Nemea River in June 394, as one contemporary reported, 'everyone knew beforehand that it must be a dangerous affair' (Lys. 16.15).

Political divisions persisted too. Political enemies may have used the prosecution of Alcibiades' son shortly after Haliartus as a means of attacking Thrasybulus. The speaker's arguments appealed to popular dislike of overly proud and overly clever young aristocrats.[3]

If indeed it did, it would have been even more effective after the dramatic battle by the Nemea River. There, on the plain of Corinth, the combined forces of the anti-Spartan league met an army of Lacedaemonians, Arcadians and Tegeans. With over 20,000 hoplites on a side, it was the greatest battle the Greeks had ever fought amongst themselves. The encounter lasted a full day until finally the Lacedaemonians prevailed. Yet their victory was not decisive, for it did not force the enemy to surrender or give up control of the Isthmus. It must have had a terrible effect on the anti-Spartan allies nonetheless, for battle casualties were high, particularly among the Athenians, who had faced the Spartans in the line of battle. The allies are said to have lost approximately

2,800 men at the Nemea, of whom the Athenians were no small part.[4]

A defeat in battle sometimes stiffens a country's will to resist and unites a wavering people. Several circumstances of Athens' defeat, however, ensured that the Nemea River would exacerbate divisions at home. Although six tribes of the Athenian army (3,600 men out of 6,000) had been beaten badly by the Spartans, four (2,400 men) had been left untouched. Perhaps the members of the six defeated tribes remembered afterwards that their victorious comrades had not attempted to regroup and turn to come to their aid. Thrasybulus may have had this failure in mind when, as is reported, he later 'reproached everyone for cowardice' (Lys. 16.16).[5]

A second controversial matter was the role of the Athenian cavalry. The allies had over 1,500 horsemen at the Nemea River, and outnumbered their opponents; the Athenians alone had 600. Yet the cavalry did nothing to prevent the Spartans from outflanking the Athenians; at Mantinea in 418, on the other hand, they had averted just such a disaster (Thuc. 5.73.1). It is possible, in fact, that only 11 Athenian cavalrymen died in the battle: such is the record of a funerary inscription of 394/93. Were the knights, too, guilty of cowardice?[6]

Neither of the two main accounts of the battle, Xenophon's or Diodorus', refers to the role of the cavalry. In Plato's *Menexenus*, written within a decade of the battle, Socrates ascribes Athens' defeat to 'bad terrain' (245e).[7] It is hard to see an explanation of Athens' cavalry failure in this remark, however, for in the likeliest reconstruction of the battle, they had the advantage of terrain.[8]

Yet the knights were not necessarily traitors to the democracy. They may have had to face the Spartan cavalry — nearly their equal in number — alone, with the allied horsemen off protecting the other flank. Or the cavalry may have lost its nerve in the face of the Spartan charge. In 394, Athens' cavalry lacked experience. Worse still, it had been demoralized by constant charges of cowardice and treason under the Thirty. Even if its intent were patriotic, therefore, the Athenian cavalry at the Nemea might have failed to carry it out.[9]

If Athens' knights were patriots, however, it is unlikely that they seemed entirely so to the *demos*, especially in the climate of distrust that had prevailed since 403. A third circumstance of Athens' defeat at the Nemea served as an unpleasant reminder of class tensions. For after the battle, the anti-Athenian party in Corinth managed to keep the gates of their city closed to the retreating allied troops (Xen. 4.2.23; Dem. 20.52–55). How many Athenians wondered if their own upper classes would not do the same after a battle in Attica?

There are several indications of popular distrust of the cavalry after the battle at the Nemea. Thrasybulus' reproach of cowardice has already been mentioned. It should be pointed out that his comments were recorded in a speech aimed at convincing the *demos* to give up its hatred of aristocrats. The speaker, one Mantitheus, criticizes Thrasybulus for making the charge: evidence, perhaps, that the butt of Thrasybulus' reproach was Mantitheus' fellow knights (Lys. 16.18). Incidentally, since Mantitheus delivered his oration sometime between 392 and 390, it may be inferred that hostility to the cavalry still existed at that date.[10]

Another side of the popular mood may be gleaned from three grave monuments of 394, which refer to the knights. One of them, a sumptuous tribute to eleven horsemen who fell at the Nemea and to another one killed at Coronea in the same year, has already been mentioned. Another is the official record of the casualties at the Nemea. Although fragmentary, this inscription has been well enough preserved to show that its relief gave great prominence to the knights. The same is true of a third monument, the grave stele of Dexileus, son of Lysanias of Thoricus, one of the knights who died at the Nemea. In superbly-carved relief, this monument shows a horseman trampling upon a hoplite.[11] In the unusual emphasis these three monuments give to the cavalry, one may detect a response to popular criticism of the knights.[12]

Consideration of an anomaly of the Dexileus monument will help strengthen this interpretation, for of the thousands of Athenian gravestones to have survived from antiquity, it is the only one that notes the date of birth or death of its subject. The stele records that Dexileus was born in the archonship of Teisander (414/13) and died in that of Euboulides (394/93). The explicit mention of Dexileus' age makes clear that a man who was 20 in 394/93 could not have had anything to do with the crimes the Thirty committed in 404/03 — an innocence which all knights did not share. Hence the funerary monuments of 394 may well reflect the tensions of contemporary Athens.

Athens' defeat at the Nemea River, therefore, stoked the fires of division that had never gone out in the city, not even in the previous summer, when the assembly voted to join the Boeotians in an alliance. It dismayed enthusiasts of the war, and convinced doubters of the soundness of their hesitation. Two months later, the anti-Spartan league met another defeat, this time in Boeotia, on the plain before Coronea.[13] Once again, the news of failure probably dampened the spirits of many Athenians. The effect may not have been as serious as that of the Nemea, for the allies lost only 600 men in the second battle (Diod. 14.84.1–2). There was no envelopment by the Spartans: a circumstance which should at least have removed suspicion of inactivity by the Athenian cavalry, even if indeed only one knight died at Coronea. Additionally, this time, Sparta had as many knights at the battle as did its enemies.[14]

Coronea, furthermore, was less than a complete victory for Sparta. Agesilaus' troops sustained great losses when he attacked the retreating Thebans head on (Xen. 4.3.19–20). More important, the Spartans failed in the objective of their campaign, the conquest of Boeotia.[15] There were some facts, therefore, in which Athenians could take comfort. Nevertheless, Coronea had been a defeat, the second of the season. The two losses probably did great damage to the political position of Thrasybulus, who had championed the anti-Spartan alliance.[16]

Another battle of summer 394, however, also affected Thrasybulus' career though he took no part. In the sea fight off Cnidos in August, the enemy fleet thoroughly destroyed the Spartan navy, the prerequisite of Spartan power in the Aegean and Asia Minor (Xen. 4–3.11–12; Diod. 14.83.4–7). Although the victorious fleet served the Persian king, it was manned in large part by Greeks, especially Athenians, including its admiral, an old political foe of Thrasybulus: Conon.[17]

Conon's Predominance

Events in the eastern Aegean made summer and autumn 394 heady days for the enemies of Sparta. After its victory at Cnidos, the Persian fleet sailed up the coast of Asia, and everywhere evicted the Spartan harmosts. The Persians, following the sound advice of Conon, made points both of not establishing garrisons and of guaranteeing each city's autonomy (Xen. 4.8.2). This generosity — combined, to be sure, with the new facts of power — succeeded admirably. The Persians persuaded most of the important states of the region to join their cause and — if the numismatic evidence has been correctly interpreted — united these states in an anti-Spartan alliance.[18]

The next spring brought even more dramatic reverses to Sparta, for the Persian fleet carried the war to Laconia itself. The fleet first sailed to the Cyclades where, based at Melos, it expelled the Spartans and overturned pro-Spartan regimes (Xen. 4.8.7). From Melos, Conon and Pharnabazus sailed to the Peloponnesus, raided the Laconian coast, and took the strategic island of Cythera, which they garrisoned (Xen. 4.8.7–8).[19]

Finally, the Persian fleet sailed to Corinth. Pharnabazus brought to the anti-Spartan allies there the Persian king's encouragement and his money. Equally important, he made a formal alliance between the Persians and their allies, on the one hand, and the league based at Corinth (the alliance of Athens, Boeotia, Argos, Corinth, etc.) on the other. In addition, the Persians set up a mercenary force at Corinth.[20]

Most Athenians probably greeted these events with cheers. Aegospotami had been avenged. More, it had been avenged by Athenians, or so many could argue. Plato's Socrates, for example, speaks of the sailors who died at Cnidos as 'our men,' just as he did of the fallen soldiers of the Nemea or the battle in 392 of the Lechaeum Long Walls (Plato. *Menex*. 245e–246a; cf. Dein. 1.75). The commander of the garrison on Cythera was no Persian, but the Athenian Nicophemus; the head of the mercenary force at Corinth was his countryman Iphicrates (Xen. 4.8.8; Harpoc., s.v. *Xenikon en Korinthoi*).

The Hero of Cnidos

Above all, the man considered most responsible for Cnidos was an Athenian, Conon. He was the hero of Greek Asia. Samos and Ephesus took down their bronze statues of Lysander and replaced them with images of Conon and his son Timotheus. Erythrae did them one better by gilding its statue of the hero and offering to erect it 'wherever it pleases Conon'.[21]

Conon's victories and honours redounded greatly to his credit at home. His political supporters made the most of the situation. Epicrates and Cephalus, for example, are likely to have turned their support for Conon in 395 into influence on the Pnyx. Epicrates' embassy (with Phormisius) to the Persian king is perhaps to be dated to the months following Cnidos.[22]

Great as was the *charis* that Conon had gathered for himself by the time his fleet sailed to the Isthmus in the summer of 393, it was nothing compared to that which he would obtain in the months ahead. For at Corinth, he convinced Pharnabazus to allow him to take the fleet to Athens and once there, to rebuild the Long Walls and the fortifications of Piraeus (Xen. 4.8.9). It would be hard to exaggerate the strategic importance of this event to Athens. Conon himself is said to have thought that 'nothing could be a heavier blow to the Lacedaemonians' (Xen. 4.8.9). Thucydides considered Themistocles' wall-building the foundation of the Athenian empire; Grote calls Conon a second Themistocles.[23]

Likewise, it would be hard to exaggerate the political consequences of the act. As sponsor of the project, distributor of funds (some of which he may have supplied himself), and supplier of much of the labour (his ships' crews), Conon was sure to obtain most of the credit. Although some of the funds for the construction were raised by the Athenians themselves before Conon's return, there is no evidence of their contributing more than a very small amount. If the victory of Cnidos had not been enough to gain Conon a reputation as the restorer of Athens, the rebuilding of Athens' walls surely was. Demosthenes, summing up Conon's achievements, called the rebuilding of the walls 'the most beautiful thing of all' (Dem. 20.68–69; cf. Isoc. 5.64). If Edmonds is right, the project made a great impression on the comic playwrights of 393: they compared Conon to Odysseus, his builders to Cyclopes or, using a colloquialism for manual workers, to 'hand-belly fillers'.[24]

In addition to the prestige it won him as an empire-builder, Conon's construction project added to his *charis* among Athenians in another humbler but significant way. The Persian king's money allowed Conon to provide jobs for the many Athenians who had not yet recovered from the economic effects of the Peloponnesian War (Xen. 4.8.10; Diod. 14.85. 2–3).

Many Athenians had the problem of poverty on their minds during the Corinthian War, from Epicrates to the characters of Aristophanes *Ecclesiazusae* and *Ploutos* to Nikarete, daughter of Damostratos, who was forced to become a wet nurse. Regaining the wealth of the empire was the solution to the problem, and Conon's efforts were the first steps in that direction.[25]

By his victory at Cnidos, therefore, by his rebuilding of the walls, by his furnishing of employment, and by his promise of renewed empire, Conon built himself a remarkable base from which to dominate Athenian politics. The extraordinary honours granted to him upon his return to Athens show that his contemporaries grasped this truth well. No one wanted to be left behind in the race to win the favour of the hero of Cnidos. Conon was voted two statues, one in bronze, making him the first Athenian to be so honoured since Harmodius and Aristogeiton. One statue stood on the Acropolis, the other in the Agora, next to the precinct of Zeus the Liberator. A bronze statue of Conon's benefactor, King Evagoras of Salamis in Cyprus, was erected next to Conon's bronze at the same time. Conon received immunity from taxation. Finally, public inscriptions referred to Conon alone as 'the liberator of the allies' (Dem. 20.69).[26]

To the ambitious, recognition is satisfying, but not sufficient. Conon did not intend to retire to the applause of a grateful country. Although little is known of Athens' activities in the year of his return (approximately, summer 393 to summer 392), enough information has survived to make clear that Conon played a leading role in them.

His return to Athens had placed Conon in an ambiguous position. Wall-builder and servant of the Great King, he had telescoped the two periods of Themistocles' long career into one year. The ancient sources unanimously say that his real loyalty lay with Athens and rebuilding its power, and that his work for Persia was but a means toward an end. Little else could have been true of a man who earned the praise of Isocrates.[27]

Yet, in 393, Conon would have been wildly imprudent to make his real loyalties clear. The Spartans later denounced him to the satrap Tiribazus for building up Athens' power at the expense of Persia's, and Tiribazus arrested him.[28] Yet, Conon had been sufficiently confident of his position to present himself to Tiribazus at Sardis: he would not have if he had been openly rebuilding the Athenian empire in 393/92 at Persia's expense. Rather, his foreign policy seems to have been to pursue the war against Sparta in a way that would help Athens without openly hurting Persia.

Thus Conon sent an embassy to Dionysius of Syracuse in 393, in the hope of winning him away from the Spartans to the alliance at Corinth (Lys. 19.19). He gave a personal subsidy to the mercenary corps at Corinth. If he used the Persian fleet to collect money from the islands, as he had told Pharnabazus he would, he is unlikely to have proclaimed the re-establishment of the Athenian empire while doing so (Xen. 4.8.9). He may have reclaimed sovereignty over Delos for Athens, but the date is uncertain. Only in the cases of Lemnos, Imbros and Scyros can one be sure that Athenian rule was openly asserted, for Athens seems to have controlled these islands at the time of the peace negotiations in Sardis in 392 (Xen. 4.8.15). Athens' relations with these three places, however, among its oldest dependencies and vital to the grain trade route, cannot be taken as typical of its relations with its former allies. Moreover, since Athenian cleruchs seem never to have been evicted from these islands, a decree in the Athenian assembly might have been sufficient to encourage patriots there to re-establish control. A naval expedition was not necessarily required.[29]

Finally, Conon may have sponsored a mission to Chios in 393/92 that offended Persia. An ancient tradition states that Isocrates went to Chios to help it draft a new democratic constitution. Biographical details about Isocrates tend to place the mission in the late 390s; Isocrates' friendship with Conon makes it tempting to see the latter as sponsor. The action risked Persia's wrath by intervening in the Persian sphere of influence, but it was far from a proclamation of the Athenian empire.[30]

While Conon conducted his balancing act abroad, he built up power and prestige at home. In Piraeus, he built a new temple to Aphrodite, goddess of Cnidos. He underwrote a festival liturgy (*hestiasis*) for the entire citizenry: a remarkable sign of generosity as well as power, considering that the liturgy was usually restricted to one's tribe. Finally, he cleared his name of Aegospotami by prosecuting another of the generals there, Adeimantus (Dem. 19.191).[31]

No other Athenian politician has left such a record of activity for 393/92: Conon dominated Athenian politics at this time. The question remains, however: how? No politician, no matter how powerful, can rule alone. Conon, no less than the meanest orator of the Pnyx, had to have allies and servants. But which allies, which servants?

Friends and Enemies

Recent scholars have advanced several different interpretations of Conon's political alliances. Two theories which invoke foreign policy may be passed over rapidly. The first sees a broad dispute over imperial policy between Conon and Thrasybulus: it makes

Conon an aggressive imperialist, Thrasybulus a moderate one. Other studies have already refuted this theory and shown that Thrasybulus was no less imperialist than Conon.[32] A second theory has argued that Conon stood for co-operation with Persia, while Thrasybulus championed all-out war with the barbarian. We have already seen, however, that Thrasybulus may have advocated co-operation with Persia during the Ionian War, and he would do so in 390 (*infra*). As far as Conon is concerned, the ancient sources agree that while he served the Persian king, he served Athens first. Of course, some other Athenian politicians will have been repelled by Conon's co-operation with Persia (*infra*), but this was not the only matter on which his friendships or enmities turned.[33]

Let us now turn to three strictly domestic political interpretations. According to the first, Conon had friends in every camp but was basically the representative of radical democracy and supported the poorer classes against the rich. This view, put forward in the nineteenth century by Beloch and Meyer, still has adherents today.[34]

A second point of view removes ideology from Conon's thinking. It argues that for reasons of expediency, Conon tied himself to the followers of Agyrrhius of Collytus, and turned on the two other main political groups of the time: the group of Thrasybulus and the group of Cephalus of Collytus.[35]

Finally, an agnostic position argues that Conon's only certain allies were the few men known to have fought with him in the Persian fleet: Aristophanes, Hieronymus, Nicophemus and perhaps Demaenetus. Nothing else can be said with certainty about Conon's political connections in 393/92.[36]

Each of these theories has points in its favour. None, however, does justice to the complexity of Athenian politics, and each has errors. Take first the view of Conon as a radical democrat. Like most Athenian politicians, Conon took pains to court 'the populist many'. By his fleet, by the renewal of empire it promised, by his building projects and by his largesses, Conon won their support. Yet they were not his sole support. Conon had close connections with the Athenian aristocracy — and with aristocracy of the bluest blood, and of less than democratic political convictions.

Lysias' nineteenth oration, *On the Property of Aristophanes*, for example, details the affairs of an unnamed Athenian family. Its members were distinguished as liturgists and as victors in the horse race at pan-Hellenic games, the upper-class sport *par excellence*

(Lys. 19.63). A sister of the speaker had been married to Phaedrus of Myrrhinus, a follower of Socrates, eponym of a Platonic dialogue — and one of the men exiled in 415 for parodying the mysteries and mutilating the herms (Lys. 19.15).[37] Yet, if Conon was a radical democrat, it is hard to imagine why he long associated himself with Phaedrus' father-in-law or why he enjoyed the support of that man's son (the speaker of Lysias 19) in 393 (Lys. 19.12–13). Why did he arrange the marriage of Aristophanes, the son of his old comrade Nicophemus, to Phaedrus' widow? (Lys. 19.13).

Likewise, the theory of Conon the radical democrat does not account for Conon's association with Callias of Alopece, no oligarch, but hardly a man of the Many.[38]

The second point of view, that Conon allied himself with Agyrrhius and turned on Epicrates and Cephalus, will not stand scrutiny either. Leaving aside for a moment the complicated question of Conon's ties to Agyrrhius, Conon's hostility to Cephalus and Epicrates rests only on the hostility between Epicrates and a relative of Agyrrhius in 392/91, when Agyrrhius' nephew Callistratus prosecuted Epicrates for his role in the Sparta peace conference (*infra*). This argument assumes that Conon, had he been in Athens at the time, would have shared Callistratus' attitude toward the peace. It also fails to consider the possibility that, although enemies in 392/91, Epicrates and Agyrrhius had earlier been *philoi*.

The third position, agnosticism, has much to recommend it. It serves at times as a useful corrective to overly speculative views, but it can be taken too far.

The case of Callias of Alopece is a good example of the problem. Two indirect links connect Callias to Conon. In 393/92, one of Conon's fellow ambassadors to Sardis was Hermogenes, who has been identified with Hermogenes, Callias' half-brother.[39] Two years later, Callias as general co-operated with Iphicrates in the latter's famous defeat of a Spartan regiment near Lechaeum (Xen. 4.5.13).

It has been objected, that fellow-ambassadors are not necessarily allies but may be competitors, and that co-operation between Callias and Iphicrates shows only that 'neither general was given to treason'.[40] Yet, balanced against these objections is a long chain of circumstantial evidence: the third colleague of Conon and Hermogenes was Callimedon, possibly a relative of Agyrrhius;

Agyrrhius and Callias were allies in the trial of Andocides in 400; Callias hated Alcibiades and, therefore, might have hated Alcibiades' *philos* Thrasybulus and supported Thrasybulus' enemy Conon.[41] The intensely personal nature of Athenian politics must be thrown into the balance, and so must the constant tendency of the Greeks to form close friendships and deathly enmities. Whatever the value of scepticism, these considerations ought to outweigh it.

Conon took his supporters not from one, but from several factions. As one of the few important Athenians not to have taken part in the civil war of 404/403, Conon had a luxury of choice which other politicians did not, as Beloch points out.[42] Conon's supporters were not restricted to 'the populist many' but included the upper classes. Politicians of many different stripes probably wanted to be attached to him, the man of the hour. Conon cultivated this diverse support, which made both good politics and sound military strategy: uniting the country was a prerequisite of rebuilding Athenian power.

Conon's ties varied in intensity from the closest and most trusted *philos* to the occasional collaborator. References to Conon's 'group' or 'party' mislead by ignoring the degree and nuance that mark human relationships.[43] Conon's *philoi* were not necessarily devoted to each other. By 387 — not to say 392 — the uneasy allies of 393 could have become outright enemies.

First, let us consider Conon's closest colleagues, the men he had worked with before Cnidos. The father of the speaker of Lysias 19 was one: he had served as a trierarch under Conon in the Peloponnesian War (Lys. 19.12). Another was Hieronymus, a close subordinate of Conon who was put in joint command of his troops in Rhodes in summer 395 while his chief was away in Caunus (*Hell. Oxy.* 15.1). He held the same position later that year when Conon went up country to consult his Persian superiors (Diod. 14.81.4). After Conon returned to Athens in 393, Hieronymus' name was not unknown on the Pnyx, as Aristophanes' *Ecclesiazusae* 201 shows.

Hieronymus' colleague in 395 was Nicophemus, an Athenian from Rhamnus (*Hell. Oxy.* 15.1). Nicophemus had fled with Conon to King Evagoras' court in Cyprus after Aegospotami (Isoc. 9.51). By 393, Conon trusted him well enough to leave him as commander of the garrison in Cythera (Xen. 4.8.8). Associated with Nicophemus in Conon's service was his son Aristophanes. In

393/92, Conon sent Aristophanes on an important diplomatic mission to Dionysius of Syracuse (Lys. 19.19–21). After Conon's death, father and son remained loyal to the old friends they had shared with him: so one would judge from the mission they organized in 391 to help Evagoras, then under attack by the Persians (Lys. 19.21–26). This vain endeavour proved to be their last, for a jealous *demos* executed them for failure (Lys. 19.7).

The lives of Nicophemus and Aristophanes illustrate one aspect of Conon's political methods. If the speaker of Lysias 19 is to be believed, before Cnidos their family was quite poor: its only property in Attica was a small plot of land in Rhamnus (Lys. 19.28). Afterwards, Aristophanes became quite rich, thanks to booty, Persian pay and a lucrative marriage. Between 393 and his death in 390, he spent a minimum of 15 talents![44]

Apparently, therefore, although Conon was himself an aristocrat, he had no qualms about drawing his closest collaborators from the lower classes. Like many a conquering general, he seems to have placed talent and loyalty before lineage.

The relationship between Conon and Iphicrates illustrates this well. In 393, the admiral appointed Iphicrates as commander of the mercenary force in Corinth, even though Iphicrates was relatively young and the son of a mere cobbler. Yet, as time would show, he was a superb general. Even before 393, he had won distinction as a marine in boarding the ship of an enemy, perhaps at Cnidos. Two bits of luck may have helped the plucky young marine win the commander's attention. First, it is remotely possible that Iphicrates and Conon were relatives, because although they came from different demes and social classes, the two men had fathers with the same name, Timotheus. Secondly, Iphicrates belonged to the same deme as Conon's lieutenant Aristophanes. Perhaps the one man from Rhamnus was his demesman's advocate with the commander.[45]

The list of names of Conon's inner circle, or of what can be known of it today, is completed with that of Demaenetus, who broke through a Spartan blockade in 395 to sail from Attica to Conon's base in Rhodes. In the last years of the Corinthian War, Demaenetus reappears as a general (*Hell. Oxy.* 6.2; Xen. 5.1.26).

Certain other Athenian soldiers and politicians attached themselves to Conon, although perhaps not as closely. Their names cut a wide path across Athenian society, from the landed aristocracy to businessmen, from sympathizers with the Thirty to champions of the Many. Such varied connections are unusual, but not entirely surprising, considering the rewards to be gained from sharing Conon's glory.

Among the aristocracy, besides Callias and his half brother Hermogenes, was Demus son of Pyrilampes, Plato's stepbrother. Demus' friendship with the speaker of Lysias 19 and his service as trierarch on Aristophanes' expedition to Cyprus suggest a connection to Conon; his family's ancestral ties to the king of Persia increase the likelihood.[46]

One Eunomus might have been in a similar position. A wealthy liturgist, he was chosen along with Aristophanes in 393 to represent Conon before Dionysius of Syracuse. Eunomus may have been picked for the mission solely because he was a guest-friend of Dionysius, rather than because of any affiliation to Conon.[47] A bit of evidence favours such an affiliation, however: Eunomus seems to have been a student of Isocrates, a strong admirer of Conon and his son Timotheus — the latter also an Isocratean pupil (Isoc. 15.93).

To the same category might belong Philomelus of Paeania, an aristocrat known in 390 'more for his nobility than his wealth,' but later a well-heeled liturgist and a general. The brother-in-law of the speaker of Lysias 19, he too may have been a pupil of Isocrates.[48]

Eurippides (sic) son of Adeimantus of Myrrhinus may also have been one of Conon's allies. In 393 Eurippides went on an embassy to Sicily, probably the same embassy as that on which Aristophanes and Eunomus served. Co-ambassadors were sometimes political rivals, but in the year of Conon's predominance, ambassador Eurippides was probably part of the team. Afterwards, sometime in the next two years, Eurippides proposed a large-scale but unsuccessful tax measure, probably an *eisphora*.[49]

One Sophilus, proposer in the assembly in 394/93 of honours for Evagoras, should also be added to the list of Conon's supporters. Conceivably, so should Cinesias of Melite, who proposed honours in 394/93 for Dionysius of Syracuse, the object of the embassy which Conon dispatched.[50]

Given his support for Conon in early 395 and his embassy c. 394 to Conon's employer, the king of Persia, Epicrates of Cephisia probably continued to support the popular hero in 393/92. One can say the same (i.e., probably) about Cephalus of Collytus.

Thrasybulus of Collytus is not recorded among Conon's supporters in 395, but his powerful antipathy toward Thrasybulus of Steiria may have impelled him into Conon's camp.[51]

Finally, Agyrrhius too may have attached himself to Conon. The evidence is unsatisfactory: Callimedon, colleague of Conon on his embassy to Sardis in 393/92, bears a relatively uncommon name, and one that is attested to in Agyrrhius' family. Agyrrhius' co-operation with Callias in 400 is a straw in the wind. Beloch suggests that Persian money, disbursed by Conon, gave Agyrrhius the wherewithal to raise ecclesiastic pay to three obols: an attractive but unproven suggestion.[52]

The safest verdict is *non liquet*. Agyrrhius the popular politician and Conon the war hero each had reason to find the other useful, and hence may have formed an alliance. At any rate, the prosecution of Conon's supporter Epicrates by Agyrrhius' nephew in 392/91 does not preclude the alliance. Even the best of friendships could break over the issues raised by Epicrates' negotiations with Sparta.

The hero of Cnidos was bound to have enemies as well as friends, and none was more likely to head the list than the hero of Phyle, Thrasybulus, and his *philoi*.[53] Conon probably had other enemies, some of them the inevitable opponents of any war leader. Farmers afraid of new invasions, potential trierarchs jealous of their wealth, former oligarchs hostile to the democracy, veterans afraid of a second Nemea River, all were perhaps still in opposition.

In addition to these opponents, however, Conon had to deal with another sort of enemy, Athenians who criticized him for fighting on behalf of Persia against fellow Greeks. This sentiment is present, for example, in Lysias' *Funeral Oration* 2.5 perhaps written in 392, which refers to the battle of Cnidos as 'the victory of the barbarians'. In his *Olympic Oration* of 388, Lysias appeals to Athens and Sparta to give up their quarrels and turn on their common enemy, Persia (Lys. 33.4–6). In his *Menexenus*, probably written soon after the King's Peace of 387/86, Plato writes bitterly of Greece's surrender to Persia. Speaking of Athens' role in the Corinthian War, Socrates says ironically that

> ashamed of the trophies of Marathon and Salamis and Plataea, it did not dare to come to the aid of the King but only allowed refugees and volunteers to help him

(245a).[54]

Alone, Lysias and Plato would not furnish evidence of popular Athenian opinion in 393. Hostility to Persia and sympathy for the Greeks of Asia Minor played an important part in Athens' rejection of the proposed peace of 392. The prosecution of Epicrates and Phormisius on their return from Persia might have come less from any misdeeds of theirs than from a basic hostility to Persia, what Demosthenes would later call 'that silliness which has often defeated you (Athenians)' (Dem. 10.33).[55]

To sum up, there were several concentric circles of followers around Conon in 393/92. Conon's closest *philoi* had fought with him before his return to Athens; they ranged from aristocrats to the son of a cobbler. Other men followed Conon only after his return. They had a variety of motives and backgrounds. Some, like Epicrates, saw Conon as the best way to restore the empire. Others, like Demus, came from along line of men who co-operated with Persia. Callias perhaps had personal ties to Conon; he certainly had soured on the family of Alcibiades, Conon's sometime rival. Finally, there were those who saw Conon as a way of getting ahead; what he stood for mattered little.

Against Conon were Thrasybulus and his *philoi*, whose enmity stemmed less from differences of policy than from personality. Oligarchs and laconophiles probably also opposed Conon. So did the enemies of Persia: Lysias and Plato are examples. If Agyrrhius supported Conon, he may have done so with reservations, for he would soon prove to be a convinced enemy of Persia. Perhaps Agyrrhius saw Conon and thought of glorious victory, while Plato thought of shameful medizing. If so, they were not the only men to see the ambiguity of the position of the hero of Cnidos.[56]

'Salvation Showed Its Face, But . . .'

Less than a year after Conon's return to Athens, the main activity in the war switched from the battlefield to the ambassador's chair. Frightened by the loss of Cythera and the refortification of Athens, the Spartans decided to try to detach Persia from their enemies in Greece. Shortly after hearing of Conon's activities in Attica, perhaps in spring or summer 392, they sent Antalcidas to Tiribazus, the Persian satrap in Sardis.[57] The Spartan came with an offer and a warning: Sparta would give up all claims in Asia Minor in return for peace, a proposition Persia should not refuse in view of Conon's dangerous rebuilding of Athenian power. If he could not obtain a separate peace, Antalcidas hoped at least to frighten Persia into withdrawing support from Conon's fleet (Xen. 4.8.12).

Conon immediately organized an Athenian counter-expedition, with himself at the head, and brought along representatives of Boeotia, Corinth and Argos (Xen. 4.8.12).[58] The Spartans had proposed a formula for the Greeks of Asia to be subjects of the king, while all other Greeks would be independent (Xen. 4.8.14). The first clause would have shamed any schoolchild who read of Salamis and Plataea. The second, while more agreeable-sounding, masked a series of concessions on the part of the Corinthian allies, entailing the loss to Athens of Lemnos, Imbros, and Scyros; to Thebes of its hegemony over Boeotia; and to Argos of its *isopoliteia* with Corinth: in short, the loss of nearly all that the allies had gained in the war (Xen. 4.8.15).[59]

Tiribazus decided to accept Antalcidas' offer, but because of the protest of the other Greeks — his allies, after all — he had to leave for Persia to obtain Artaxerxes' approval. Before going, he secretly financed a Spartan fleet. Moreover, he arrested Conon on the grounds that the Spartans' charge was true: Conon was using the king's fleet to build up Athens' power. Tiribazus thus deprived Athens of the architect of its naval revival, and incidentally rid himself of a formidable rival for royal favour (Xen. 4.8.16, Diod. 14.85.4).

He may have done more as well. Before going to Susa, Tiribazus quite possibly issued a statement in the king's name that ordered the Greeks to make peace on Antalcidas' terms. This hypothesis goes far toward explaining Philochorus' characterization of the peace proposal of 392 as 'the peace which the king sent down' (*FGrH* 328 F 149a).[60]

When Tiribazus eventually saw the king, about three months later, Artaxerxes expressed his opinion of the proposal by his decision to send the pro-Athenian Struthas to Ionia as satrap, where in another three months, the latter worked to undo Tiribazus' mischief (Xen. 4.8.17, Diod. 14.99.1).[61] In the meantime, however, Tiribazus' policy had a resounding effect. In autumn or winter 392, Athens sent a peace embassy to Sparta, probably a continuation of the process Tiribazus had dared to begin.[62] Why should the Athenians, recently such steadfast opponents of peace, now show such enthusiasm for negotiation?

Between the negotiations at Sardis and those at Sparta the battle of Lechaeum Long Walls took place.[63] This Spartan victory was an incentive toward negotiation, for it hurt the allies in several ways. It cut off Corinth from its main outlet to the sea, and gave its enemies a base from which to harry the land (Xen. 4.4.17). The allies suffered many casualties at Lechaeum; in *Menexenus* 245e, Socrates mentions Lechaeum alongside the Nemea River as one of the worst defeats of the war. Finally, the Spartan breach in the walls, combined with the capture of two Saronic Gulf towns, Sidus and Crommyon, opened the road to an invasion of Attica (Xen. 4.4.11–13; Diod. 14.86.4; And. 3.18). Not long after, Athens showed how seriously it took this danger by marching its hoplites to Corinth in full force and rebuilding its walls, the western one in haste, then the eastern one more leisurely (Xen. 4.4.18). In sum, the military balance had tilted against Athens.[64]

The dramatic arrest of Conon was just as serious. Imagine the uproar in the agora when the news of Tiribazus' perfidy reached it. Conon was soon released from prison, but nevertheless he died later in 392, apparently of an illness in Cyprus.[65] The death of Conon removed the keystone of Athenian politics. His followers were suddenly leaderless. In turmoil over the events of Sardis, they seem to have split into two factions. One concluded that, for the moment at least, peace with Sparta and Persia was necessary. Epicrates represents, and perhaps led this faction. The other group decided to avenge Conon and carry out the war. Nicophemus and Aristophanes belonged to this group, if their anti-Persian expedition to Cyprus in 391 is any indication (Xen. 4.8.23–24). So did Agyrrhius, who may have been associated with Conon.

Conon's death had another effect: it opened the political stage to men who had not been his associates. Andocides may belong to this category, for nothing ties him to Conon. Thrasybulus certainly fits the bill: an enemy of Conon, he spoke out against peace with Sparta.[66]

The treaty negotiated at Sparta must be considered before examining Athens' reaction further. Andocides and his fellow ambassadors negotiated better terms than those at Sardis.[67] Athens could keep its three island stepping-stones to the Black Sea, and Thebes could maintain its rule over all of Boeotia except Orchomenus (And. 3.12–14). The rest of the cities of mainland Greece, however, would be autonomous, which meant that Argos and Corinth would have to give up their isopolity (And. 3.24–27). Apparently, Struthas had not yet reversed Tiribazus' policy; Andocides assumes (or asserts?) that Persia is still on Sparta's side. He says:

> shall I be told that we must continue fighting until we have crushed Sparta and her allies? We are not adequately equipped, in my opinion, for a campaign of such a scale; and if we are successful, what must we ourselves expect from the *barbaroi* afterwards?
> (And. 3.16)

Andocides says nothing about surrendering the Greeks of Asia Minor to Persia, but he had every reason to pass over this embarrassing concession, upon which Persia presumably continued to insist.[68]

Perhaps that is why the Athenian *demos* not only rejected the treaty, but charged Andocides and his colleagues with treason. Convicted and condemned to death, they had to flee Athens.[69] Still, their treaty had not been without its supporters. With the help of Andocides' speech and of other contemporary orations and comedy, one can form an idea of the groups on either side of the debate.

First, there were the proponents of peace. Andocides begins his speech with a promise that peace with Sparta will not necessarily bring an oligarchy as in 403 (And. 3.1). Later, he says that the supporters of the peace were contemptuous of the bumbling *demos*, which, in the past, had been unable to 'save itself,' i.e. make peace (And. 3.33). These two remarks are inconclusive, but other indications in contemporary speeches suggest that there *were* laconophiles in Andocides' Athens, men who would have welcomed an alliance with Sparta, friend of oligarchy. Andocides himself bends over backwards to praise Sparta for granting peace to the Athenians; he conveniently neglects the battle of Cnidos in order to assert that Sparta was undefeated in the Corinthian War (And. 3.8).[70] A few years earlier, the son of Alcibiades also had kind words for Sparta. In defending himself against a suit for a sum of five talents, he berates his opponents with these words:

> now they blame [my father] for what happened; and say that he taught the Lacedaemonians how to fight; the Lacedaemonians, who can teach this art to others!
> (Isoc. 6.11)[71]

The pamphlet *Against Alcibiades*, which was written between 396 and 380, praises the Spartans for generally accepting their defeats graciously, even defeat at the hands of their allies (Ps.-And. 4.28).[72] At the same time, it attacks the Athenians for their slaughter on Melos in 416: one of those very charges which, according to Isocrates, former Athenian oligarchs employed to contrast their city with Sparta (Ps.-And. 4.22; cf. Isoc. 4.110–114). Whether or not he was an oligarch, the speaker shows himself to be far removed from Athenian democracy, declaring those institutions to be best which 'fit both the many and the few' (Ps.-And. 4.6).

Hence in 392 some antidemocratic Athenians probably were anxious for a reconciliation with Sparta as a counterweight to the power of the *demos*. Those of them who were wealthy enough to be eligible for the trierarchy had additional reason for pacifism: the greatly-increased expense of a war without Persian subsidies. Even with Persia's help, the war had already necessitated one *eisphora*, in 393 (Isoc. 17.41).[73]

Another group of doves was made up of the war weary. If Aristophanes' *Ecclesiazusae* is anything to judge by, there were many people so minded by winter 392: mothers who worried about their sons (233–35), or men who, like the voters of Aristophanes' imaginary assembly, would agree to turn the state over to women because 'this was the only thing that the city had yet to do' (456–57).[74]

Oligarchs, stingy liturgists and the war weary are plausible supporters of Andocides' peace. Perhaps they seem strange companions for Andocides' fellow-ambassador, Epicrates of Cephisia: in 395, more of a hawk than Thrasybulus, and a leader of the 'populist many' (*Hell. Oxy.* 1.3). Epicrates' pacifism can be satisfactorily explained, however, without positing a complete change in his politics. Together with Andocides and perhaps Epicrates' co-ambassador to Persia *c*. 394, Phormisius, he may be taken as the representative of a fourth group of supporters of the peace: pragmatists. A pragmatist could hardly fail to notice that Boeotia, Athens' first and most important ally, favoured peace (And. 3.20, 24, 28). Nor would he let sentiment govern his attitude toward Persia.

By his very early support of Conon's fleet, and by his embassy to Artaxerxes, Epicrates had shown that he was willing to collaborate with Persia. It is not odd, therefore, that he should sell out the

Greeks of Asia as the price of continued co-operation. Nor does his position mean that he or even Andocides had given up the hope of rebuilding the empire. For all his concessions to philolaconian sentiment, and for all his chiding of those who wanted to regain 'the Chersonese, the colonies, the landed property and the debts,' Andocides declares himself a supporter of empire (And. 3.15). He represents his peace as a tactical retreat, a means of allowing Athens to build up its strength in order to acquire someday the same empire as it once had (And. 3.37–38). Andocides sums up his proposal by describing it as an *arche ton agathon*, taking advantage of a pun in Greek which makes the slogan both 'the beginning of good things' and 'the empire of good things' (And. 3.37–38).[75]

Now for the opponents of the peace and their motives. Andocides underlines one: fear that peace with Sparta would mean oligarchy (And. 3.1). Certainly, a small minority of Athenian oligarchs hoped for such a result. Nor was it impossible — not if the fates of Thebes and Corinth after 386 are any examples.[76]

A second crucial point was Athens' betrayal of the Greeks of Asia Minor. Philochorus implies that this was the official charge in Callistratus' indictment of the ambassadors (*FGrH* 328 F14a; cf. Plato *Menex.* 245b–d). In five years the Athenians would indeed be troubled by the abandonment of the Greeks of Asia Minor which the King's Peace demanded (Diod. 14.110.4).

Third, more selfish motives also seem to have been at work. Andocides accuses his opponents of wanting to fight to regain the empire: on the evidence, a justifiable charge. While empire would bring long-term benefits, some *penetes* may have had their immediate needs in mind: the booty which Thrasybulus placed so much emphasis upon in his campaign of 390, or even the salary of an oarsman (And. 3.25, Xen. 4.8.28). While Conon's largesses and the gradual recovery of agriculture probably eased the plight of Athens' poor, their problems had not disappeared. Fourth, the war against Sparta had not yet been won.[77]

Whatever the motive, the means by which Athenians would implement their will against Persian opposition was a question mark. The hawkish *demos* of 392 had lost its head, or so many scholars write. Pan-Hellenism, empire and poverty, they argue, led Athens to exaggerate its strength and thus irresponsibly oppose Persia and Sparta.[78]

But the *demos* might have indeed known what it was doing. When the assembly voted to reject Andocides' peace, some of its leaders might have suspected the truth: that Artaxerxes intended to pull the rug out from under Sparta. Perhaps they already knew of the appointment of Struthas; perhaps they were merely gambling on Persian court intrigues.[79]

Some of the leading opponents of peace can be identified. Callistratus moved the indictment against Andocides and his colleagues. Callistratus was a young man, between the ages of 20 and 30, and this prosecution is his first known political act. He probably had the support of his famous uncle, Agyrrhius, not merely because of their kinship, but also because later tradition connects the two men (both were associates of the banker Pasion) and because Agyrrhius' generalship of 389/88 makes him an unlikely pacifist.[80]

If Agyrrhius was indeed a colleague of Conon in 393, then Conon's former supporters were now divided over peace; Epicrates, for example, supported it. There has been much speculation over Cephalus' attitude. The sources are silent, but given Cephalus' lifelong opposition to Sparta, he too was probably a hawk in 392/91.[81]

One is on slightly firmer ground with Thrasybulus. By 390, he had made enough of a comeback to be appointed commander of Athens' new fleet (Xen. 4.8.25–31), a position which in itself permits the assumption of support for war. Lysias' *Funeral Oration* 2.63, which curiously ascribes the rebuilding of the Long Walls to 'the men of Phyle' rather than to Conon, may reflect Thrasybulus' return to favour. It has, moreover, been suggested that when *Ecclesiazusae* says that Thrasybulus was angry at 'salvation' (202–203) and that he 'spoke a wild pear [a constipatory agent] to the Spartans' (356 + scholiast), the play refers to the peace of 392. Thrasybulus' sometimes colleague Aesimus was also active at the time of *Ecclesiazusae* (208); did they pursue a common policy?[82]

With the rejection of Andocides' peace, a period — approximately a year — of dizzying changes in Athenian politics came to an end. Conon was dead and his supporters in disarray.

The major factional leaders in Athens were now a resurgent Thrasybulus of Steiria, Agyrrhius of Collytus (supported by his nephew Callistratus of Aphidna), Thrasybulus of Collytus, Aesimus, and Cephalus of Collytus. Whether the surviving *philoi* of Conon — Aristophanes, Nicophemus, Eunomus, Demaenetus and Iphicrates were all active in the next few years — followed one, or several or none of these leaders is an open question. Similarly, we cannot name the leaders of that amorphous but important tendency: the friends of Sparta, enemies of democracy, penny-pinching liturgists, and those who were simply tired, all who had united in support of peace in 392/91. This tendency had lost its leaders, Epicrates and Andocides, but was likely to regroup.[83]

Some Athenians may have felt certain about the future. Others, however, watching Sparta rebuild a navy, remembering the hesitancy of Boeotia, the weakness of Corinth and the treachery of Persia, were less sure. The diffident mood of Aristophanes' *Ecclesiazusae* may reflect this spirit. The voice of the disillusioned speaks at lines 193-96:

This league again, when first we talked it over,
It seemed the only thing to save the state.
Yet when they'd got it, they disliked it.
He who pushed it through was forced to cut and run.[84]

The play, certainly a product of the Corinthian War, is notoriously difficult to date. A production in winter 392/91, however, is one of the likeliest suggestions.[85] Scholars have long debated the import of Praxagora's regret (*Eccl.* 202-203) over the recently-missed opportunity of 'salvation': the peace negotiations of 392, the battle of Cnidos, the eclipse of Thrasybulus have each been suggested.[86] Aristophanes' allusions are, indeed, often hard to grasp today. In this case, however, perhaps the ambiguity was intentional.

Notes

1. Dem. 18. 118; Polyb. 30.18; Strabo 9.30. See also Rogers, *Aristophanes*, vol. 5 xv.
2. After Haliartus, the Argives, Corinthians, and Locrians joined the Atheno–Boeotian alliance. The allies proclaimed their aim as the overthrow of Spartan hegemony. To this end, they formed a common council at Corinth, gathered an army, and dispatched ambassadors to win allies, who succeeded in gaining all of Euboea, Leucas, Acarnania, Ambracia and the Chalcidice. See Diod. 14.83.1–3; Tod, *GHI*, vol. 2, no. 102–3. At the same time, allied forces snatched Pharsalus in Thessaly and Heracleia-in-Trachis from the Spartans. They also defeated the Phocians in a battle in Locris. See Diod. 14.82.5–10.
3. The prosecutor complained that young Alcibiades wanted to be acquitted because of his noble birth (Lys. 14.18) and the public services of his ancestors (24).

He placed him in that class of men who constantly broke the law, flouted religion and took *hetairai* (41–46): in other words, among the *jeunesse dorée* who had mutilated the Herms and parodied the Mysteries in 415. Cf. *supra*, chap. 4, n. 71.

4. Xen. 4.2.9–23; Diod. 14.82.10, 83.1–2; Lys. 16.14–15; Strabo 8.6.25; Dem. 20.52–53; Plato *Menex*. 245e. The best modern accounts are H. Delbrück, *History of the Art of War Within the Framework of Political History, Vol. 1: Antiquity*, trans. Renfore (Westport, Conn.: 1975 [1920]), 155; J. Kaupert in J. Kromayer and G. Veith, *Schlachten-Atlas zur Antiken Kriegsgeschichte* (Leipzig: 1922), 30ff.; *Idem, Antike Schlachtfelder*, vol. IV (Berlin: 1931), 595–7; W. K. Pritchett, *Studies in Ancient Greek Topography*, vol. 2: *Battlefields* (Berkeley: 1969), 73ff.; J. K. Anderson, *Military Theory and Practice in the Age of Xenophon* (Berkeley: 1970), 144, 147–50. For the number of hoplites, see Kromayer-Veith, *Schlachten-Atlas* 31. For the casualties, see Diod. 14.83.2. An outflanking motion could cause particularly heavy losses to an army: Thuc. 5.73.1.

5. Sparta's defeat near Lechaeum in 390 stiffened the morale of the Spartan army, Xen. 4.5.7–18. Thrasybulus' reproach, Lys. 16.16: τοῦ σεμνοῦ Στειριῶς τοῦ πᾶσιν ἀνθρώποις δειλίαν ὠνειδεκότος. On the identity of ὁ σεμνὸς Στειριεύς, see L. Gernet and M. Bizos, *Lysias, Discours*, vol. 2 (Paris: 1926), 12.

6. Cavalry at battle: Xen. 4.2.16–17, who gives these figures for the allied cavalry, attributes 600 horsemen to the Spartans. Diod. 14.83.1 states that each side had 500 cavalry, but against his figures, Kromayer-Veith, *Schlachten-Atlas* 31. Cavalry casualties: Tod. *GHI* vol. 2, no. 104, plus commentary *ad loc*.

7. Plato *Menex*. 245e: τῶν τε ἐν Κορίνθῳ χρησαμένων δυσχωρίᾳ.

8. The best reconstruction is Pritchett, *Studies* 82–3 which places the battle on the Corinthian plain between the stream Rachiani and a point about one mile to the west. To the south was the steep scarp at the edge of the plain; to the north, two miles away, the sea. The allied line faced west, and the Athenians stood on its left flank. In order to outflank the Athenians, therefore, the Spartans must have marched between them and the scarp. I walked this space in May, 1979, and could find no sign of any obstruction that might have allowed the hoplites but not the cavalry to operate.

9. Hdt. 4.123–28; Anderson, *Military Theory and Practice* 148. For Athenian attitudes toward the cavalry, Xen. 3.1.5.

10. For the date, see Gernet and Bizos, *Lysias*, vol. 2 7.

11. Nemea: *IG* II[2] 5221. For a photograph, J. Travlos, *A Pictorial Dictionary of Athens* (New York: 1971), 321. Dexileus: Tod, *GHI* vol. 2, no. 105. For a photograph, see Travlos, *Pictorial Dictionary*, 315.

12. I follow the arguments of Colin Edmondson's '*IG* II[2], 6217: A Footnote to the Restoration of the Athenian Democracy', a paper read at the American Philological Association meeting in December, 1974.

13. Xen. *Hell*. 4.3.15–21, *Ages*. 2.6–16, *Anab*. 5.3.6; Diod. 14.84.1–2; Plut. *Ages*. 18–19; Polyaenus 2.1.3, 5, 19; Pausanias 9.6.4, 3.9.13; Nepos *Ages*. 4.5; Frontinus 2.6.6; Strabo 9.2.29. The best modern accounts are Kaupert in Kromayer-Veith, *Schlachten-Atlas* 31–3; Pritchett, *Studies* 85–95; Anderson, *Military Theory and Practice* 152ff.

14. One knight died: Tod, *GHI* vol. 2, no. 104, line 5. Numbers at battle: Xen. 4.3.15 states that the two sides had the same number of horsemen (without saying how many that was).

15. Anderson, *Military Theory and Practice*, 155.

16. See, among others, Seager, 'TCAI,' 99.

17. *Hell. Oxy*. 1.25, 16.30. Cf. B. Jordan, *CSCA* 2 (1969), 200, on the composition of Conon's crews.

18. Only two Hellespontine cities, Sestus and Abydus, remained faithful to Sparta (Xen. 4.8.3–6). Of the other Greek cities of Asia, some expelled Sparta and maintained their freedom, while others joined Conon's forces. See Diod. 14.84.4, who lists in the latter group Cos, Nisyros, Teos, Mitylene, Ephesus and Erythrae.

The Politics of War, 395–391 BC 145

Sometime in the early fourth century, seven or eight Greek cities of Asia issued silver coins stamped with the legend ΣΥΝ, i.e. 'AL (liance)'. These states are Rhodes, Cnidos, Iasus, Ephesus, Samos, Byzantium, Cyzicus, and perhaps Lampsacus. The coins were minted on the Persian weight standard and all bear the type of Heracles strangling two snakes, attested elsewhere as a symbol of liberation. G. L. Cawkwell argues convincingly that these coins were issued by a Persian-sponsored alliance against Sparta, formed shortly after Cnidos. See Cawkwell, 'A Note on the Heracles Coinage Alliance of 394 BC', *NC* 6th ser. 16 (1956), 69–75 and C. M. Kraay, *Archaic and Classical Greek Coins* (London: 1976), 248–9. *Contra* J. M. Cook, *JHS* 81 (1961), 67–72, with a convincing refutation by Cawkwell, 'The ΣΥΝ Coins Again', *JHS* 83 (1963) 152–4.
    19. For contemporary conditions in two Cycladic islands, Siphnos and Paros, see Isoc. *Aeginiticus*, especially 18–20, 38–40, the plaint of a Siphnian aristocrat forced into exile. Cythera: Lewis, *Sparta and Persia* 144.
    20. Xen. 4.8.8; Diod. 14.84; Harpocration s.v. Ξενικὸν ἐν Κορίνθῳ. Alliance: G. Busolt underscores its importance in *Das Zweite Athenische Seebund* (Leipzig: 1877), 669–70.
    21. Paus. 6.3.16; Dem. 20.71; *SIG*[3] no. 126.
    22. *Supra*, chap. 4, n. 36. For the date, I. A. F. Bruce, 'Athenian Embassies in the Early Fourth Century BC', *Historia* 15 (1966), 277–8.
    23. Thuc. 1.93; Grote, *History of Greece* vol. 9, 323.
    24. Conon's contributions: Xen. 4.8.9; Diod. 14.85. 2–4; see *APF* 509. Athenian contribution minor: see Tod, *GHI* vol. 2, no. 107 and Pritchett, *Greek State at War* vol. 2 (Berkeley: 1974), p. 120 n. 21. *Contra*, Seager, 'TCAI', 99. Comic playwrights: J. M. Edmonds, *The Fragments of Attic Comedy* (Leiden: 1957) pp. 861, 875, 899, 933, 937 (οἱ ἐγχειροψογάστορες).
    25. Epicrates: *supra*, n. 24 and chap. 4, p. 103 and n. 29. Aristophanes' plays: *infra*, chap. 6, 'The Testimony of Aristophanes'. Nikarete: *supra*, chap. 2, p. 56.
    26. Conon's Honours: Dem. 20. 68–71. Acropolis: Paus. 1.3.2; Tod, *GHI* vol. 2, no. 128. Agora: Paus. 1.3.1; Isoc. 9.57; Dem. 20.70; Aesch. 3.243; Nepos. *Timoth.* 2.3. Evagoras: Isoc. 9.57, D. M. Lewis and R. S. Stroud, 'Athens Honors King Evagoras of Salamis', *Hesperia* 48 (1979), 192–3. Cf. Beloch, *Attische Politik* 118–19; Sealey, 'Callistratos', 183; Pritchett, *Greek State at War*, vol. 2 p. 120 n. 21; Strauss, 'Thrasybulus and Conon', 39–40.
    27. Isoc. 4.142, 5.62–64, 9.52–57; Nepos *Conon* 5.2; Justin 6.3.
    28. Xen. 4.8.16; Diod. 14.85.5; Nepos *Conon* 5.3–4.
    29. Mercenary corps: Androtion, *FGrH*, 324 F 48 = Philochorus, *FGrH*, 328 F 150. Delos: *IG* II[2], 1634 makes clear that Athens had re-established control of Delos by 390. F. Courby, 'Notes . . . sur le sanctuaire d'Apollon délien', *BCH* 45 (1921), 178–83, gives Conon credit. Seager, 'TCAI', 101–3, 115, is more sceptical. No naval expedition: Seager, 'TCAI', 102, n. 66. The Carpathus decree (Tod, *GHI*, vol. 2, no. 110) has often been taken to prove that Athens re-established its empire in the late 390s. The decree is imperialist (lines 18–20, 27, 31) but Tod's date of *c.* 393 (p. 30) is conjectural. M. Jameson now proposes a late fifth-century date. See Lewis, *Sparta and Persia*, 105, n. 3.
    30. Ps.-Plut. *Vit. X. Orat.* 837B. Cf. Münscher, 'Isokrates', *RE* 9 (1916), col. 2170. A thorough study of the not-always-reliable *Vitae* would be useful.
    31. Temple to Aphrodite: *IG* II[2], 1425, line 284; Dem. 22.72, 24.180; Paus. 1.1.3. *Hestiasis*: Athenaeus 1.3d. Cf. *RE* 8 (1913), col. 1315. On the general subject of Conon's wealth and expenditures, *APF*, 508–9.
    32. Dispute over imperial policy: S. Accame, *Richerche intorno alla Guerra corinzia* (Naples: 1951), 241–53; Idem 'Il problema della nazionalità greca nella politica di Pericle e di Trasibulo', *Paideia* 11 (1956), 250. Refutation: Seager, 'TCAI', 99 n. 34, 110–11; Perlman, 'Athenian Imperialistic Expansion', 264–6; Cawkwell, 'Imperialism of Thrasybulus', 270, n. 6.

33. Dispute over Persia: Cawkwell, 'Imperialism of Thrasybulus', 275–6. Refutation: *supra*, chap. 4, n. 66; *infra*, p. 153; Strauss, 'Thrasybulus and Conon', 45–8. Served Athens first: *supra*, n. 27.
34. Meyer, *Geschichte des Altertums*, vol. 5, 241–2; Beloch, *Attische Politik* 119; Chiara Pecorella Longo, *'Eterie'* 58.
35. Sealey, 'Callistratos', 183–5; Perlman, 'Athenian Imperialistic Expansion', 263.
36. Seager, 'TCAI', 93–4. Funke, *HA* 126–7, argues that it is impossible to identify Conon's allies; only the political enmity of Conon and Thrasybulus is provable.
37. Cf. *APF* 201.
38. On Callias, *supra*, chap. 4, p. 102.
39. Xen. *Hell*. 4.8.12, *Mem*. 4.8.4; Plato *Crat*. 384a, 391b–c. Cf. Sealey, 'Callistratos', 183.
40. Seager, 'TCAI', p. 103, n. 79.
41. Callimedon: Sealey, 'Callistratos', 183. Callias and Agyrrhius: And. 1.132–136. Callias and Alcibiades: Ps.-And. 4.13–15.
42. Beloch, *Attische Politik* 119.
43. E.g., Beloch, *Attische Politik*, 99, 119.
44. Lys. 19.28. Cf. *APF* 201–2.
45. On Iphicrates' appointment: Harpocration, s.v. Ξενικὸν Κορίνθῳ. Age: According to Justin 5.1 Iphicrates was only 20 years old in 394. He died *c*. 354: Nephos *Iphic*. 3.3; Dem. 23.130, 136. As Nepos states, he lived until old age (*senectus*). Even had he reached 75, however (no mean feat after the rugged life of a mercenary general!), Iphicrates would only have been 35 in 393. Cobbler's son: Arist. *Rhet*. 1367b18; Plut. *Mor*. 186f, 187b; *Suda* 1:772. *APF* 248, defends the accuracy of this tradition. Distinction as marine: Plut. *Mor*. 187a. Cf. Pritchett, *Greek State at War*, vol. 2, 62. Fathers: Conon's deme as Anaphlystus, as *IG* II² 3774 shows. Iphicrates came from Rhamnus, as Aesch. 1.157 shows. On Conon's father, see, among others, Tod. *GHI*, vol. 2, no. 128; on Iphicrates', Paus. 9.14.6. On Conon's aristocratic background, *APF* 506–8. Aristophanes' deme: Lys. 19.28. Iphicrates' deme: Aesch. 1.157.
46. Ar. *Ach*. 61–3; *Wasps* 98; Lys. 19.25; Plato *Gorgias* 481d, 513b. Cf. *APF*, 329–32.
47. Seager, 'TCAI', 104.
48. Lys. 19.15; Isoc. 15.93–94. Cf. *APF* 548–9.
49. Arist. *Rhet*. 1384b15 + schol.; Ar. *Eccl*. 823–29 + schol.; Thomsen, *Eisphora* 184; Ussher, *Ecclesiazusae* comm. ad loc.; *APF* 202–3.
50. Sophilus: *IG* II² 20; Lewis and Stroud, 'Evagoras', 192–3. Sophilus also proposed honours in 394/93 for one Phil——, *IG* II² 19.4–5. Cinesias: *IG* II² 18.5; Seager, 'TCAI', 103; Funke, *HA* 112 n. 27.
51. Epicrates and Cephalus: *Hell. Oxy*. 1.3; Embassy; *supra*, n. 22. Collytus: *supra*, chap. 4, p. 103.
52. Callimedon: Xen. 4.8.13; Athen. 8.340e. Cf. Sealey, 'Callistratos', p. 185; *APF*, pp. 278–9. Callias: Andoc. 1.132–36. Beloch: *Attische Politik*, 120.
53. *Supra*, chap. 4, p. 103.
54. In general, see Seager, 'TCAI', 108ff.; Cawkwell, 'Imperialism of Thrasybulus', *passim*. On the date of Lysias' *Olympic Oration*, 'TCAI', 114, n. 186. On the *Menexenus* as a bitter protest against the King's Peace of 387/86, see Kahn, 'Motive of the Menexenus', 220ff.
55. Cf. Cawkwell, 'Imperialism of Thrasybulus', 276.
56. The affiliations of some politicians *c*. 393 are too obscure for speculation. I therefore pass over Herakleides of Klazomenae (*supra*, chap. 4, p. 101); Gnathios, proposer of the Eretria alliance in 394/93(*IG* II² 16, 1. 6; Funke, *HA* 112

n. 26); Neocleides, the *rhetor* lampooned in Ar. *Eccl.* 254–55, 398–407, *Ploutos* 665, 716 + schol., 747; Ar. frg. 439. Cf. *PA* 10631.

57. To have time to visit the Cyclades, Laconia, and the Isthmus, Conon cannot have reached Attica before summer 393. To judge by Xen. 4.8.12, not long after his arrival, his activities began to alarm Sparta. See T. T. B. Ryder, *Koine Eirene, General Peace and Local Independence in Ancient Greece* (London: 1965), 166.

Antalcidas may have reached Sardis as early as winter 393/92. Spring 392 is likelier, though, because when the other Greeks reached Sardis shortly after Antalcidas, Corinth was already in revolution (cf. the reference to the Argo –Corinthian isopolity at Xen. 4.8.15 and Funke, *HA* 86 n. 48.) to be dated to early 392 (n. 62). A reasonable estimate is that the Sardis negotiations began in spring 392 and lasted through summer (Funke, ibid.).

The relationship between the Sardis conference and the following negotiations at Sparta is exceedingly complex. I follow the argument that the two meetings were part of a single negotiating process, and that Sardis predated Sparta by several months. Complete arguments for these points can be found most cogently in Ryder, *Koine Eirene* 165–9. Cf. Beloch *GG*² vol. 3.2, 81–2; P. Treves, 'Note sulla guerra corinzia', *RdFi* 65 (1937), 120–40; V. Martin, 'Le traitement de l'histoire diplomatique dans la tradition littéraire du IVᵉ siècle', *MH* 1 (1944), 13–30; F. Jacoby, *FGrH*, commentary *ad* Philochorus 328 F 149; S. Accame, *Ricerche intorno*, 111ff.

For a different point of view — that the two conferences were not part of a single process — see Hamilton, *SBV* 234–55; Funke, *HA* 141.

58. Conon's Athenian colleagues were Hermogenes, Dion, Callisthenes and Callimedon. On Hermogenes, *supra*, n. 39. On Callimedon, *supra*, n. 52. Dion was a well-known orator of the time (Plato *Menex.* 245e). Callisthenes (*PA* 8038) is otherwise unknown. On the possibility that Conon was not officially an Athenian ambassador, see Funke, *HA* 137, n. 8.

59. On Argos' isopolity with Corinth, see G. T. Griffith, 'The Union of Corinth and Argos', *Historia* 1 (1950), 236–56.

60. For the theory, see Barbieri, *Conone* 179.

61. According to Hdt. 5.50–54, the trip from Ionia to Susa took three months; a round trip therefore took six. If Struthas did not leave for Susa until summer 392 (n. 57) he did not return to Sardis until winter 392/91.

62. One *terminus post quem* of the conference at Sparta is summer 392. According to And. 3.20, at the time of the conference the Boeotians had been fighting for four years. Since the war began in summer 395, the conference must have taken place after summer 392. See Griffith, 'Union of Corinth and Argos', p. 242, n. 6.

A second *terminus post quem* is probably the battle of the Lechaeum Long Walls (text, *infra*). This battle took place within weeks or months of the revolution at Corinth and subsequent isopolity with Argos. The revolution broke out at the Corinthian festival of the Eukleia, i.e. in the first few months of 392: O. Jessen, 'Eukleia', *RE* 6.1 (1905), col. 1052. Some date the battle to summer 392: e.g., Hamilton, *SBV* 249–51. One detail, however, rules out this date. The prelude to the battle was the defection of two Corinthian aristocrats to the Spartan army at Sicyon, which they reached by wading through a torrent, Xen. 4.4.7. They could not have done this in high summer, when all the torrents in the Corinthia would be dry. Hence their defection must have occurred in the spring or fall. Assuming the battle postdates the Sardis conference (n. 57), one should choose the fall. The Sparta conference took place shortly afterwards, probably before Struthas' arrival in Sardis in winter 392/91. This date is attractive because it both removes Struthas from the scene when Athens was willing to negotiate and provides a reason — his return — for Athens' ultimate rejection of the treaty.

63. On dating the battle between the two conferences see previous note and Hamilton, *SBV* 251–3.

64. Two references in contemporary oratory indicate the Athenian fear of enemy

invasion. Lysias 2.70, praises the soldiers who had died at Corinth for having kept the war from Attica. And 3.20's detailed account of the suffering of Boeotian land at the hands of the enemy recalls Attica's similar plight in the Peloponnesian War.

65. See H. Swoboda, 'Konon', *RE* 11 (1922), cols. 1332–3.

66. Opened the stage: Beloch, *Attische Politik* 123. Thrasybulus: *infra*, p. 142 and n. 82.

67. Andocides led the mission. His colleagues were Epicrates of Cephisia, Cratinus of Sphettus and Euboulides of Eleusis. See hypothesis to And. 3; Philochorus, *FGrH*, 328 F 149a. Euboulides may have been the archon of 394/93. See Diod. 14.85.1; *PA* 5325. Epicrates was probably the well-known politician, associate of Conon. See Sealey, 'Callistratos', 185. Cratinus is not otherwise known. See *PA* 8757a. I have preferred the arguments of Cawkwell, 'Imperialism of Thrasybulus', p. 276, n. 25, to Bruce's attempt to redate the aftermath of Epicrates and Andocides to the aftermath of the King's Peace of 387/86 ('Athenian Embassies in the Fourth Century BC', 273ff.), for the testimony of Philochorus, even as preserved in Didymus, is preferable to that of Aristides and his scholiast.

68. Philochorus explicitly says that the proposed peace left the Greeks of Asia 'in the house of the king'. If, as has been suggested, the conference at Sparta was part of a continuing process that had begun at Sardis, then Sparta could hardly have retracted this concession to Persia which it had already made. Cf. Jacoby, *FGrH*, Suppl. b. 518.

69. Hypothesis to And. 3 *De Pace*; Philochorus, *FGrH* 328 F 149a; Ps.-Plut. *Vit. X Orat.* 835.

70. Note too Andocides' charge at 3.21–23 that Athens had violated its alliance of 404 by going to war against Sparta in 395. The two statements moved Jacoby to complain of Andocides' 'nauseating philo-Laconism'. See *FGrH* 3b Suppl. 2, p. 413, n. 7.

71. Blass, *Die Attische Beredsamkeit* vol. 2 (Leipzig: 1898), 225, dates the speech to 397.

72. Date: G. Dalmeyda, *Andocide, Discours* (Paris: 1930), 109–10.

73. Funke (*HA* 148, n. 56) vigorously asserts — without argument — that compared to power politics, neither socio-economic, domestic political or philolaconian considerations mattered in the debates on war and peace in 393/92. Yet he offers no evidence — and foreign policy is not made in a vacuum.

Eisphora: for date of Isocrates 17, see L. Van Hook, *Isocrates*, vol. 3 (Cambridge, Mass.: 1968), 211. On *eisphora* by 392, cf. Isaeus 5.37, Lys. 19. 24, 42; Funke, *HA* 170 n. 15.

74. Date of *Ecclesiazusae*: *infra*, n. 85.

75. Epicrates: see the argument of Cawkwell, 'Imperialism of Thrasybulus', 276. Andocides: Seager, 'TCAI', 106–7; J. Ober, 'Views of Sea Power in the Fourth-Century Attic Orators', *AncW* 1.3 (1978), 120.

76. After the King's Peace, Corinth became an oligarchy again: Xen. 5.1.34. In 382, Spartans seized the Theban acropolis and imposed oligarchy: Xen. 5.2.29–31.

77. Roberts, *Accountability* 89–93 argues unpersuasively that most of Andocides' enemies were not hawks but doves, angry that he had failed to secure his proposed peace.

78. See Beloch, GG^2 vol. 3.2, 82; Seager, 'TCAI', 105, 107.

79. Knew of Struthas: Beloch, *Attische Politik* 124. On the chronology, *supra*, nn. 57, 62.

80. Callistratus: *APF* 278. Agyrrhius, kin and tradition: Dem. 24.135; Pasion: Isoc. 17.31, Dem. 49.47; Business: And. 1.133. Cf. Funke, *HA* 146 n. 48. *Contra*, Roberts, *Accountability* 92–93.

81. Dove: Sealey, 'Callistratos', 185. Hawk: Beloch, *Attische Politik* 123. *Non liquet*: Funke, *HA* 146 n. 51. Opposition to Sparta: Kounas, 'Prelude to hegemony' 164–6.

82. Thrasybulus' command: for the date, *infra*, chap. 6 n. 1. Lysias: Seager, 'TCAI', 108. Ar. *Eccl.*: Seager, 'TCAI', 106–107; *infra*, n. 85; Funke, *HA* 146, n. 49. Aesimus: *supra*, p. 96.
83. Post-392 activity: *infra*, chap. 6.
84. Trans. Rogers, *Aristophanes* vol. 5 60. Ar. *Eccl.* 193–96:

τὸ συμμαχικὸν αὖ τοῦϑ', ὅτ' ἐσκοπούμεϑα,
εἰ μὴ γένοιτ', ἀπολεῖν ἔφασκον τὴν πόλιν.
ὅτε δὴ δ'ἐγένετ', ἤχϑοντο, τῶν δε ῥητόρων
ὁ τοῦτ' ἀναπείσας εὐϑὺς ἀποδρὰς ᾤχετο.

85. Many date the play on the basis of scholiast's statement (*ad Eccl.* 193) that two years before its production 'the Lacedaemonians and Boeotians' — emended to the Athenians and Boeotians — made an alliance. Some take this as a reference to the Atheno–Boeotian treaty that preceded the battle of Haliartus in summer 395, and hence date the play to winter 393. E.g., Ussher, *Ecclesiazusae*, pp. xxi, nn. 2–3; xxv. Others prefer the alliance forged at Corinth after the battle and, therefore, winter 392. E.g., V. Coulon and H. Van Daele, *Aristophane*, vol. 5 (Paris: 1930), 5.

The scholiast of the *Ecclesiazusae*, however, is not always trustworthy. For instance, he identifies the unnamed mover of Athens' alliance (195) as Conon — although Conon was not in Athens at all in 395/94. In finding a date for the play, therefore, one need not follow the scholiast's lead.

An alternative comes from Seager's suggestion (*supra*, n. 82) that the *Ecclesiazusae* makes reference to the peace negotiations of 392, and so must postdate them. He posits a date in either 392/91 or 391/90. Funke (*HA*, 170) argues against 391/90, on the grounds that Thrasybulus could not be described as 'not called upon' in that year of his naval command. He refuses to rule out 393/92, and suggests either that year or 392/91. But Aristophanes' illusions are difficult to pin down: hence, although 392/91 is the most attractive, any of these three years seem possible.

86. Seager, 'TCAI', 106–7, sees a reference to the peace negotiations. Rogers, *Aristophanes* vol. 5 xvii, thinks the battle of Cnidos is meant. Ussher, *Ecclesiazusae* xxv, takes it as a warning to return to the wise counsels of Thrasybulus.

6 Division and Defeat, 391–386 BC

By their rejection of Andocides' treaty in 392/91, Athenians showed that they were not yet ready to make peace. Now they had to show how they would pursue war. Several questions stand out. Would they concentrate their efforts against Persia or Sparta? Who would lead Athens' campaigns? Who would pay for them? Few could afford war tax, but few could afford to give up the dream of empire. Would Athenians be able to overcome these and other divisions and pursue a consistent policy? Before Athens could frame its response, actions by Sparta and Persia did much to set its terms.

Thrasybulus' Last Mission

In the spring of 391 the war resumed. Sparta dealt Athens a serious blow at Lechaeum by capturing both the Lechaeum Long Walls (recently rebuilt by Athens) and its dockyards and Corinthian ships. The way to Attica was open again (Xen. 4.4.19). Even more dramatic, perhaps, were events in Asia Minor. The new satrap, Struthas, had reached the coast and strongly favoured Athens. Sparta sent an army under Thibron to oppose him; it captured Ephesus and several cities in its hinterland, which it plundered (Xen. 4.8.17–19).

Before the summer was out, however, Persia recouped, killing Thibron and routing his army. At the same time as Sparta sent out a new commander, it intervened further south, in a civil war in Rhodes. Small fleets under Ecdicus and Teleutias, respectively, made for Rhodes, probably in 390. On his way, Teleutias ran into an enemy fleet: ten Athenian ships sent to help Evagoras of Cyprus against Persia. The plucky Teleutias captured all ten and continued to Rhodes (Xen. 4.8.20–24).[1]

The capture moved Xenophon to remark on Athens' folly: an ally of Persia helping a Persian opponent (4.8.24). Had the assembly let its heart outweigh its head? The organizers of the expedition were Conon's close friends Aristophanes and his father

Nicophemus. They had been Persian officers but repayment of the hospitality (*xenia*) of Evagoras, who had sheltered them after Aegospotami, was evidently more important.[2]

They probably had a strategic consideration in mind as well. After the arrest of Conon, it was evident that Persian friendship was unsteady and dependent on personalities. Persia's surprise attack on Evagoras had taught Nicophemus and Aristophanes to act accordingly.[3]

Not everyone in Athens agreed. Thrasybulus, for one, would make the most of Persia's friendship on his expedition to Asia Minor the same year. One may posit, therefore, a conflict in the assembly over Athenian policy toward Persia, which the aftermath of the mission to Cyprus illustrates.

Aristophanes and Nicophemus managed to escape Teleutias, but on their return to Athens, they were impeached for their failure and convicted. Their property was confiscated, and the generals were executed (Lys. 19.7). The punishment was grave; given Athenian finances in 391, the loss of ten ships was no small crime. Nevertheless, perhaps some Athenians voted less out of anger over failure than out of fear of success, which would have jeopardized the alliance with Persia. To another group of jurors, the issue might have been not policy but revenge. A year before, Athens had condemned two other politicians to death (*in absentia*) Andocides and Epicrates. Aristophanes' and Nicophemus' votes then are not recorded, but one can guess. Epicrates and Andocides wanted to strike a deal with Persia; Aristophanes and Nicophemus, the opposite. Hence, the former supporters of Andocides and Epicrates might have had a personal reason to have Aristophanes and Nicophemus executed.

Another man who is likely to have supported the vote for execution was Thrasybulus. He had probably not supported Andocides' peace in 392/91, but he did not want a complete break with Persia. Furthermore, he had no love for men as close to Conon as Aristophanes and Nicophemus once were. Nor did he need rivals for power in Athens, not now when his own career was on the rise again. In response to Sparta's intervention in Rhodes, the *demos* sent Thrasybulus to the island in charge of a fleet of 40 ships, probably in summer 390 (Xen. 4.8.25).

It was a remarkable moment in Athenian history. Thrasybulus' fleet was the largest Athenian navy to sail from Piraeus since 405. Conon had commanded *Persian* armadas. To the patriot,

Thrasybulus' sailing was a moment of pride; to the historian, it raises several interesting questions.

Thrasybulus' comeback must be considered first. By spring 390 (perhaps earlier) Thrasybulus had regained the position he had lost in 394 and 393, and apparently still lacked at the time of the peace negotiations of 392/91. One reason for his success was the death of Conon. Funke points out another: Thrasybulus was now the only successful and experienced admiral whom Athens had left.[4] Besides which, Thrasybulus was probably more palatable to the propertied than such alternatives as Agyrrhius or Cephalus.

The number of ships, 40, was a respectable one against the fleet of Teleutias, grown to 37 ships by the time he reached Rhodes (Xen. 4.8.24). But it was hardly half the size of Conon's 90-ship fleet at Cnidos and less than a quarter of the 180 Athenian triremes at Aegospotami (Diod. 14.83.4; Xen. 2.1.20). An Athens without imperial tribute could not compete with the resources of Persia or even of the limping Athenian empire of 405. Persian subsidies to Athens had almost certainly stopped with Conon's death; even if a trickle of Persian gold continued, the Athenian war effort required *eisphorai* and trierarchies.[5]

To be fully effective, the war effort also required energetic and enthusiastic tax-payers. But there was a significant peace tendency in Athens in 390, its members less than enthusiastic about war taxes. Hence, when Lysias complains about *eisphorai* and Aristophanes jokes about tax evasion — he quips that the Athenians are a nation of takers and not givers (in Athens, even the statues of the gods had their palms out) — they may be engaging in more than the usual, formulaic wartime complaints. The efforts of the doves in 392/91 suggest that there was fire beneath this smoke. Indeed, tax evasion may have damaged the Athenian war effort considerably.[6]

Thrasybulus' purpose remains in question. Although he was sent to Rhodes, he never reached it. Instead, he turned north to the Asian coast, the Hellespont, and Thrace.

It has recently been argued that the fleet was Thrasybulus' idea. He intended to restore Athens' fifth-century empire, and he meant to do it even if the price was war with Persia: that is why he opposed the peace of 392/91. The evidence is Thrasybulus' extensive achievement during his campaign: alliances made with two Thracian Kings and a dozen Greek cities in Asia Minor and the North Aegean, and an alliance with the cities of the Thraceward region in prospect; the establishment of a democracy in Byzantium; re-establishment of the 10 per cent tax on ships in the Hellespont, earlier imposed in the Ionian War; 5 per cent taxes in Thasos and Clazomenae; and various money-raising expeditions. These imperialistic measures belie any theory of Thrasybulus as a more moderate imperialist than Conon. That Thrasybulus himself was proposer of the expedition of 390 is implied by Lysias 28, and seems likely (Lys. 28.4).[7]

Nevertheless, the restoration of empire was only Thrasybulus' ultimate aim: his immediate purpose was to win the war against Sparta. 'To make the city great and free,' the speaker of Lysias 28.14 puts it, in an apt rallying cry (cf. Lys. 25.32, 27.14). The proclamation of a new Athenian empire would have meant open war with Persia, as Thrasybulus knew. Yet he expected to have Persia's co-operation in this Spartan campaign.

When Thrasybulus went to Asia Minor in 390, as Xenophon 4.8.27 writes, he found 'cities in Asia favourably disposed on account of the king's being a *philos* to the Athenians' (tr. Loeb). A year later, Sparta found that the Hellespontine cities were still inclined toward the Athenians 'because Pharnabazus was their *philos*' (Xen. 4.8.31, tr. Loeb). Nor did Sparta think it was worth the effort to woo Artaxerxes until 388, long after Thrasybulus' mission, and only in the wake of Athens' help, under Thrasybulus' successors, to the two Persian enemies, Cyprus and Egypt.[8]

Cawkwell has argued that whereas Conon remained a Persian admiral and believed in the necessity of friendship with Persia, Thrasybulus paid no attention to Persian feelings. On the contrary, Thrasybulus was no enemy of Persia. He pushed for the recall of Alcibiades in 411 precisely because of the Persian aid that might come with him. In 408–407 he may have helped negotiate the treaty of Chalcedon, a pact between Athens and the Great King. As for his aggrandizements in 390–389, they could all be justified as part of the common war effort. Busolt first argued, long ago, that the alliances made in 390–389 did not belong to a revived Delian League but to a wartime effort against Sparta. Thrasybulus' taxes and imposts could be represented as wartime measures, as could his raids on Lesbos or Aspendus. Nor are Thrasybulus' domestic politics irrelevant. A man who had friends among the Few as well as the Many could afford to pursue empire slowly.

Finally, as Busolt argues, if Athens did restore the empire, or part of it, between 391 and 387, it is odd that Xenophon does not mention its dissolution at the time of the King's Peace, as he does the dissolution of the Boeotian League (Xen. 5.1.36). To sum up, Thrasybulus was willing to test Persian power in order to build up Athens, but he had no wish to break with Persia by proclaiming a new Athenian empire.[9]

Thrasybulus turned away from his original course to Rhodes because there was little he could do there to dislodge the oligarchs from their forts, and because the Spartans could do little harm to the democrats in his absence. He never lost sight of his mission's purpose, however, and when he was killed at Aspendus in 389, he was on his way to Rhodes (Xen. 4.8.25, 30).

There was nothing glorious about Thrasybulus' death: he was killed in his tent at night by Aspendians avenging an Athenian booty raid (Xen. 4.8.30). Still, his bones were brought back to a place of honour, in first place among the public graves outside the Dipylon Gate, next to Pericles and Phormio (Paus. 1.29.3).

Had Thrasybulus lived, however, he might have encountered serious political difficulties. While off Lesbos, he had lost 23 ships in a storm (Diod. 14.94.3). His subordinate commanders were later called back to Athens; the charge was embezzlement, but perhaps the *demos* also had the loss of the ships in mind (Lys. 28.1-5, 10-12; 29.2). Although Thrasybulus himself was not recalled, the prosecutor of his subordinate Ergocles threatens that Thrasybulus' day would have come too, had he lived (Lys. 28.8). Indeed, the prosecutor depicts Ergocles warning Thrasybulus of enemies 'plotting against you and your *philoi*' (Lys. 28.6).[10]

It cost Thrasybulus' enemies little to see him buried with honour; that concession is no proof of Thrasybulus' political prestige had he lived. Despite his achievements, a man who had lost half of his fleet in a storm, who had never reached his ostensible goal (Rhodes) and who could not prevent the recall of his lieutenants, was a man in political trouble. 'As for Thrasybulus, men of Athens,' the prosecutor of Ergocles says,

> he did well to end his life as he did: for it was not right for him to live in the prosecution of such schemes or to suffer death at your hands with his repute of having served you well in the past, but rather to settle his account with the city in that sort of way
> (Lys. 28.8).

This is probably an exaggeration, but one with a grain of truth. Recognizing this, many scholars have argued that Thrasybulus' replacement, Agyrrhius, was probably his enemy.[11] In the past, Agyrrhius had been associated with Archinus, Callias, and possibly Conon, but never with Thrasybulus or Alcibiades. His advocacy of ecclesiastic pay is more of a populist gesture that one would expect from Thrasybulus. Assuming he shared his nephew Callistratus' support for the Greeks of Asia, Agyrrhius was probably more openly anti-Persian than Thrasybulus.[12]

The comic playwrights were merciless to Agyrrhius. Aristophanes describes him in winter 388 as 'farting from wealth'. Plato Comicus depicts the *demos*, apparently as a pregnant woman, begging for help before she 'gives birth' to Agyrrhius, i.e. elects him general. Agyrrhius, however, could hardly have been sanguine about the job.

Money was one of Athens' greatest problems in 389, and Agyrrhius, with his financial expertise, is likely to have been sensitive to the manifold aspects of the matter. First, Athens' fleet and army had to be financed. Second, and more serious, Athenians were still suffering severely from the losses of the Peloponnesian War, as Aristophanes' last plays demonstrate (*infra*, 'The Testimony of Aristophanes'). The founder of ecclesiastic pay would not be ignorant of the plight of the poor; would it be surprising if his oratory spurred them on to war, empire and prosperity?

Political reality was likewise challenging for Agyrrhius. In 390, events in the Corinthia established a new Athenian hero, Iphicrates. By his destruction of a Spartan regiment near Lechaeum that summer, he wiped out the effects of recent Spartan victories and gave new health to the ailing Atheno–Boeotian alliance. His recapture of Sidus and Crommyon closed the road to Attica.[13]

Iphicrates' victory secured him immortality in the history of Greek warfare. It could hardly have hurt his standing in Athenian politics either. Whether he used this influence on behalf of Agyrrhius, some other leader or simply himself is unclear. Callias — Iphicrates' co-partner at Lechaeum in 390 and Agyrrhius' partner against Andocides in 400 — provides a link between the two men, but it is a weak one. Diotimus, general in 388/87 and 387/86, might have been a *philos* of Iphicrates. In the first year

Diotimus was sent to Corinth to replace Chabrias, probably a rival of Iphicrates (*infra*) as head of the mercenary corps. That autumn he was transferred to the Hellespont, where he helped Iphicates maintain a naval blockade of Abydus. Likewise, perhaps Eunomus and Demaenetus the Bouzygid, both generals in 388/87, were also *philoi* of Iphicrates, because of their common connection to Conon. One might even consider adding Cleobulus son of Glaucus of Acharnae, a general who commanded a fleet with Demaenetus, perhaps in 388, and whose nephew Philochares would in later years serve as a soldier under Iphicrates.[14]

If Iphicrates' friends are unclear, it is certain at least that he attracted enemies. He had to wait until 371 before he was properly honoured for his victory of 390. In winter 390/89, his plans rejected by the *demos*, Iphicrates resigned his command in Corinth. His influence and military reputation were strong enough to win him a command in the Hellespont shortly afterwards, but he had seen the limits of his power (Xen. 4.8.34, Diod. 14.92. 1–2).[15]

Iphicrates began his career under Conon, and perhaps his current enemies included the former *philoi* of Thrasybulus. It is plausible that Chabrias son of Ctesippus of Aexone claimed to pick up that fallen leader's mantle. Destined to have a great military career, Chabrias served his first term as general under Thrasybulus in Thrace in 390/89, where he negotiated a treaty with the Thracian princes Seuthes and Medokos. Co-operation with Thrasybulus does not demonstrate *philia*, but it is striking that, soon afterwards, Chabrias was chosen by the *demos* to replace a protégé of Conon in a moment of disgrace: Iphicrates. In 389/88, Chabrias was appointed new commander of the Athenian mercenary corps at Corinth, perhaps as a continuation of the rivalry between Thrasybulus and Conon. If Thrasybulus' former faction indeed regrouped rather than simply dissolved, another member might have been Aesimus, still active in 384 as one of several ambassadors to Chios.[16]

Another prominent orator and general about 390 was Thrasybulus of Collytus. In 387/86 he was a general in Thrace and the Hellespont where he would lose his squadron of eight ships to Antalcidas (Xen. 5.1.26–27, Lys. 26.33, Dem. 57.38). If Thrasybulus' nephew Thrason of Erchia was old enough to take part in public life about 390, he probably supported his uncle. Both men were known for their pro-Theban position.[17]

Cephalus of Collytus also continued to be active. Cephalus was sufficiently well-known to be poked fun at by Plato Comicus at about the time of Agyrrhius' command in 389. In 386, he moved a bill which bestowed *proxenia* on one Phanocritus of Parium and also implied a criticism of the Athenian generals deceived by Antalcidas: Demaenetus, Dionysius, Leontichus and Phanias (Xen. 5.1.26). Note that the common support for Conon which bound Cephalus and Demaenetus in 395 did not restrain Cephalus in 386. In 384, Cephalus was one of the ambassadors who swore alliance between Athens and Chios. His political *philoi* are uncertain: one might have been Phormisius, co-ambassador to Persia about 394 with Epicrates (Cephalus' colleague of 395) and along with Cephalus, one of the men who helped Thebes in 378 (Dein. 1.38).[18]

Pamphilus of Keiriadai, general in 389/88, was also a friend of Thebes, as is shown by the name he gave his son, Boeotus. Pamphilus was wealthy and political: a scholiast calls him *demagogos* and gives him a hanger-on, 'the needle seller'. Before 387, Pamphilus married his daughter Plangon to the orator and politician, and later trierarch and general, Mantias son of Mantitheus of Thorikos. The dowry was either 10,000 dr. or 1 tal. Mantias himself was a well-known figure, lampooned along with Cephalus and Agyrrhius by Plato Comicus about 389. Pamphilus first appears at Haliartus in 395 as a hipparch. His hostility to Alcibiades' son there, taken in connection with his pro-Theban opinions, suggests a connection to Thrasybulus of Collytus.[19]

In sum, in the final stages of the Corinthian War, as in earlier periods, faction and disunity continued in Athens. At least three major factions can be discerned after the death of Thrasybulus of Steiria: those of Agyrrhius, Thrasybulus of Collytus and Cephalus — and at least five if one reckons as independent leaders Iphicrates and Chabrias, both more military than political figures. Agyrrhius, Cephalus, Thrasybulus of Collytus, and perhaps Pamphilus, are likely to have championed the Many, whose impecunity demanded the wealth of empire. The Few, or at any rate an anti-war tendency, complained of *eisphorai* in 389/88 (Lys. 28.3–4). Who were their leaders?

Agyrrhius vs. Artaxerxes

Neither nature nor man had been kind to Athens on Thrasybulus' last campaign. With their rapid dispatch of Agyrrhius to replace the murdered Steirian, however, the Athenians showed that they had lost none of their famous boldness of spirit. In fact, the next year saw them more reckless and aggressive than had the last.

If their opponents had been equally true to their reputed national character, the Athenians might have succeeded. Agesilaus was no Archidamus, however, and his subjects were not the slow and cautious Spartans of the fifth century. His army retaliated quickly to Iphicrates' slaughter by cutting down trees in the Corinthiad (Xen. 4.5.10).

In the same spirit, Anaxibius was sent to the Hellespont. With Abydus as a base, he raided the territories of the allies of Athens and Persia and stopped any Athenian or allied ship he found at sea (Xen. 4.8.32–34). In 390/89, the Athenians in turn sent Iphicrates and his mercenaries to the Hellespont. Eventually, that clever general managed to ambush Anaxibius, killing him and some 260 men — as many as Iphicrates had slaughtered near Lechaeum (Xen. 4.5.18, 8.34–39).

Thwarted at the Isthmus and struggling in the Hellespont, Sparta resolved to open new theatres of combat. Agesilaus spent the summer of 389 ravaging Acarnania, ally of Athens and Boeotia, and by the next spring, he had obtained a suit for peace and alliance (Xen. 4.6.1–7.1). The next Spartan initiative was closer to home. The navarch Eteonicus sailed to Aegina, and there declared his willingness to help anyone who wished to plunder Attica. Pamphilus of Keiriadai led a force of hoplites to Aegina to retaliate. Pamphilus managed to hold a fortress at first, but within five months, he was forced to abandon it. He appears to have paid for his defeat with a trial for embezzlement, condemnation, and the confiscation of his property; he died still owing the state 5 tal. If they were indeed *philoi*, it was a setback for Thrasybulus of Collytus too.[20]

Athens now widened its commitments, and turned to an all-but-open anti-Persian policy. This was neither a knee-jerk anti-Persian reaction nor reckless imperialism, but rather a judicious anticipation of an inevitable Persian betrayal. According to Aristophanes' *Ploutus*, produced in winter 389/88, Athens had made an alliance with King Acoris of Egypt, a rebel from Persia. It was an insult to one Athenian ally — Persia — but a boon for another — Evagoras of Cyprus.[21]

The Persians soon responded: by summer 388 they had sent Tiribazus back to Sardis as satrap. The Spartans did not miss the

Division and Defeat, 391–386 BC   159

significance of the replacement of the pro-Athenian Struthas, and they sent Antalcidas to Ephesus as navarch, thinking, as Xenophon writes, 'that by doing this they would please Tiribazus very much' (Xen. 5.1.6). For their part, the Athenians sent a new expedition to Cyprus later in the year: ten triremes under Chabrias. New lines of loyalty were being drawn (Xen. 5.1.10).

Through fall 389 and spring 388 the two sea wars continued, one in the Saronic Gulf and the other in the Hellespont. Perhaps in autumn 389 the Athenians sent 13 ships to refortify Aegina, under the command of Eunomus. Not long afterwards, he met the Spartan Gorgopas in a sea battle near Cape Zoster (Attica). Gorgopas won, and captured four ships (Xen. 5.1.6–9).

Whether or not Eunomus was punished is not known; he was not sent back to Aegina. Instead, Chabrias, en route to Evagoras late in 388, stopped at Aegina. There, with his peltasts and a body of hoplites under Demaenetus, he laid an ambush for the Spartans and their Aeginetan allies and won the victory. Moreover, they cleared the Saronic Gulf of all raiders and were able to sail it 'just as in time of peace' — at least for a while (Xen. 5.1.10–13).

Iphicrates did not suffer long from his recall. The *demos* perceived that, although no diplomat, he had great military talents, and sent him to the Hellespont and his victory against Anaxibius (*supra*). In late 388, he faced a new challenge from a Spartan fleet of 25 ships under Nicolochus. With the help of the general Diotimus, Iphicrates was able to gather 32 ships and blockade the Spartans at Abydus (Xen. 5.1.6–7). The next year, 387, however, saw dramatic Athenian defeats. First, the Spartans on Aegina dared a raid on Piraeus with only 12 triremes. Not only were they able to wreak havoc in Piraeus, but, sailing afterwards down the coast of Attica, they captured incoming merchant ships, some full of grain. Athenian unpreparedness made an ominous contrast to the stubborn resistance against Lysander in 404 (Xen. 5.1.13–24).

Worse was yet to come. In summer or fall, Antalcidas returned to the coast of Asia with the prize he had long sought: Artaxerxes' agreement to jettison Athens and impose peace on the Greeks, the kind of peace Sparta and Tiribazus had negotiated five years earlier. When Antalcidas heard of Nicolochus' plight at Abydus, he sped there with a relief force (Xen. 5.1.25).[22]

Now other Athenian generals hurried to the Hellespont for the showdown. In addition to Iphicrates and Diotimus, there were

Demaenetus, Dionysius, Leontichus, Phanias, and Thrasybulus of Collytus (who had been in Thrace). They were not enough, not now that Artaxerxes had made up his mind. The pro-Athenian satrap of Phrygia, Pharnabazus, had been recalled to Susa — 'kicked upstairs,' to use the language of American politics. Artaxerxes had given Pharnabazus his own daughter in marriage, but had replaced him in Phrygia with Antalcidas' friend Ariobarzanes. Dionysius of Syracuse, moreover, had returned to friendship with Sparta, and was sending 20 ships to the Hellespont.

Even before these reinforcements arrived, Antalcidas had tricked most of the Athenians into leaving the western Hellespont, while he managed to capture Thrasybulus' fleet of 8 ships with his own of 25. Soon afterwards, Antalcidas had a fleet of 80 ships against 24 Athenian. Sparta controlled the Hellespont and Athens' grain supply. Peace was at hand (Xen. 5.1.25–29).[23]

The peace which Antalcidas had negotiated allowed Athens to keep Lemnos, Imbros and Scyros. There could, of course, no longer be the benefits of the Athenian tax on ships at the Bosphorus, nor of its 5 per cent taxes at Thasos or Clazomenae. Moreover, the power of Athens' allies was to be broken. Thebes had to give up its hegemony of Boeotia, and Argos of Corinth. The parties to the treaty had to acknowledge Persia's rule of Cyprus. Finally, the treaty turned the cities of Asia over to Artaxerxes.[24]

Athens hesitated at the surrender of so much, especially of the Ionians. In the end, however, as Xenophon points out, it had no choice. Antalcidas prevented the grain ships from the Ukraine from sailing to Athens; as in 404, the result, eventually, would have to be famine. Nor had the raids from Aegina ended. Hence, in winter 387/86, oaths to abide by the treaty were sworn.[25]

Athens had not gained all it hoped to from the Corinthian War, but it had made gains. Money had poured into the city from Persia, plunder and taxation. The walls were rebuilt and a small fleet was in being. Lemnos, Imbros and Scyros, guardians of the grain route, were Athenian again. The empire had not been re-established but notice had been served: Athens was back.

Still the cup was as empty as it was full, and one would expect a price to be paid for failure. Indictment was one ordinary consequence of defeat; in the last phase of the Corinthian War alone, at least five men (Aristophanes, Nicophemus, Ergocles, Philocrates and Pamphilus) had suffered it. There is considerable justification, therefore, for the usual practice of dating the trials of Thrasybulus of Collytus, Dionysius and Agyrrhius to the months following Athens' defeat. None of these trials is dated in the sources, but each of the defendants (assuming Dionysius is the general of 387/86) played a part in the débâcle of 387/86. Of Thrasybulus and Dionysius it is known simply that they were convicted. In the case of Agyrrhius, there are the further details of a lengthy stay in prison of several years, until he could repay what he was suspected of having embezzled; apparently he was ruined for life.[26]

Several other signs of the time should be taken into account. In 386, a bill of Cephalus obliquely criticizes the previous year's generals in the Hellespont. In the same year, both Iphicrates and perhaps Chabrias preferred mercenary service to Athens'. Although each man might have simply been going where the jobs were, they might also, as Sealey suggests, have feared the consequences at Athens of defeat in the Hellespont.[27]

These indications further strengthen the traditional case for political trials in 386. If the evidence were copious, it might reveal in these trials an element of the struggle between the Many and the Few; it might, but it probably would not. In the crisis of defeat, Athens' politicians were more concerned with blaming others for military failure and with saving themselves than with inflaming class conflict. Besides, there were champions of the Many both among the prosecuted (Agyrrhius) and the prosecutors (Cephalus).[28]

What was the shape of Athenian politics after these scores had been settled? It is remarkable how many of the leaders of the past decade were gone: Agyrrhius, Andocides, Conon, Epicrates, Thrasybulus of Steiria and probably Anytus were either exiled, imprisoned or dead.

Nevertheless, there was no retreat from the aggressive policies pursued by all of these men save Andocides; the peace of 387/86 was not a triumph of Athenian doves, but merely the recognition of reality. In short order, Athens was looking for new openings and new allies.[29]

From the little that the relevant sources — epigraphical and oratorical — reveal, the three leading figures in Athenian politics for the first five years after the peace were familiar names: Cephalus, Aesimus and Thrasybulus of Collytus. If Thrasybulus had been convicted about 386, he had recovered enough of his influence by 382 to block the eponymous-archon-elect Leodamas at his scrutiny and replace him with one Euandros, himself called a former supporter of the Thirty (Lys. 26.10, 13, 21–24). This Euandros was no unimportant person, since even his opponent admits that Euandros and his father had 'spent much on the city, performed liturgies with competitive generosity, and won many fine victories under the democracy' (Lys. 26.3–4). Davies identifies him with Euandros, son of Euithalion of Euonymon, secretary to the treasurers of Athens in 411 under the oligarchy of the Four Hundred (whence the smear about the Thirty?). He might also be the same Euandros who proposed a decree in 386/85 to honour the Odrysian King Hebryzelmis.[30]

Aesimus was one of the five Athenian ambassadors sent to administer an oath of alliance to Chios in 384. Cephalus was one of the others. Also, as previously noted, it was Cephalus who moved the bill in 386 grating the proxeny to Phanocritus and criticizing the Hellespontine generals.[31]

This is less evidence than one needs to justify Sealey's statement that Cephalus was probably the most influential man in Athens during these years. More evidence, though, comes from the next five years, 381–76, when Cephalus proposed the important decree in 378 which sent an army to Thebes to help it against Sparta. The next year, Aesimus was still important, because he was sent with ships to administer an oath of alliance to Methymna. Thrasybulus also shows up in 377 on a similar mission to Thebes. In this same period, a man first heard of in 404 also supported Thebes: Phormisius.[32]

Another rising figure of the era had first appeared in 392/91: Callistratus, chosen general in 378/77, when he would organize the finances of the Second Athenian League. Perhaps the fate of his uncle Agyrrhius had contributed to his apparent eclipse in the intervening years. Another general for 378/77 had also revived a flagging career: Chabrias.[33]

New names, though, begin to appear. A third general of 378/77 was Timotheus, Conon's son. The man who proposed the decree establishing the Second League and who immediately went (with Thrasybulus) on a mission to Thebes, was Aristotle of Marathon, who acquired a reputation as a writer of forensic speeches. The third member of the mission to Thebes was Pyrrhandrus of Anaphlystus — probably a young man, since he was still alive in 330. He had been sent on a similar mission to Byzantium the year before, in 378, and in 377 he would also propose an alliance with Chalcis. Another zealous supporter of Thebes in 378 was a *philos* of Thrasybulus of Collytus: his nephew Thrason of Erchia.[34]

To sum up, war and politics — but mostly politics — took a heavy toll of the Athenian political elite from 395 to 386. At list of the major political figures of the period includes Andocides, Aesimus, Anytus, Agyrrhius, Callias, Callistratus, Cephalus, Conon, Epicrates, Phormisius, Thrasybulus of Steiria and Thrasybulus of Collytus: 12 in all, or 14 if one includes Chabrias and Iphicrates, primarily military men. Of these, two had died in wartime service abroad (Conon and Thrasybulus of Steiria) and four had been exiled or irreparably disgraced by the Athenians themselves (Andocides, Anytus, Agyrrhius and Epicrates). Only six (or eight) men survived in public life, which means an attrition rate of about 40–50 per cent. It also means that during the Corinthian War, the leading politicians and generals were more likely to be destroyed in domestic politics than to be killed in battle. One might buttress this conclusion with the statistic that at least 17 different public figures (orators, generals, ambassadors) are known to have been tried for high crimes (bribery, embezzlement or treason) during the Corinthian War, one of them on two separate occasions, and at least 13 were convicted.[35] By contrast, it is hard to think of any important public figures besides Conon and Thrasybulus of Steiria who had died in wartime service abroad. It is not surprising that a new generation of leaders had begun to emerge within ten years of 387/86.

The Testimony of Aristophanes

Two extant plays of Aristophanes, *Ecclesiazusae* and *Ploutos*, were produced in the later Corinthian War, and indicate both what the poet considers funny and what he considers pressing public problems. Hence the historian must interpret these plays with caution and sensitivity. (Two mythological parodies by Aristophanes, *Cocalus* (387) and *Aelosicon* (386), also date from this period, as does perhaps his *Storks*; none is extant.)[36]

Consider first that, in marked contrast to *Archarnians*, *Peace* or *Lysistrata*, neither *Ecclesiazusae* nor *Ploutos* is primarily concerned with the war in which Athens was then embroiled. This is striking, but not unique, since the same could be said for the six other extant Aristophanes plays, all produced during the Peloponnesian War. *Ecclesiazusae* focuses on politics, if not as exclusively or vehemently as do *Knights* or *Wasps*. In *Ploutos*, the interest in politics fades away almost entirely; indeed, the play has been called the beginning of Middle Comedy, that apolitical genre.[37]

We must, however, resist the temptation to conclude, as some have, that Athenian politics itself had lost its vigour. There were no longer any ideals, any worthy politicians to champion them, or patriotic citizens to rally around them: so conclude the editors of the Budé edition of Aristophanes, Coulon and van Daele. They write: 'The city vegetates in a sleep which already has the appearance of death.'[38] Yet Aristophanes himself was sufficiently active politically to serve on the Council in the early fourth century. Moreover, escapist comedy from the pen of a writer nearing the age of 60 does not declare an entire society moribund.[39]

A second blind alley leads out from the one subject the two plays certainly do have in common: economics. In *Ecclesiazusae* the focus is macroeconomic, with such themes as the greed of the *demos*, the inability of the polis to raise money, and the contrast between rich and poor receiving most attention. In *Ploutos* the focus is microeconomic, on the poverty of individual citizens, specifically farmers. As Mossé writes, both plays address 'the shameful inequality of fortunes and the destitution of the majority'.[40]

We ought not, however, to conclude with Ehrenberg that the plays demonstrate a shift 'from a political to an economic outlook, from the political consciousness of a citizen to the economic purpose of an individual human being'.[41] There is, first, the methodological fallacy of characterizing an era on the basis of two comedies. Second, *Ecclesiazusae* is shot through with 'the political consciousness of a citizen'. Third, our *Ploutos* is the revised version of a play first performed in 408: hence, if Athens had abandoned politics, it had done so 20 years before, even before, even before the political clash of oligarch and democrat in 404–403.

We should likewise avoid the widespread conclusion that, since the hero and chorus of *Ploutos* are very poor farmers, the Attic peasant in 388 had been reduced to proletarian misery, perhaps even revolutionary ferment (cf. the dethroning of the gods at the end of play), and certainly suffered far more than his urban counterpart. Aristophanes wrote about farmers because he admired them and found them funny. However poor their real condition, comic license allowed the poet to exaggerate it greatly.[42]

What *can* be said is that *c*. 391–388 Aristophanes was very concerned with the theme of money. As he describes them, contemporary Athenians were divided into a small number of rich and much larger group of poor, some desperately poor. What both groups wanted was prosperity (*eudaimonia*, cf. *Eccl*. 240, *Ploutos* 802) and in order to get it, the local morality (*to epichorios tropos*, *Ploutos* 47) left no holds barred (*to meden askein hygies en toi nun bioi*, *Ploutos* 50). The polis was just as bankrupt as its citizens, both financially and — in the person of its leaders — ethically (*Eccl*. 135–139, 174–88, 208, 250–56; *Ploutos* 171–72, 174–76, 1192–93). The only hope was a radical change, either through the communism of *Ecclesiazusae* or the divine intervention of *Ploutos*. But in the first case the cure was worse than the disease and in the second a miracle was required.

Aristophanes is much less troubled by Athens' aggressive military and diplomatic policies than by its economic policies. Not surprising, considering the Athenian economic decline since the days of his antiwar plays. The poet's new theme fits in very well with the facts: Athens' losses in the Ionian and civil wars, the financial burdens of the Corinthian War, and the impecunity evidenced by Thrasybulus' money-raising raids in 389. It is striking that what one observer found most noteworthy about Athens *c*. 390 was its economic (and consequent ethical) problems.

Both plays, particularly *Ploutos*, describe the poverty of the ordinary citizen and the huge gap, financial and moral, between rich and poor. *Ecclesiazusae* mentions men who have no beds, no cloaks in winter, and suffer from pleurisy (408, 415–21, 566). In addition to the problems of clothing, shelter and health, both plays lay great emphasis on hunger — indeed, *Ecclesiazusae* is obsessed with food, as E. David demonstrates. A less emphatic, but more pathetic problem, also mentioned in both plays, is the burden of burial expenses (*Eccl*. 592, *Ploutos* 555). The protagonist of *Ecclesiazusae*, Praxagora, promises reform: she will abolish poverty (566) and the crimes it occasions (605). She will free the debtor (567, 659–661). She will abolish the gap between rich and poor, landed magnate and landless wretch, slavocrat and one-slave yeoman (591–94). Praxagora also testifies to the class-consciousness of the *penetes*, when she promises that her reform will allow them to brush aside their 'well-heeled' social superiors (631–34).[43]

The Job-like hero of *Ploutos*, Chremylus, is frustrated because, in spite of being god-fearing and law-abiding, he is a *penes* and luckless. His *philoi* and demesmen are old farmers, poor enough to find thyme root a tempting victual (253–58, 283). They have trouble finding a living (751–52). These were the kind of men who scavenged the crossroads shrines of Hecate once a month to eat the offerings to the goddess (594–97) and who looked forward to the 'workhouse meals' of porridge and barley-meal at the feast of Theseus (627–28).[44] They cringed at the bad news 'no barley in the bin!' (763). They knew the curses of poverty: hunger, lack of proper clothes and shelter, insects (535–47, 841–49). Politicians, generals and informers, on the other hand, seemed only to get richer (174–76, 180, 850–958).

The *Ecclesiazusae* has much to say on two related themes: (a) Athenian selfishness and greed and (b) the problem of raising revenues. Praxagora makes the *demos* and its greed responsible for Athens' varied problems: although they earn a public wage (ecclesiastic pay) all each member of the *demos* wants is his private advantage (205–208). As a result, the common good 'reels' (208, cf. 135–36). The politicians are wicked and the people corruptible (175–76, 185–89). Ecclesiastic pay is simply a matter of greed and not of principle (185–86, 309–310). The polis is in crisis and in need of salvation (106–109, 174–75, 209, 395–97). Praxagora's solution is to put the polis in the hands of the women — after all, the Athenians had tried everything else (*Eccl.* 445–47). More substantively, she commends women for their skill at *oikonomia*, as stewards (*epitropoi*) and treasurers (*tamiai*), words which in Attic Greek have the double connotation of public or private office (211–212).[45] Of great relevance to the Athenian treasury, women were superlatively resourceful at raising money (236). They would not be cheated, since they were cheats themselves (237) — not merely a male chauvinist joke, since Aristophanes' Athenians evaded taxes, let alone turned in their property to the new communist regime (601–602, 730–876).

The Athens that Aristophanes describes, therefore, is needy, greedy, class-ridden, money-crazy and confused. Comic writers usually exaggerate, but they need a substratum on which to build. Hence, if there were no serious concern about economic and financial matters in Athens *c*. 390, no poverty and no communist theorizing, the plays would have fallen flat. The concern might have been considerably less obsessive, however, the poverty less pressing, and the theorizing less radical than Aristophanes depicts. It is nevertheless clear that by the standards of classical Athens, wealth and poverty were unusually pressing topics *c.* 390. In other words, the Corinthian War and the legacy of the Peloponnesian and civil wars were still heavy economic burdens.[46]

Notes

1. En route to Rhodes, Ecdicus captured Samos from Athens (Diod. 14.7.3; Seager, 'TCAI', 108).
Chronology: I follow Seager, 'TCAI', 109, n. 27 and Funke, *HA*, 95, n. 87, 96, n. 91. Cawkwell redates Teleutias' and Thrasybulus' missions to late 391 ('Imperialism of Thrasybulus', 271–75) but the dating of the Athenian fleet to Cyprus at Lys. 19.28–29 'in four or five years' since the battle of Cnidos rules out a date before 390/89.
2. Aristophanes was ambassador (Lys. 19.23), Philocrates son of Ephialtes commanding general (Xen. 4.8.24), Plato's step-brother Demus one of the trierarchs (Lys. 19.25). Nicophemus' position is unclear.
3. See E. Costa, 'Evagoras I and the Persians, ca. 411 to 391 BC', *Historia* 24 (1975), 40–56.
4. Funke, *HA* 151.
5. The last known Persian distribution of money to Athens in the Corinthian War is Pharnabaus' in 393 (*supra*, chap. 5, n. 20). If Persian subsidies continued afterwards, ancient sources do not record them. The death of Conon — so important a liaison between Athens and Persia, Persia's interest in keeping Athens from growing too powerful, and Artaxerxes' notorious cheapness (*Hell. Oxy.* 15), all add weight to the argument from silence.
6. Lys. 28.3–4; 29.4, 9; Ar. *Eccl.* 197–98, 779–83.
7. Thrasybulus' goals: Seager, 'TCAI', 110–11; Cawkwell, 'Imperialism', 275–7; Hamilton, *SBV* 294–6. For an older, but similar view, see Beloch, *Attische Politik*, 125; Cloché, 'Conflits', 184–7.
Thrasybulus' achievements: Xen. 4.8.26–31; Diod. 14.94.2–4; Dem. 20.59–60; *IG* II² 21 (= Bengtson, *Staatsverträge*, no. 238, pp. 185–7), 24 (= Tod, *GHI*, vol. 2, no. 110). Earlier, between 395 and 393, Athens had made alliances with Thebes (Xen. 3.5.16), Boeotia, Corinth, Argos, Locris, Leucas, Acarnania, Ambracia, the Thracian Chalcidice (Diod. 14.82.1–3; Tod, *GHI*, vol. 2, nos. 101–3), Cos, Nisyros, Teos, Mitylene, Ephesus, Erythrae (Diod. 14.84.4) and possibly Eretria (Tod, *GHI*, vol. 2, no. 103; cf. P. Krentz, 'Athens' Alliance With Eretria', *AJP* 100 [1979], 398–400; D. Knoepfler, 'Sur une clause du traité de 394 avant J. C. entre Athènes et Erétrie', *AJP* 101 [1980], 462–9). The seven or eight Greek cities of Asia in the Heracles coinage alliance of 394 may have also adhered to the anti- Spartan cause; *supra*, chap. 5, n. 18.
For the interpretation of Thrasybulus here, see Strauss, 'Thrasybulus and Conon', 45–8.
8. Persian support: Funke, *HA* p. 149, n. 60. Antalcidas woos Artaxerxes: Xen. 5.1.6, 25. Chabrias' mission to Evagoras of Cyprus in 388: Xen. 5.1.10. By winter 389/88, the date of Ar. *Ploutos*, Athens had made an alliance with the Persian rebel Acoris of Egypt: *Ploutos* 178 and *schol.*; Bengtson, *Staatsverträge* no. 236, pp. 183–4.
9. Cawkwell: 'Imperialism', 276; similarly, Seager, 'TCAI', 105–13; Funke, *HA* 115–7. Alcibiades, Chalcedon: *supra*, chap. 4, n. 66. Busolt: *Das zweite athenische*

Seebund (Leipzig: 1877), 673–6. Similarly, G. T. Griffith, 'Athens in the Fourth Century', in P. Garnsey and C. R. Whittaker, eds, *Imperialism in the Ancient World* (Cambridge: 1979), 128–33.

10. Saur, 'Thrasybule' 230, n. 83; Funke, *HA* 158–9. Roberts (*Accountability*, 97ff.) argues on the strength of Lys. 28.5, that Thrasybulus was recalled too. Cf. Accame, *Ricerche* 138.

11. Replacement: Xen. 4.8.31, Diod. 14. 99.5. Enemy: *infra*, next paragraph.

12. Archinus: Ar. *Frogs* 367, schol. *ad Eccl.* 102. Callias: And. 1.33. Conon: *supra*, chap. 5, p. 135. Enemies: Beloch, GG^2 vol. 3.1, 91; Accame, *Ricerche* 136; Sealey, 'Callistratos', 185 all argue for enmity. Seager, 'TCAI', p. 110, n. 143 and Funke, *HA* 160 object because of the lack of evidence. Anti-Persian: Beloch, *Attische Politik* 127–8.

13. Aristophanes: *Ploutos* 176 + schol. Plato Comicus, *The Ladies' Return from Worship*, frg. 185 Edmonds, *Attic Comedy*. Cf. Plut. *Praec. Reip. Ger.* 801a–b. Iphicrates: Xen. 4.5.6, 7–18. For the topography of Iphicrates' campaign, see J. Wiseman, *The Land of the Ancient Corinthians* (Göteborg, Sweden: 1978), 99.

14. Immortality: Pritchett, *Greek State at War*, vol. 2, 117. Callias: Xen. 4.5.13; And. 1.18, 133; *supra*, chap. 4., p. 102. Diotimus: Schol. Aristid. *Panath.* 3.274–75 Dind.; Polyaen. 5.22; Lys. 19.50–51; Xen. 5.1.7, 25; *APF* 162–63. Eunomus: Xen. 5.1.5–9; *supra*, chap. 5, p. 134. Demaenetus, general 388/87 (Xen. 5.1.10, 26) had also been associated with Conon (*infra*, n. 18). In 388 he was Chabrias' colleague (Xen. 5.1.10); whether he was Chabrias' or Iphicrates' *philos* is unclear. Cleobulus: Aesch. 2.78, 149; *APF* 544–5.

15. Honours in 371: Dem. 23.10; Aesch. 3.243; Arist. *Rhet.* 1397b; Lys. frg. 7 Gernet and Bizos *Lysias*. Cf. Pritchett, *Greek State at War*, vol. 2, 124.

16. Iphicrates and Conon: *supra*, chap. 5, p. 133. Chabrias: Xen. 4.8.34, 5.16; Diod 14.92.2; *IG* II^2 21.1, lines. 21–2. Seager, 'TCAI', 114. Aesimus: Tod, *GHI* vol. 2, no. 118, line 41. Anytus, the grain commissioner of 388, was probably not Anytus, son of Athemion of Euonymon, but rather his son or someone else entirely. See Lys. 22.8,9; *APF* 41; *supra*, p. 96.

17. Thrasybulus: Aesch 3.138; *supra*, pp. 103–4, 134–5. Thrason: Aesch 3.138; Dein. 1.38; *APF* 239.

18. Cephalus: Tod, *GHI*, vol. 2, no. 116, lines 6, 10–15; n. 118, line 40; *supra*, chap. 4, p. 102. Demaenetus: *Hell. Oxy.* 1.1, 3.1–2; Xen. 5.1.10; Aesch. 2.78. Dionysius, Phanias, Leontichus: nothing is known of their political connections. Phormisius: *supra*, chap. 4, p. 99.

19. Pamphilus: Lys. 15.5, Xen. 5.1. 2–5; schol. *ad* Ar. *Ploutos* 174; Dem. 40.20–22. Boeotus. Dem. 39.32, 40.23. Plangon: Dem. 39.2, 23; 40.6–7, 14, 20, 22. Mantias: Dem. 39.3; Arist. *Rhet* 1398b2; *IG* II^2 1609, line 61; Diod. 16.2.6–3.5. Cf. *APF* 364–368; Seager, 'TCAI', 113.

20. Pamphilus; previous note and cf. Beloch, *Attische Politik* 329; *APF* 365.

21. *Supra*, n. 8. The scholiast says Athens made the alliance to obtain grain from Egypt.

22. Xenophon records Antalcidas' return immediately after describing Teleutias' victory, 5.1.24–25. Among the ships Teleutias captures were some full of grain; hence, the harvest of May–June must now have been over. Antalcidas' return, therefore, should be dated to summer or fall.

23. Hamilton, *SBV* 308–10; F. Graefe, 'Die Operationen des Antalkidas im Hellespont', *Klio* 28 (1935), 262–70.

24. Xen. 5.1.31; Diod. 14.110.3; Justin 6.6.1–3; Aelius Aristides *Panath*, 172.10, ed. Dindorf. Cf. Bengtson, *Staatsverträge*, nos. 241–2, pp. 188–92. The most important modern interpretive discussions are those of U. Wilcken, 'Über Entstehung und Zweck des Königsfriedens', *Abh. Preuss. Akad.* 15 (1941); V. Martin, 'Le traitement de l'histoire diplomatique dans la tradition littéraire du

IVe siècle avant J.-C.', *MH* 1 (1944), 127–39; Ryder, *Koine Eirene*, 34–6, 122–3; Hamilton, *SBV* 301–25.

25. Athens' sympathy for the Ionians: Diod. 14.110.4. Aegina and the grain blockade: Xen. 5.1.29 and Lysias 22 *Against the Grain Dealers*, which seems to refer to Athens' difficulties at this time. Cf. Seager, 'Lysias Against the Corn Dealers', *Historia* 15 (1966) 172–84. On the oaths: Xen. 5.1.20–35; for the date, see Wilcken, 'Königsfriedens', 17.

26. Earlier trials: *supra*, pp. 40n.88, 151, 154, 158. Thrasybulus of Collytus: Dem. 24. 134, Lys. 26.23f. Dionysius: Dem. 19.180. Agyrrhius: Dem. 24.135; *APF* 278. Roberts has argued that the impeachment trials of the Corinthian Wars were by and large attacks on radical democrats by conservatives (*Accountability* 84, 96, 106). The reality was simpler: in most cases they were attacks on unsuccessful generals by an angry *demos* (egged on by factional enemies).

27. Cephalus: Tod, *GHI* vol. 2, no. 116 lines 7–16. Iphicrates: Nepos. *Iph*. 2.1; U. Kahrstedt, *RE* 9 (1916), 2019–20; *APF* 249–50. Chabrias: Diod. 15.29.2; Dem 20.76; Nepos. *Chabr*. 2.1; cf. J. Kirchner, *RE* (1899), 2017–18.

28. *Contra* Cloché, 'Conflicts', 188–92; Hamilton, *SBV* 311.

29. P. Cloché, *Politique étrangère* 45–54; Funke, *HA* 164–5.

30. *APF* 177–8; Tod, *GHI* vol. 2, no. 117, lines 5–6.

31. Aesimus: Tod, *GHI* vol. 2, no. 118, 1. 41. Cephalus: ibid., 1.40; no. 116 lines 7–16.

32. Sealey: 'Callistratos', 185. Cephalus: Dein. 1.39; cf. A. P. Burnett, 'Thebes and the Expansion of the Second Athenian Confederacy: *IG* II^2 40 and *IG* II^2 43', *Historia* 11 (1962), 16. Aesimus: Tod, *GHI* vol. 2, no. 122 line 20. Thrasybulus: Aesch. 3.138. Phormisius: Dein. 1.38; *supra*, pp. 99, 157.

33. Callistratus: Diod. 15. 29.7; Theopompus *FGrH*, 2B 115 F 98. Cf. Cloché, La Politique de l'Athénien Callistratos (391–361 avant J. C.)', *REA* 25 (1923), 8–11; Sealey, 'Callistratos', 185–7.

34. Timotheus: Diod. 15.29.7. Aristotle: Tod, *GHI* vol. 2, no. 123, lines 7, 76; D. L. 5.35. Pyrrhandrus: Tod, *GHI* vol. 2, no. 123 lines 76–7; no. 121 line 21; no. 124 line 8. Thrason: Aesch. 3.138; Dein. 1.38.

35. For the details in the following cases, *supra*, chap. 1, n. 88: Adeimantus, Anytus (possibly); Polyaenus and Theomnestus; Epicrates and Phormisius; Mantitheus; Aristophanes and Nicophemus; Epicrates, Andocides, Cratinus and Euboulides; Epicrates and his fellow envoys; Ergocles and Philocrates, Pamphilus, Agyrrhius, Dionysius, Thrasybulus of Collytus.

36. Edmonds, *Fragments*, vol. 1, 573, 670, 692; Rogers, *The Plutus of Aristophanes* (London: 1907), xxiii–xxiv.

37. V. Coulon and H. Van Daele, *Aristophane*, vol. 5 (Paris: 1930), 81; Ehrenberg, *Aristophanes* 69.

38. Coulon-Van Daele, *Aristophane* vol. 5, 7; cf. Rogers, *Plutus* 14.

39. Council: *IG* II^2 1740, line 24.

40. Mossé, *Athens in Decline* 13.

41. Ehrenberg, *Aristophanes* 72; cf. Coulon-Van Daele, *Aristophane* vol. 5, 81; Lévy, *Athènes devant la défaite* 8.

42. Croiset, *Aristophanes and Political Parties* 177–8; Coulon-Van Daele, *Aristophane* vol. 5, 79; Ehrenberg, *Aristophanes* 70. Mossé, *Athens in Decline*, 13–14. See *supra*, chap. 2, pp.61–3.

43. On hunger, disease, burial and crime see E. David, *Aristophanes and Athenian Society of the Early Fourth Century* BC (Leiden: 1984), 6–12 — a thorough analysis, but one without sufficient allowance for comic exaggeration.

44. Rogers, *Plutus* 70.

45. Attic Greek: Ussher, *Ecclesiazusae* 104. On Athenian selfish materialism, see David, *Aristophanes and Athenian Society* 32–8.

46. David, *Aristophanes and Athenian Society* 33–4.

Conclusions

This book began with the conviction that by studying Athens after the Peloponnesian War, we could understand an important and absorbing 20 year period, and, as well, reach general conclusions about the nature of politics in classical Athens. It is time to summarize those conclusions. In the preceding chapters it was necessary to define terms and propose a theory before considering the details; here, we may begin with the specific and proceed to the general. Hence, the following conclusions are divided into four main subjects: unity and disunity in Athens during the period 403–386, the relation of socioeconomic to political developments in the period 403–386, the light shed by this period on the nature of Athenian politics, and the importance of the period in the broad sweep of classical Athenian history.

The first conclusion is that Athenian political unity between 403 and 386 was fragile, at times tenuous. This stands counter to the prominent thesis that once the storm of the Thirty was weathered, only superficial and relatively unimportant political divisions existed in Athens. There were several causes of disunity.

First and foremost was the legacy of the civil war over the Thirty. In spite of the amnesty and its observance, deep hostility between the men of the City and the men of Piraeus continued throughout the period of the Corinthian War. One ground for hatred was tangible: the property of democrats that oligarchs had purchased and never returned. Other, less material, reasons were no less important, however: betrayals and executions, invective and threats, mismanagement of the war or kowtowing to the enemy after surrender, and finally, fear that the other side would misbehave again.

A second cause of disunity — related to the first, often equated to it in rhetoric, but not the same — was the hostility between the *penetes* and the *plousioi*, that is, between the ordinary working people and the leisured rich. Always a factor in Athenian politics, this hostility had been exacerbated by the widening of the gulf between have and have-not as a result of the Peloponnesian War. It was one thing to go from super-rich to merely rich, quite another to go from middle class to destitute. The newly-destitute were more ready than ever to make demands of the rich, but the rich were less able than ever to meet them, for even their wealth had shrunk. The *eisphora*-paying class was in no condition to finance a war, but the loss of the empire demanded its contributions.

Without the hostility between City and Piraeus and *plousioi* and *penetes*, the course of Athenian history in this period might have been different. If, for example, the *demos* distrusted former oligarchs less, it might have been willing to accept the peace that Andocides negotiated in 392/91. If the Few could have trusted the Many, they might have been sincere in voting for war in 395 and not merely too frightened to voice their opposition. If the knights had not suffered so much abuse and hostility after 403, they might have put up better resistance at the Nemea. With more wealthy Athenians enthusiastic about the war, more than one Mantitheus might have susbsidized poor hoplites in 394: fewer men might have shirked the duty to pay *eisphora* or liturgies, and Thrasybulus might have had a bigger fleet.

A third cause of disunity was the rancor of defeat, the imperative of finding shoulders on which to lay blame for losing first the Peloponnesian War and then the Corinthian War. There were scores to settle, which helps to explain Conon's prosecution of Adeimantus in 393/92 for losing Aegospotami, Andocides' prosecution of Archippus for mutilating a Herm, the execution of the generals Aristophanes and Nicophemus in 391 for their loss of ten ships, the prosecution of Thrasybulus' subordinate commanders in 389 for losing a fleet off Lesbos, the trials of the generals in 386, and even, in part, Anytus' prosecution of Socrates in 399.

Losing two wars within 20 years sharpened the prospects of political divisiveness in Athens, but these were already considerable because of the atomistic tendencies inherent in Athenian political culture — a fourth cause of disunity. Athenian political culture in the late fifth and early fourth centuries had taken traditional values, which already put little emphasis on compromise, and toughened them in war. Hence, politicians tended to value loyalty to friends before loyalty to country, and ambition before morality. They found it natural to seek scapegoats as a way of saving face. They considered vengeance not merely acceptable, but a moral obligation. These values have much to do with the statistic that over 20 generals, trierarchs, magistrates, ambassadors and orators are known to have stood trial in Athens between 403 and 386; more than half are known to have been convicted, and five to have been executed. It is noteworthy that Athens' leaders during the Corinthian War were more likely to fall in domestic politics than in battle.

Manifestly, and in spite of these disadvantages, Athens was able to muster considerable unity after the Peloponnesian War, enough to abide by the amnesty and to prosecute the Corinthian War, from which Athens did profit, if hardly to the degree of its war aims. Three factors account for this unity. First, neither the division between *plousioi* and *penetes* or between country and city outweighed the appeal of a war to regain the Athenian empire. The *penetes* needed empire more desperately than did the *plousioi*, the *plousioi* grumbled about war tax and feared the political consequence of an imperial *demos*, but on balance, both groups stood to profit enormously. Likewise, the country had suffered more from foreign invasion during the Peloponnesian War than the City had, indeed certain trading interests in the City had even prospered, but many in the City had suffered from invasion, and until the walls were rebuilt, they could look forward to suffering even more. The urban–rural division that has been built upon Aristophanes *Ecclesiazusae* 197–98 turns out, upon closer analysis, to dissolve in smoke.

Second, however much the *demos* might have wanted to violate the amnesty and take revenge, at first the power of Sparta to invervene and then the necessities of wartime unity held it in check.

Third, the demographic consequences of the Peloponnesian War were decisive. Although there were roughly as many hoplites as thetes in 431 (about 20,000 each), thetes suffered over twice as many casualties in the Peloponnesian War: an estimated *c.* 12,600 to an estimated *c.* 5,160. Moreover, hoplites suffered nearly all of their casualties before 412, thetes very few before 415 and nearly half after 413. While hoplites therefore suffered little during the Ionian War, thetes were devastated. By the beginning of the fourth century, there were roughly 9,250 hoplites and 5–7,000 thetes in Athens, hence a total citizen population of 14,250–16,250. While the numbers of hoplites and thetes had been roughly equal in 431, by the beginning of the fourth century, hoplites outnumbered thetes by on the order of 20 per cent, if not more. If the *demos* was comparatively quiescent after 403, a major reason is that so many of its potential leaders were dead.

174 *Conclusions*

This discussion has already illuminated the second subject of these conclusions, the relationship of socioeconomic to political developments. Postwar politics were shaped by both (a) the economic consequences of Peloponnesian invasion, loss of empire and property confiscation under the Thirty and (b) the demographic consequences of battle casualties, epidemic, hunger, poverty and perhaps birth control. A set of conditions was created under which class conflict would be a major element in politics, but not always a decisive one. The *demos* was too depleted in both numbers and wealth to compete with the *plousioi*. Moreover, self-interest united these groups more than it divided them. A majority of the *plousioi* wanted, like the *demos*, to regain the empire and to keep Sparta out of Athenian affairs.

To explain postwar politics, one needs to work on two levels, to employ two models: class and faction. This leads, of course, to the third general conclusion, the nature of Athenian politics. This dual analysis is, I trust, not a matter of ambivalence or indecision, but rather of the dichotomous character of Athenian politics in Athens. In a society in which personal relationships were more important than legal ones, politics without factions was unthinkable.

A judicious reading of the literature in political anthropology provides the student of Athenian politics with a workable model of a faction: a more accurate and satisfactory appellation for Athenian elite political groups than either 'party' or 'group'. Athenian factions were small, informal, competitive groups. They were held together by loose, diverse, non-corporate ties: collegiality was among these ties, but in the last analysis the factions were clientelist, i.e., the leader–follower tie was crucial. Politicians spoke often of *philia*, but what they had in mind was usually rather instrumental friendship, with its tangible and mutual obligations, than emotional friendship. Examples of factions from our period are Thrasybulus and his followers, Conon and his followers, Agyrrhius and his followers, Cephalus and his followers, and many others.

Around the year 400, the faction was still the basic building block of elite politics, an effective instrument of power. On the other hand, from the early fifth century on, if not earlier, class-interest politics played an increasingly important role in Athens. It slowly became clear that one could organize — however informally or, by our standards, shoddily — a following by appealing to class interests, to those of either *hoi polloi kai demotikoi* or *hoi epieikeis kai ousias echontes*, to use P's categories.

Clientelism was crucial to elite politics, but it played only a limited role in the political community. No doubt a faction leader or his lieutenants could count on personal ties to deliver some votes in the assembly — some, but not enough. To win, a leader had to invoke personal charisma or appeal to class interests. Under the rubric of charisma may be understood a reputation for military skill, financial expertise, or family talent, as well as oratorical or personal magnetism. A few Athenian politicians may have built their careers on these qualities alone, but most politicians had to appeal to class interests.

Thrasybulus, for example, had a reputation for military skill, and for courage, loyalty and pluck. Although he was not a great orator, he staked out a position as a democrat who was moderate and a conservative. Archinus held a similar position in the political spectrum, but unlike Thrasybulus, he had supported Theramenes in 404, and in 403 he placed more emphasis than Thrasybulus on co-operating with former Therameneans. Although he had served as a general, Archinus was famous as an orator. Conon returned to Athens in 393 after a prudent exile with a stunning if spotted military record. It included having made the best of a bad business at Aegospotami, but also the smashing victory of Cnidus. Moreover, Conon had his finger on the Persian purse-strings. Hence a wide assortment of Athenians followed him enthusiastically. Among them may have been Agyrrhius, who built his career as a financial expert and a supporter of *hoi polloi*, advocating assembly pay and foreign conquest.

Agyrrhius held his positions consistently during the postwar period, but not all politicians were so steadfast. Epicrates of Cephisia, for example, changed from warhawk to peace negotiator, although this was perhaps only a tactical change, a temporary response to war reverses by a consistent imperialist. Phormisius, on the other hand, did an about-face, from proposing a limited oligarchy in 403 to supporting democratic Thebes' rebellion from oligarchic Sparta in 378.

To different degrees, therefore, different politicians appealed to charisma or class. Hence, there is no formula for analyzing particular politicians or political conflict. In each case, men and circumstances varied.

Too often, Athenian political conflict has been seen simply as a clash of faction or ambition, as simply a power struggle. Reality was more complex. For example, when Epicrates and Cephalus clashed with Thrasybulus over sending support to Conon in 395 during the Demaenetus affair, they were not merely attempting to outbid him for the favour of the *demos*. That was one of their motives, of course, but they were also far more impatient than Thrasybulus about the problems of the poor, which the Persian aid promised by Conon might alleviate. To take another example, when Agyrrhius' nephew Callistratus attacked the peace negotiators of 392/91 (among them Epicrates and Andocides) it was not merely to launch his own career and rid his uncle and patron of powerful rivals. It was also, to judge by Agyrrhius' generalship in 389/88, a vote against postponing the struggle to rebuild Athenian power.

Political conflict in Athens, therefore, was a matter of principle, policy and class as well as of power. This statement is true not only of the years between 403 and 386, but of any period in classical Athens from the 460s on, and perhaps earlier. Strengthened by numbers and imperial prosperity, the *penetes* were more assertive in the fifth century than in the fourth, but their struggles did not cease in the year 400. Likewise, the exertions of the *plousioi* came to a head in the oligarchies of 411, 403 and 322, but their activity was prodigious in other years too.

All things considered, slightly more of the political struggles of the period 403–386 were a matter of faction than of class. This state of affairs is less of a reflection of the inappropriateness of the class model to Athenian political history than of the peculiar stalemate of classes in postwar Athens. Again, as a result of the Peloponnesian War, the voice of the *penetes* had been weakened (although not, of course, silenced).

The specifics of the period 403–386 reveal a pattern to factional politics. A successful, popular general could dominate the political scene and unite conflicting factions, but only temporarily. Conon, victor of Cnidus, is the prime example: he dominated Athens in 393/92 in a manner reminiscent of Cimon or Pericles. Thrasybulus, victor of Phyle, is a second example, although his prominence from 403 to 394 was far less secure than Conon's. Thrasybulus was challenged by factions representing the tendencies both of the Few and the Many: most prominently by Archinus on the one hand and by Epicrates and by Cephalus on the other. Had Thrasybulus been a better orator or more of a champion of the *penetes*, he might have had a firmer grip on power. His failure after a year of military defeat in 394 is a reminder, as Aristophanes might have put it, that *demos* was an animal requiring constant feeding.

After Conon's death, the disintegrative tendencies of Athenian politics asserted themselves. Thrasybulus and Agyrrhius neutralized Andocides and Epicrates in their efforts to make peace in 392/91. After Thrasybulus re-emerged as a naval commander in 390, his hold on power was so tenuous that he could not prevent the recall of his lieutenants. His successor, Agyrrhius, was unable to secure victories, and ended his career in prison. He faced many challengers for power in the final phase of the Corinthian War, among the Iphicrates, Thrasybulus of Collytus and Cephalus. After the King's Peace, power continued to be divided many among competitors.

The place of the postwar period in Athenian history is the fourth subject of these conclusions. Chronologically, the fourth century began during these years, but substantively, the postwar period has ties to the fifth century. Both at home and abroad, the issues of the Peloponnesian War still set the stage for Athenian politics. Through a process which Ober aptly calls 'generational hangover,' Athenians continued to believe in the empire; they lacked the defensive mentality of the fourth century.[1] Neither the separation of generals and politicians nor the abandonment of political munificence which characterize the fourth century obtained in the postwar period. Most of the leaders of the postwar period had been active before 404; very few of these same leaders survived past 386. In intellectual affairs, Aristophanes, Socrates and Thucydides were still alive during at least part of the postwar era.

Of course, the postwar period does display many differences with its predecessor: the loss of the Athenian empire and the decline of the thetes are the most significant. The drop in the number of thetes played an important role in the history of Athenian politics. Jones suggests that fourth-century Athens displayed an 'increasingly bourgeois tone' because of the reduction of the thetic class in the Peloponnesian War.[2] His was an unsubstantiated suggestion, but the *prima facie* evidence and, I trust, the statistical calculations of this book indicate that it is correct. Incidentally, my figures for the thetes in 403 lend credence to Plutarch's statistic of 12,000 thetes in 322 (*Phoc.* 28) and render Diodorus' 22,000 implausibly large (18.18.5); a rise from 5–7,000 to 12,000 thetes in 80 years is impressive, to 22,000 astounding.

On balance, therefore, while the postwar period is closer to the fifth century, in demographic terms as in other ways it is the beginning of the fourth. That trite term, a transitional period, seems to be unusually apposite.

A few words ought to be said, in closing, about the direction of future research. A subject that requires further investigation is ideology in the postwar period. Having examined Aristophanes, for instance, one would like to know the extent to which other contemporaries perceived postwar Athens as a weaker, poorer place. Did the Athenians think of themselves as a divided people? Here one must re-examine Lévy's theory that after the defeat of 404 Athenians began to abandon their ideology of power and imperialism and slowly move toward Panhellenism and pacifism.[3] One might find evidence of this change in a Thucydides, a Socrates, even a Lysias. The man in the street, however, or practising Athenian politicians, are another matter.

I would like to add a few personal and possibly controversial observations about methodology. Generally speaking, one can find two kinds of studies in ancient Greek historiography today. The first aims at investigating sources, evaluating facts and refining details; its model is positivism. The second tries to explain what happened and to describe the general pattern. These studies range from neoconservative to Marxist to poststructuralist, but they all use models, derived either from a comprehensive understanding of ancient history, from a comparison to other periods of history, or from other disciplines. Good research requires both kinds of studies, the specific and the general. I would hope however, that ancient history might see more of the second.

Positivism, unfortunately, discourages discourse with historians who study other eras, and it is incomplete: given the fragmentary, lacunary nature of the evidence, any attempt to 'let the facts speak for themselves' without some carefully-thought-out framework is doomed to fail. The process of verifying the facts is where the study of the past should begin, not end. Thucydides wrote history not merely because the facts were verifiable, but because he could use those facts to teach a lesson. Historians today would do well to follow the founder of our discipline.

Notes

1. Ober, *FA* 209.
2. Jones, *AD* 10.
3. Lévy, *Athènes devant la défaite* 209–22.

Appendix: Hoplite and Thetic Battle Casualties in the Peloponnesian War

Hoplites

I include Spartolus where 430 were killed (Thuc. 2.97.7); Aetolia, where 120 *epibatai* serving with Demosthenes were killed (Thuc. 3.98.4); the *epibatai* were normally hoplites, p. 82 n. 12; Corinth, where *c*. 50 died (Thuc. 4.44.6, Diod. 12.65.6); Delium, where 1,000 died (Thuc. 4.101.2); Amphipolis, where *c*. 600 died (5.11.2); Mantinea, where 200 Athenians (including settlers on Aegina) fell (5.74.2); Sicily, where of 2,700 hoplites, 280 knights and (at most) 170 trierarchs sent out, 'only few out of many came home' (Thuc. 7.87.6; cf. 6.43, 7.20; Diod. 13.2.5, 8.7, 9.2), say 20 per cent, i.e., 630; Cyzicus, where, at a guess, 25 hoplites fell on land (Diod. 13.51.2, 6; Xen. 1.1.18); Ephesus, where 100 hoplites and ?100 *epibatai* of hoplite status fell (Diod. 13.64.2, Xen. 1.2.9); a raid into Lydia, where 7 Athenian soldiers (hoplites?) were killed (Xen. 1.2.5); Arginusae, where it is not unreasonable to postulate 500 hoplite deaths (Xen. 1.6.34, Diod. 13.100.3–4; see Busolt *GG* 3.2 1596–97); Aegospotami (*infra*), where it is fair to guess that 6 per cent of the 3,000 Athenians executed (10 *epibatai* plus 1–2 trierarchs per ship, plus several generals and taxiarchs) were of hoplite or higher status, i.e., 180 men; 95 *epibatai* of hoplite status estimated among the dead at the Corinthian Gulf, Sicily (425), Syme, Euboea, Cynossema and Notium (*infra* a, c, g, h, i, k) — for a total of 5,470 hoplite casualties. We must also keep in mind the several instances where we know that there were some hoplite casualties, but not how many: Methone (Thuc. 2.25.2, Diod. 12.43.2); the garrison at Delium (Thuc. 4.100.5, Diod. 12.70.6); some of the 400 hoplites attacking Sicyon (Thuc. 4.101.4); Pylos (Diod. 13.64.7); Agis' raid in Attica (Diod. 13.72.4, Xen. 1.1.33–35); the sea battle in Mitylene harbour before Arginusae (Diod. 13.79.2).

Thetes

I have culled the following thetic casualties mainly from Thucydides, Xenophon and Diodorus Siculus. The ancient trireme carried *c*. 200

180   Appendix

men, of whom 170 were rowers, on the average 10 marines (*epibatai*), 4 archers, 6–8 petty officers, 2 gangs of 5 seamen each reporting to the helmsman and bow officer, and the trierarch(s). Although Pericles boasts that the skilled men were all citizens, inscriptions demonstrate the presence of metics and foreigners in their midst as the Peloponnesian War wore on. See Thuc. 1.143.1; L. Casson, *Ships and Seamanship in the Ancient World* (Princeton: 1971), 304–5; Jordan, *Athenian Navy* 142, 150–1; J. S. Morrison, '*Hyperesia* in Naval Contexts in the Fifth and Fourth Centuries BC', *JHS* 104 (1984) 54–6. The casualties are:

a. Thuc. 2.90.5: In the Corinthian Gulf, 9 Athenian ships were disabled, and all those who did not swim ashore were killed. If, at a guess, 20 per cent of the men died, the thetic casualties would have been 125, hoplite 17.

b. 4.14.4: some men probably died at the battle of Pylos, say 25 thetes.

c. 4.25.4–5: Athens and Rhegium lost 2 ships in Sicily. In one case, the entire crew escaped; in the other, an Athenian ship, assuming that 20 per cent of the crew died, 14 thetes and 2 hoplites were lost.

d. 4.101.2, Diod. 12.70.4: A 'great number' (πολὺς ἀριθμός) of 'the metics and foreign allies as well as Athenians' who accompanied the hoplites to Delium were killed; or, as Diod. says, total (incl. hoplite) Athenian losses were 'many times' the 500 Boeotian dead. Originally, there may have been as many as 30,000 of these citizen thetes and poor metics and other foreigners (4.93.3–94.1; cf. French, *Growth* 137; *contra* Beloch, *Bevölkerung* 73), but very few remained until the start of the battle (4.94.1). In order to account for the 'great number' of the dead, Gomme argued that the Boeotian cavalry followed up after the battle, and attacked the unarmed masses (*HCT ad* 4.101.2). If this is right, then there may have been thousands of casualties among the unarmed: at a guess, say that 1,000 Athenian thetes died.

e. 6.43: In 415, Athens sent 60 triremes and 40 troop-transports to Sicily, carrying, among others, 700 thetic *epibatai*. By the system of calculation used here, they held about 5,020 thetes, including the *epibatai*. As for the troop-transports, I have followed Dover's theory (*HCT ad loc.*) that they were rowed by hoplites and carried a skeleton crew of sailors, say 10 per ship; that is 144 citizen thetes. According to Thucydides, few of these men ever returned to Athens (7.87.6). If, say, only 20 per cent of the citizen thetes survived, some 4,100 would have been killed.

f. 7.16, 20.2: In the winter of 414/13, Athens sent reinforcements in 50 ships. Thucydides did not specify how many were triremes, how many transports, but a rough calculation is possible. He explained that with the help of 13 allied ships, the Athenians brought 5,000 fresh hoplites to Sicily. If the allies supplied no troop transports, Athens would have had to furnish 29. Assuming the allies came forth with just a few such ships, Athens would have supplied about 25, as well as 35 triremes. Applying to these figures the system of calculation used above, some 2,500 thetic casualties are obtained. Cf. Beloch, GG^2, vol. 3.2, 394.

g. Thuc. 8.42.4: At Syme in 411, Athens lost 6 ships. If 20 per cent of the crews died, Athens lost 86 thetes, 12 hoplites.

h. 8.95.7: In 411 off Euboea, the Peloponnesians captured 22 Athenian ships and killed or made prisoners of the crews. If 20 per cent of the men were killed, 317 thetes and 44 hoplites were lost to Athens.

i. 8.106.3, Diod. 13.40.5: At Cynossema, Athens lost 15 ships according to Thuc. or 5 sunk according to Diod. If 20 per cent of the men on the 15 ships died, 216 thetes and 30 hoplites would have been killed.

j. Xen. 1.1.18, Diod. 13. 51.2, 6: Of the 'many' *epibatai* and archers whom Diod. says fell on land in the battle of Cyzicus, I make a guess of 25 hoplites and 25 thetes.

k. Xen. 1.5.14, Diod. 13.71.4: Xen. says that 15 ships were lost at Notium, but most men escaped. Diod. says that 22 ships were lost, but makes no mention of casualties. If one follows the lower figure and assumes a death rate of 20 per cent, 216 thetes and 30 hoplites were killed.

l. 1.6.34: The Athenian side lost 25 ships, crews and all, at Arginusac. Of the 150 ships present, 110 Athenian, so it is probably fair to multiply the total casualty figures by two-thirds to obtain Athenian losses: 3,300 men. See Beloch, GG^2 vol. 3.2, 395. If 36 per cent were thetes, Athens would have lost 1,147 thetes.

m. Xen. 2.1.28, Diod. 13. 105–106, Plut. *Lys.* 13.1, Paus. 9.32.9: According to Xenophon, Lysander executed all the Athenians whom he captured at Aegospotami; Plutarch provides the figure of 3,000, Pausanias of 4,000. Diodorus makes no mention of any executions. C. Ehrhardt has argued in favour of

Diodorus' authority, which goes back to the Oxyrhynchus historian (*Phoenix* 24 (1970) 225–8) but I have defended the tradition of the other three authors (*AJP* 104 (1983) 24–35). If, to be conservative, we use Plutarch's figure, after subtracting an estimate of hoplite casualties (*supra*), a sum of 2,820 thetic casualties is reached.

The total estimate of thetic casualties in the Peloponnesian War is 12,591. This is a minimum: there were certainly losses in the battle of Mitylene harbour before Arginusae (Diod. 13.79.2) and probably on other occasions too.

Select Bibliography

(I include only those works which are fundamental to the central themes of this book, excluding studies of individual points, which appear in the notes, and works already cited under Abbreviations.)

Audring, G. 'Über Grundeigentum und Landwirtschaft in der Krise der athenischen Polis'. E. C. Welskopf, ed., *Hellenische Poleis, Krise — Wandlung — Wirkung*, vol. 1 (Berlin: 1974)
Bailey, F. G., *Strategems and Spoils, A Social Anthropology of Politics* (New York: 1969)
Boissevain, J. 'Factions, Parties, and Politics in a Maltese Village', *American Anthropologist* 66 (1964), 1275–1287
—— *Friends of Friends, Networks, Manipulators and Coalitions* (Oxford: 1974)
Bolkestein, H. *Economic Life in Greece's Golden Age* (Rev. Jonkers. Leiden: 1958)
Calhoun, G. M. *Athenian Clubs in Politics and Litigation* (Austin, Tex.: 1913)
Campbell, J. K. *Honour, Family and Patronage. A Study of Institutions and Moral Values in a Greek Mountain Community* (Oxford: 1964)
Cawkwell, G. 'The Imperialism of Thrasybulus', *CQ* 26 (1976), 270–77
Cloché, P. *La restauration démocratique à Athènes en 403 avant J.-C.* (Paris: 1915)
—— 'Les conflits politiques et sociaux à Athènes pendant la guerre corinthienne (395–387 avant J.-C.)' *REA* 21 (1919), 157–92
—— *La Politique Étrangère d'Athènes de 404 à 338 a. C.* (Paris: 1934)
Dover, K. J. *Lysias and the Corpus Lysiacum* (Berkeley: 1971)
Finley, M. I. *The Ancient Economy* (Berkeley: 1973)
—— 'Athenian Demagogues'. Finley, ed. *Studies in Ancient Society* (London: 1974)
—— 'The Fifth-Century Athenian Empire: A Balance Sheet', in Finley, *Economy and Society in Ancient Greece*, ed. B. D. Shaw and R. P. Saller (New York: 1981)
—— *Politics in the Ancient World* (Cambridge: 1983)
French, A. *The Growth of the Athenian Economy* (London: 1964)
Gouldner, A. *Enter Plato. Classical Greece and the Origins of Social Theory* (London: 1967)
Grote, G. *A History of Greece*, 4th ed. (London: 1869)
Hansen, M. H. 'The Athenian "Politicians", 403–322 BC'. *GRBS* 24 (1983), 33–55
—— '*Rhetores* and *Strategoi* in Fourth-Century Athens'. *GRBS* 24 (1983), 151–80
—— 'Demographic Reflections on the Number of Athenian Citizens 451–309 BC' *AJAH* 7 (1982), 172–84
Hanson, V. *Warfare and Agriculture in Ancient Greece* (Pisa: 1983)
Harding, P. 'In Search of a Polypragmatist'. *CC* 41–50
Hignett, C. *A History of the Athenian Constitution to the End of the Fifth Century* (Oxford: 1952)
Humphreys, S. C. 'Economy and Society in Classical Athens'. *AdSNSdP* 2nd series 39 (1970), 1–26
—— *Anthropology and the Greeks* (London: 1978)
—— *The Family, Women and Death, Comparative Studies* (London: 1983)
Hutter, H. *Politics as Friendship* (Waterloo, Ont.: 1978)

184 Select Bibliography

Isager, S. and Hansen, M. H. *Aspects of Athenian Society in the Fourth Century* BC Trans. Rosenmeier (Odense: 1975)
Kluwe, E. 'Die Soziale Zusammensetzung der athenischen Ekklesia und ihr Einfluss auf politische Entscheidungen'. *Klio* 58 (1976), 295–33
—— 'Nochmals zum Problem: Der soziale Zusammensetzung der athenischen Ekklesia. . . .' *Klio* 59 (1977), 45–81
Kounas, D. D. A. 'Prelude to Hegemony: Studies in Athenian Political Parties from 403 to 379 BC Pertaining to the Revival of Athenian Influence in Greece' (Diss. Illinois: 1969)
Lévy, E. *Athènes devant la défaite de 404: Histoire d'une crise idéologique* (Paris: 1976)
Lintott, A. *Violence, Civil Strife and Revolution in the Classical City* (Baltimore: 1982)
MacDowell, D. *Andokides. On the Mysteries* (Oxford: 1962)
Meiggs, R. *The Athenian Empire* (Oxford: 1975)
Michell, H. *The Economics of Ancient Greece*, 2nd edn (Cambridge: 1957)
Mossé, C. *La fin de la démocratie athénienne* (Paris: 1961)
—— *Athens in Decline, 403–386 BC* trans. Stewart (London: 1976)
Nicholas, R. W. 'Factions: a Comparative Analysis', in M. Banton, ed. *Political Systems and the Distribution of Power* (London: 1965) 21–61
Nicholson, N. K. 'The Factional Model and the Study of Politics'. *Comparative Political Studies* 5 (1972), 291–309
Pecorella Longo, C. *'Eterie' e Gruppi Politici Nell'Atene del IV secolo a. c.* (Florence: 1971)
Perlman, S. 'The Politicians in the Athenian Democracy of the Fourth-Century BC' *Athenaeum* n. s. 41 (1963), 327–55
—— 'Political Leadership in Athens in the Fourth Century BC' *PP* 22 (1967), 153–72
Reverdin, O. 'Remarques sur la vie politique d'Athenes au Ve Siecle'. *MH* 2 (1945), 200–12
Rhodes, P. J. 'Athenian Democracy After 403 BC' *CJ* 75 (1980), 305–23
—— 'On Labelling 4th-Century Politicians'. *LCM* 3 (1978), 207–11
Roberts, J. *Accountability in Athenian Government* (Madison:1982)
Saur, L. 'Thrasybule de Stiria: une certaine idee d'Athènes' (Diss. Liège: 1978)
Strauss, B. S. 'Thrasybulus and Conon: A Rivalry in Athenian Politics in the 390s BC' *AJP* 105 (1984), 37–48
Walcot, P. *Greek Peasants Ancient and Modern.* (Manchester: 1970)
Wolf, E. 'Kinship, Friendship, and Patron–Client Relationships in Complex Societies', in M. Banton, ed. *The Social Anthropology of Complex Societies* (London: 1966)

Index

Abydus 156–9 *passim*
Acarnania 158
Acharnae 59
Achilles 32
Adeimantus of Scambonidae 19, 32–4, 53
  is friend of Alcibiades 119n71
  prosecution of 108, 129
Adkins, A.W.H. 3, 30
Aegina 77, 79, 105, 110
Aegospotami 50, 56, 77, 126, 132, 152
  casualties at and after 179–81
  Conon's role in 32, 34, 129
Aeschines (orator) 3, 95, 102, 104, 109
  on Archinus 97, 116n25
  versus Demosthenes 26, 30
Aeschines (Socratic) 95
Aesimus (politician) 19, 89–91, 96, 142, 156, 162
Agesilaus (Spartan king) 75, 107, 109, 158
Agoratus (alleged informer for Thirty) 33, 89, 102
Agyrrhius of Collytus 31, 104, 112, 175–7
  and Andocides 49, 101
  and Callistratus 12, 142
  and Conon 130–8 *passim*
  farms taxes 20, 49, 114
  introduces ecclesiastic pay 14, 91, 100–1
  trial of 161
Alcibiades of Scambonidae 26–7, 30–4, 94–6, 102–4, 114
  and Athenian economy 46, 55
  and Callias 136
  philoi 19
  returns to Athens 23, 108
  supported by Thrasybulus 92–3, 153
Alcibiades, son of Alcibiades 139, 157
  prosecution of 96, 98, 104, 112, 122, 143n3
Alcmeonids 11–12
Amit, M. 71
amnesty (403 BC) 90, 96, 114
Amphipolis, battle of 46, 51–2, 179
Andocides of Kydathenaion 14, 50–7 *passim*, 121

peace mission (392/1 BC) 138–43 *passim*, 148n67, 172
  political activity 99–103 *passim*
  prosecuted in 400 BC 34, 95, 98–100
  prosecuted in 392/1 BC 132, 150–1, 155, 176
  prosecutes Archippus 100, 114, 172
Antalcidas (Spartan politician) 136–7, 159–60
Peace of Antalcidas *see* King's Peace
Antiphon (orator) 27, 53
Antisthenes (Socratic) 95
Anytus of Euonymon 14, 19, 55, 89–92 *passim*, 100, 161
  faction of 94–6
  prosecutes Socrates 36, 47, 172
Apaturia 29
Archedemus (orator) 93
Archestratides
  prosecutes Alcibiades, son of Alcibiades 33, 104
Archidamian War 44, 62, 77
Archinus of Coele 14, 26, 89–92 *passim*, 98, 101, 175
  faction of 96–101
Archippus
  prosecuted by Andocides 100, 114, 172
Arginusae, battle of 29, 46, 82n7, 93, 179, 181
Argos 122, 137, 143n2, 160
Aristarchus (Socratic) 48
aristocrats 26, 30, 53, 122–4 *passim*, 130–4 *passim*
  see also epieikeis kai tas ousias echontes, oligarchs, *plousioi*
Aristophanes 34, 74, 80, 108, 152, 177
  discusses Athenian economy 46–8, 127, 155, 163–7
  Ecclesiazusae 34, 108, 132, 140, 142
  date 86, 143, 149n85
  lines 197–8 5–6, 58, 61–3
  on Athenian economy 45, 56, 163–7
  on Cleon 16
  on ecclesiastic pay 91, 99, 101

Index

on peace negotiations (392/1 BC) 140–3 *passim*
on town and country 61–3, 68n95, 127
Ploutos 32, 57, 155, 163–7
Aristophanes of Rhamnus 19, 126, 132–4, 138, 150–1
Aristotle 19, 47, 79
  on Archinus 96–7
  on Athenian rowers 60, 71
  on civil war (404–3 BC) 3, 42, 54–5
  on Conon and Thrasybulus of Steiria 108
  on ecclesiastic pay 100–1
  on pragmatism and policy 27
  on thetes 80
  on Thrasybulus of Collytus 103
  political terminology of 19
Aristotle of Marathon 162
assembly, Athenian 24–30
Artaxerxes 137, 153
Athenaeus
  and bigamy 74
Audring, G. 4, 5, 63
Aulus Gellius 127

Beloch, K. J. 15, 75–7, 110, 130–5 *passim*
birth control 73–4, 83n18
Boeotia 104–13 *passim*, 122, 155
  see also Thebes
Boissevain, J. 18
Burn, A. R. 78
Busolt, G. 153

Callias of Alopece 19, 34–5, 56, 66n47, 102, 114
  Conon's link to 131–6 *passim*
  partner of Iphicrates 155
Callimedon
  philos of Conon 131, 135
Callistratus of Aphidna 14, 131, 141–2, 162, 176
cavalry, Athenian 26, 49, 56, 98–102 *passim*, 105, 122–5
  and Athenian manpower 75–7
Cawkwell, G. 153
Cephalus of Collytus 47, 100
  and Epicrates 90, 102–6 *passim*, 109–12 *passim*, 130–1, 134, 176
  in later Corinthian War 142, 156–7, 161–2, 177
  populist 26, 90, 102–3, 109
Cephisophon of Paeania 91, 106
Chabrias of Aexone 156–62 *passim*

Chalcedon, treaty of 118n66, 153
Chambers, W. N. 15
Charicles (oligarch) 20
cheirotechnai (skilled workers) 47, 64n20
Chios 129
Cimon, son of Miltiades 24–7 *passim*
Cinesias of Melite 134
City Men 57, 89–92 *passim*, 97–8, 113–14, 171
civil war (404–3 BC) 1, 42, 54–5, 74–5
class 174–5
  conflict 55–9
  consciousness 26
  divisions 42, 59–63
Clearchus (Spartan mercenary) 25
Cleobulus (Athenian general) 156
Cleon, son of Cleaenetus 12, 14
clientelism 30–1, 175
cleruchs 52, 58, 60, 77, 81, 84n36, 129
Cnidos, battle of 108, 125, 143, 152
  and Conon 14, 34, 126, 135, 139
Connor, W. R. 16, 21, 24
Conon of Rhamnus 13–14, 175
  and Thrasybulus 4, 108, 114, 135, 152–3
  other enemies 135–6
  arrest and death 137–8, 151–2, 161, 163
  exile in Cyprus 77
  faction 19, 112, 129–35, 142, 156, 174–6
  hero of Cnidus (394–2 BC) 125–9, 137–8
  in Persian service (397–4 BC) 78, 103–11 *passim*
  prosecutes Adeimantus 32, 34, 108, 129, 172
  tendency 127–32 *passim*, 175–6
Corinth 122–8 *passim*, 137–43 *passim*, 160
  garrisoned by mercenaries 126, 133, 155–6
  joins anti-Spartan alliance 122, 143n2
Corinthian War (395–86 BC) 4, 92
  Aristophanes on 61–3, 163–7
  Athenian politics and 111–13, 122–9, 139–43, 154–63 *passim*, 171–3 *passim*, 177
  narrative of 109–10, 121–6, 136–9, 150–4, 157–60
  see also eisphora
Coronea, battle of 14, 124–5
Coulon, V. and Van Daele, H. 164

Critias (oligarch) 20, 93–5 *passim*, 114
Crito of Alopece 45, 109
Critobulus of Alopece 45, 58
Critodemus of Alopece 109
Cynossema, battle of 179, 181
Cyrus (Persian prince) 25
Cythera 126, 136
Cyzicus, battle of 181
David, E. 165
Davies, J. K. 13, 42, 53, 162
debt cancellation 57
Decelea 44–9 *passim*, 53, 60, 73–4
Decelean War 47–8, 59, 105
  see also Decelea, Iono-Decelean War
Deinarchus 99, 126, 157
Delium, battle of 72, 80, 179–80
Demades (orator) 49
Demaenetus
  and Conon 133
  and Demaenetus affair 103, 107–11 *passim*, 119n73, 176
  general 388/7 BC 156–70 *passim*
democrats 3–4, 7n12, 15, 77, 89, 93, 105, 170
demos (political community) 16–17, 19, 27–8, 38n26, 139–40 *passim*
Demosthenes 27, 103, 124, 136, 156
  on Conon 108, 127–9
demotikoi 26, 100, 102
Demus, son of Pyrilampes 134
Dexileus Monument 124
Diodorus Siculus
  on Athenian battle casualties 71, 178–82 *passim*
  on Athenian plague 84n26
  on Athenian politicians 132, 154, 156
  on Conon 108, 125, 127, 137, 152
  on Corinthian War 121–5 *passim*, 137–8, 141, 154–7
Diodotus (investor) 50
Diogeiton (money-lender) 49
Diogenes Laertius 74
Dionysius (general) 160–1
Dionysius of Syracuse 19, 128, 133, 160
Diotimus (general) 155–9 *passim*
disunity, Athenian 3–4, 89, 114, 150, 157, 171–3
Dodds, E. R. 3, 32
Dover, K. J. 3, 25, 30

ecclesiastic pay 91, 100–2
economy of Athens 4
  agriculture 43–6
  banking 49

commerce 48–51
culture 51
domestic rural 43–6
domestic urban 46–51
effect of Peloponnesian raids 44–6
farmers 44–5, 60–2
finance 49–50
light industry 46–8
loss of empire 50–3
mining 45–6
postwar depression 45–6
timema 54
Ehrenberg, V. 58–62 *passim*, 164
eisphora 46, 54–8, 74, 105
  in Corinthian War 57, 140, 152, 157
  payers of 43, 51
  proposal of Eurippides 134
Eleusis 19, 56, 92, 105
Elis 105
empire, Athenian 51–3
envy 34–5
Ephesus 126
Ephialtes (Athenian politician) 26–7
Epichares (oligarch) 91, 98
Epicrates of Cephisia 175–6
  and Cephalus 89–90, 102–3, 176
  and Conon 19, 112, 131, 134
  champion of the Many 26, 89–90, 109
  death sentence 151
  embassy to Persia 99, 126, 157
  faction 102–3, 106
  on Athenian poverty 103, 127
  Persian subsidy 100
  prosecution of 135–6, 161
  role in peace of 392/1 BC 138–43
Eraton (wealthy farmer) 45, 49
epidemic *see* plague
epieikeis kai tas ousias echontes, hoi 29, 90–1, 175
Eratosthenes (Lys. Orat. 1) 32
Eratosthenes (Lys. Orat. 12) 41n88
Ergocles (*philos* of Thrasybulus) 23, 34, 89, 154
Euandros (alleged oligarch) 162
Euboea 42, 53, 179, 181
Eunomus (general and politician) 19, 134, 156, 159
Euripides' *Orestes* 23–4
Euripides of Myrrhinus 134
Eutheros (ex-cleruch) 56, 84n36
Euthyphro (Socratic) 84n36
Euxitheos (politican) 30, 56
Evagoras of Cyprus 128, 132–4, 150, 158–9

Index 187

Index

faction 2, 17–28, 174
  and *hetairia* 20
  and *philia* 20–4
  Athenian examples 19
  definition 17–18
    connotation 18
    pragmatism and policy in 24–7
    size 24
Few, the 90–1, 96–101, 114, 157
Finley, M. I. 11, 28, 36n1, 68n89
Fisher, N. R. E. 21
Five Thousand, the 79
Foster, G. 21
Four Hundred, the 19, 79, 92, 99, 162
friendship
  see philia
Funke, P. 3, 28, 152
  evaluates Archinus 96–7
  on class 4–5, 58, 63
  on politics as power struggle 25

generalship, and politics 14
Gilbert, G. 15
Gomme, A. W. 70–6 *passim*
Gorgopas (Spartan general) 159
Gouldner, A. 3, 30
Grote, G. 15, 113, 120n83, 127
guilt culture 32

Hagnias (wealthy Athenian envoy) 109
Hagnon of Steiria 76
Haliartus, battle of 112, 121–2
Halimous, deme of 30
Hansen, M. H. 36nn4,8, 37n26, 81n2, 118n51
Hanson, V. 44
Harding, P. 68n92
Heracleides of Clazomenae 14, 101, 106
Hermogenes (politician) 131, 134
Herms, desecration of 34, 95, 99, 114, 131
hetairia 20–1, 24
Hieronymus (Conon's subordinate) 132
honor 31–2
hoplites 57, 61, 74
  battle casualties 5, 71, 75–6, 173, 179
  and thetic casualties 58, 80
  class 12, 26, 43
  in battles of 395 BC 121–2
  numbers of 78–81, 173
Hopper, R. J. 50
Humphreys, S. C. 27, 38n39, 39n53

Hyperbolus (ostracized politician) 30, 91

idiotai (politically inactive) 17
'invisible property' 55
Ionian War 74, 80, 92, 108, 153
Iono-Decelean War 42, 53, 58
  see also Decelean War
Iphicrates of Rhamnus 158–9, 177
  commands mercenaries in Corinth 126
  hero of Lechaeum 131, 155–6
  philos of Conon 133, 146n45
Irwin, T. H. 116n21
Ischomachus (landed magnate) 45, 56
Isocrates 1, 97–8, 132
  on Conon 127–8
  on Lochites *see* Lochites
  on Thrasybulus of Steiria 93–4
  pupils of 134

Jones, A. H. M. 14, 43, 58, 76, 78, 177

Kagan, D. 39n65, 40n70, 68n89
King's Peace (387/6 BC) 135, 141, 160
knights *see* cavalry
Krentz, P. 67nn71–4, 116nn21,26

laconophiles 100, 136, 139–40
Lauffer, S. 46
Lechaeum
  destruction of Spartans at 155–6
  Long Walls, battle of 126, 131, 138, 147nn62–3, 150
Leites, N. 24
Leodamas (archon-elect, 382/1 BC) 162
Leon of Salamis 55, 95, 98
Lesbos 79
Lévy, E. 178
liturgies 13, 42, 45, 74, 129
Lochites (wealthy young man) 26, 57, 102, 117n45
Locris 110, 143n2
Long Walls, Athenian 14, 127
Lycurgus of Boutadai 55
Lysander 50, 73–4, 111, 126, 159
Lysias 1, 4, 47, 56, 65n26, 178
  on Andocides 95, 99–100
  on Athenian economy 45–50
  on Athenian population 79, 181
  on civil strife 3–4, 26, 54–7 *passim*, 114
  on Conon 107, 128, 135–6
  on Corinthian War 121–3
  on *eisphora* 58, 152, 157

on *hetairia* 20
on Mantitheus *see* Mantitheus
on minor Athenian politicians 22, 33, 89–90, 96, 99
on *philia* 22–3, 33
on political culture 33–5
on Thraysbulus of Collytus 103, 156, 162
on Thraysbulus of Steiria 16, 35, 142, 153–4
Property of Aristophanes 109
see also Aristophanes of Rhamnus, Nicophemus of Rhamnus

Macedon 26
manpower, Athenian
 after Peloponnesian War 5, 70–85, 173–4
 political significance 5, 58, 81, 173–4
 and battle casualties 71, 73, 80–1, 173–4, 179–82
 and birth rate 73–4
 see also birth control
 and children 73
 and malnutrition 73, 82n16, 83n17
 and metics 71–5 *passim*, 78–81 *passim*, 82n5, 83n23
 and military strength 81–2
 and oligarchs 74
 and plague 73–4, 81n3
 and poverty 73–4
 and women 73–4, 81n3
 effects of immigration and emigration 77–8
Mantias of Thorikos 157
Mantinea, battle of 123
Mantitheus (Athenian knight) 49, 98, 122, 124
Many, the 26–9 *passim*, 90–1, 96, 131, 134, 157
 factions after 404 BC 101–4
McCoy, W. J. 115n16
Meiggs, R. 54, 80–1
Meletus (oligarch) 98
Melos 140
metics 49, 51, 55, 66n51
 see also manpower, Athenian
Meyer, E. 130
Middle Comedy 164
Mossé, C. 4–5, 63, 68nn89, 93, 164
Mytilene 77, 179, 182

Nathan, A. J. 18, 20, 25

Nemea River, battle of 80, 122–6, 138, 144nn4–12
Nepos, Cornelius 111
Niceratus, son of Nicias 55
Nicholas, R. W. 18
Nicholson, N. K. 24
Nicias, son of Niceratus 30
Nicias (Isoc. Orat. 20) 55
Nicomachus (alleged oligarch) 102
Nicophemus of Rhamnus 19, 126, 132–3, 138, 150–1, 172
Nikarete, daughter of Damostratos 56, 127
Notium, battle of 103, 108, 181

Ober, J. 177
Oionias of Atene 53
Old Oligarch (Ps.-Xenophon) 85, 95, 98
oligarchs 15, 20, 26, 55, 74, 89
 against Conon 135–6
 and cavalry 102
 and oligarchy 26–7, 89, 93–4, 99, 102
 and Phormisius 99, 114, 175
 in amnesty and aftermath 59, 90–1, 96–9, 103–6 *passim*, 109, 112–14 *passim*
 in 404/3 BC 90–9 *passim*, 103–5 *passim*
 in peace of 392/1 BC 139–40, 143
 political tendency 17, 90
 versus democrats 3–4, 113
Oropus 105
ostracism 19
Oxyrhynchus historian 1, 4
 on Cephalus of Collytus 102–3, 106
 on Conon 132
 on Demaenetus affair 107–12 *passim*, 119n73, 133
 on Epicrates of Cephisia 99–103 *passim*, 106, 140
 on the Few 100, 112
 on Thrasybulus of Steiria 93
 political terminology 19, 26, 29, 90–1, 175

Pamphilus of Keiriadai (general) 157–8
Pausanias (author) 103–7 *passim*, 110–13 *passim*, 154, 181
Pausanias (Spartan king) 111
Pecorella Longo, C. 28
penetes 4–5, 58–9
 and *plousioi* 57, 61–3, 171–6 *passim*
 definition 42–3, 63n1

Index

Pericles 11–13 *passim*, 31–2, 52, 72, 154
  citizenship law suspended 74, 77
  democratic principles 27
Perlman, S. 37n22, 38n26, 119nn76–7
Phaedrus of Myrrhinus 109, 131
Phanocritus of Parium 157, 162
Pharnabazus (satrap) 126–8, 153, 160
Phidias (sculptor) 13
philia 2, 21–4, 174
  responsibilities of 23–4
  size of group 24, 29–36 *passim*
Philochares (Athenian soldier) 156
Philochorus (historian) 54, 137, 141
Philocrates (Thrasybulus'
  subordinate) 34
Philomelus of Paeania 134
Philon of Acharnae 104
Phlius 55
Phocis 110
Phormisius (politician) 14, 89, 92
  embassy to Persia 126, 136, 157
  proposes limiting citizenship 90, 97, 99
  reverses policies 99, 162, 175
Phyle, battle of 15, 89, 92, 97, 107
Piraeus 14, 63, 66n53, 129
  and trade 48, 50
  Piraeus men 89–92 *passim*, 97–9, 112, 171
  refortification 63, 127
  Spartan threat to unwalled 111, 121
plague (430–27 BC) 72–81 *passim*
  nature of 83n24
  see also Athenian manpower
Plato 31, 112, 123
  on Socrates' conviction 23, 94–5
  anti-Persia 135–6, 141
Plato Comicus 155, 157
plousioi 5, 42–3, 63n1
  and *penetes* 57, 61–3, 171–6 *passim*
Plutarch 19, 24, 32, 72, 103, 181–2
Pnyx 126, 129, 132
politeuomenoi, hoi 17, 24, 29, 38n26
politics
  community 17, 28–9, 48
  elite 17–20, 48, 174–5, 163
  following 17, 28–30
  generosity 13–14
  geography 42, 59–63
  group, inadequate term 16
  party, inadequate term 1–2, 15–17, 91
  political culture 2–3, 31–6, 172
  political trials 36, 172–3
  politicians 11–14

pragmatism and policy 24–7
tendency 17
see also faction, class, clientelism, democrats, *demotikoi, epieikeis kai tas ousias echontes*, envy, generalship, *hetairia*, oligarchs, *polloi kai demotikoi*, populists
polloi kai demotikoi, hoi 29, 90–1, 102, 175
Polyaenus (politician) 22–3, 104
Polycrates (rhetorician) 95
poor
  see penetes, ptochoi
populists 14, 91, 94, 102–3
postwar period 1–6, 12, 26, 35, 90–2, 177–8
Potidaea 76, 79
Pseudo-Andocides 140
ptochoi 43, 59
Pyrrhandrus of Anaphlystus 162–3

Rhinon of Paeania 91, 98
Roberts, J. 148n77, 168n10, 169n26
Rhodes 106–7, 11, 150–2
Rhodes, P. J. 46n85, 78, 115n7
rich and poor 42–3, 56–9 *passim*, 63n1, 109, 164–5
Ruschenbusch, E. 72–3, 82n11, 99

Ste. Croix, G. E. M. 4–5, 58, 63
Samos 98–9, 106, 126
Sarakatsani 14
Saur, L. 94
Sealey, R. 24–5, 28, 101, 104, 161–2
Second Athenian Confederacy 14, 162
shame culture 32
Sicilian Expedition 29, 77, 113, 179–81
slaves 45–6
society, Athenian
  see aristocrats, class *epieikeis kai tas ousias echontes*, manpower, *penetes, plousioi, polloi kai demotikoi*, rich and poor
Socrates 36, 74, 131, 177–8
  and Athenian economy 47, 51, 56
  and Corinthian War 123, 126, 135, 138
  philoi 94–6
  prosecution of 1, 3, 13, 94–6, 114
Solon 11, 27, 35
Sophilus (supporter of Conon) 134
Sophocles 35

Index 191

Sparta 126, 139, 173
stasis 16
Struthas (satrap) 137–42 *passim*, 158–9
Syme, battle of 179, 181

Tanagra, battle of 24
taxes 49, 93, 153, 160
  see also eisphora, liturgies
Teisis (oligarch) 98
Teleutias (Spartan general) 150, 152
Ten Thousand, the 31
Thasos 92
Thebes 122, 141, 148n76
  see also Boeotia
Themistocles 127–8
Theopompus (buccaneer) 50, 66n44
thetes 12, 78, 173
  and politics 110, 114
  battle casualties 5, 71–3, 179–82
  and hoplite casualties 58, 80
  definition 43
  numbers 80–1, 177
Theozotides (politician) 10, 14, 100, 102, 117n45
Theramenes of Steiria 26, 29–30, 89–93 *passim*, 96, 101, 175
Therameneans 14, 89, 92–9 *passim*, 175
Thibron (Spartan general) 77, 150
Thirty, the 89–98 *passim*, 106, 124, 162
  and Socrates 3, 95
  confiscate property 47, 54–5, 93–4
  execute Athenians 5, 54
  in amnesty and aftermath 90–1, 102–3, 124, 162, 171
  see also oligarchs
thranitai 73
Thrason of Erchia 156
Thrasybulus of Collytus 14, 89, 91
  in late Corinthian War 156–61 *passim*
  political loyalties 103–4, 112, 135, 177
Thrasybulus of Steiria 14, 34, 174–7
  and Alcibiades 19, 33, 92–3, 96
  and Anytus 94, 96
  and Archinus 89–90, 96–7, 116n25
  and other enemies 102–4, 155
  and Athenian society 42, 47, 55–7
  and Boeotia 103–4, 111
  and Conon 4, 33, 107–9, 114, 129–30, 135–8 *passim*

and Persia 107, 153
at Phyle 89
attacks on 112, 122–4, 154, 172
citizenship bill 97
death 154, 163
faction 16, 90–4 *passim*
in Corinthian War 110–12, 121–5 *passim*, 150–4, 157
political eclipse 96, 108
tendency 27, 91–4 *passim*
Thrasyllus (politician) 93, 115n15
Three Thousand, the 42, 54–9 *passim*, 63, 91, 97, 109–14 *passim*
Thucydides 1, 3, 35, 51, 53, 123
  on Athenian battle casualties 71, 179–82
  on Athenian plague 75–6
  on Athenian politics 20, 27, 29, 31, 113
  on Athenian society 44, 52–3
  on *eisphora* of 428 BC 54
  on hoplite numbers 78–9, 84n33
  on Pericles 27, 31, 52, 72
  on Thrasybulus of Steiria 92
Thucydides, son of Melesias 27, 30, 53
Timotheus of Rhamnus 162
Tiribazus (satrap) 128, 136–8, 158
trierarchies 74, 152

vengeance 34
'visible property' 55, 63
Voltaire 18

Walcot, P. 3, 30
Whibley, L. 15

Xenophon 4, 23, 103, 133, 142, 150, 156–60
  on assembly-packing 29
  on Athenian battle casualties 179–82
  on Athenian economy 45–9
  on Athenian unanimity (395BC) 110–13 *passim*
  on Conon 108, 125–32, 137
  on famine (405/4 BC) 73
  on Iphicrates 156–9, *passim*
  on Nemea River battle 80, 123
  on oligarchs 42, 55, 98, 105
  on political culture 25–6, 31–5 *passim*
  on Socrates 35, 47–9, 58, 94–5
  on Thrasybulus of Steiria 34, 92–4, 104, 107, 121, 141–2, 151–4